Dramatic Concepts
Greek and Indian

Dramatic Concepts
Greek and Indian

A Study of
the *Poetics* and the *Nāṭyaśāstra*

Bharat Gupt

PRINTWORLD
Publishers of Indian Traditions

Cataloging in Publication Data — DK
[Courtesy: D.K. Agencies (P) Ltd. <docinfo@dkagencies.com>]

Gupt, Bharat, author.
Dramatic concepts : Greek and Indian : a study of the poetics and the Nāṭyaśāstra / Bharat Gupt.
pages cm
"First published in India in 1994" – Title page verso.
Includes bibliographical references and index.
ISBN 9788124600252

1. Aristotle. Poetics. 2. Bharata Muni. Nāṭyaśāstra. 3. Poetics. 4. Drama. I. Title.

LCC PN1040.A7G87 2022 | DDC 808.1 23

ISBN: 978-81-246-0025-2
First Published in India in 1994
Second impression in 1996
Third impression in 2006
Fourth impression in 2016
Fifth impression in 2022

Printed and published by:
D.K. Printworld (P) Ltd.
Regd. office : "Vedaśrī" F-395, Sudarshan Park
(Metro Station : ESI Hospital)New Delhi – 110015
Phones : (011) 25453975; 25466019
e-mail: indology@dkprintworld.com
Web: www.dkprintworld.com

for

Yukti

Preface

THE primary aim of this book is to confront the rival theories of dramatics, Greek and Indian, with a view to draw conceptual parallels and differences. It is argued here that the Greek system of poetics, of which drama was one part, began semiotically but in its later European application tapered into the lexical. On the other hand, the Indian system has remained semiotic through and through. Both systems, however, had a beginning in a semiotic structure which was based and sustained by what I have called hieropraxis.

There have been many partial and some complete studies on this subject. Most of them have resulted in broad generalizations. Their approach invariably has been to take a concept from Aristotle and juxtapose it with a parallel from Bharata Muni. This way only a logocentric comparison is achieved. I have adopted a different method. I have placed the two dramatic theories within the broad framework of ancient Indo-European culture and the art of hieropraxis or sacred drama for which they were formulated. In other words, much of the similarity between the theories owes to the fact that they both emerge from a common Indo-European world-view. Ancient Greeks and Indians not only upheld some common metaphysical and epistemological concepts, but they also regarded theatre as a sacred action meant to please gods as well as men. Moreover, for them theatre was not, as is often erroneously argued, meant for the ruling elite, or merely the worldly audience, it was for the whole cosmos which was its raison d'etre.

I have also argued that sacred drama required the perfection of certain production techniques which were synesthetic. Music, dance and semiotized gesture were all unified to produce a performance text and the *Poetics* and the *Nāṭyaśāstra* are, above all, manuals that present theories for the production of such performance texts. Thus, in this study, the emphasis is on techniques of production or elements of theatrical representation. It is not upon dramatic genres such as tragedy, comedy or *daśarūpakas*. These genres as lexical structures, have been the basis of comparison between Greek and Indian dramatic theories all too long.

Besides pointing out the common Indo-European factor and the hieropraxic nature of the two ancient traditions, I have also emphasized that with the rise of post-Renaissance drama in Europe, the Greek tradition tapered from the semiotic to the word-centered performance text. This change was a departure from the hieropraxic towards the secular. Only the Byzantine period in Europe had achieved some sort of a synthesis between the sacred and the secular. From the Renaissance onwards, the sacred was too often redefined and at times even isolated from daily life under Humanistic and Individualistic ideologies. This resulted in the break-up of the aural-visual unity of the hieropraxic kind which was primarily an expression of human and cosmic unity.

The Russian semiotician Yuri Lotman has noted the difference between Classical and European sensibility and formulated his theory of two kinds of aesthetics, that of "identity" and that of "opposition." For Lotman, all folklore, Middle Ages in Europe, Classicism and the Asian cultures practise the first, and Romanticism, Realism and Avant-garde follow the second. The aesthetics of identity, holds Lotman, rests upon the identity or nearness of the code of the sender with that of the receiver. Its absence generates the aesthetics of opposition. While accepting all this, I would further add that the opposition to the code of the sender or the absence of nearness to it always results in a desemiotization of gesture and opsis in theatre. The gap created between the sender and the receiver needs to be filled by laborious means. In European theatre, extensive verbal discourse was used to fill in the gap. Later on, naturalist scenery and costume were used for the same purpose. And still later, a breakdown of verbal discourse was used as a device for reflecting the Absurdist universe. This method of filling in the gap created a total dependence upon logocentric means in theatre and reduced the synesthetic unity of the classical techniques. It may also be pointed out that, in the aesthetics of identity, the sender's code works instantly upon the spectators and creates in them a deep emotional arousal resulting in an aesthetic pleasure which has been termed katharsis in one tradition and *rasa* in another. On the other hand, in the aesthetics of opposition, emotional arousal is replaced by intellectual reflection. The plays of Ibsen, Shaw and Brecht are the high point of this intellectual stimulation meant to lead one to certain ideologies. Quite in contrast to this, a major aim of hieropraxis was to provide a deep emotional relief or bliss, in which the psyche of the spectator was transformed from the ordinary state to a special state, just as on the stage the worldly reality was transformed into a unique reality produced through multi-discourse techniques.

Before beginning to 'confront' the two systems with each other, I offer a revaluation of the *Nāṭyaśāstra* from a modern critical perspective. Its basic tenets are redefined in a modern intelligible language not for the sake of establishing a false analogue between it and the *Poetics* but for using it as a lexical site for interpreting its semiotic import. For the same reason I have put in a whole chapter on the date of the *NŚ* which in my reading brings it closer to the *Poetics* historically as well as conceptually.

The book is divided into three parts. The first part opens with an Introduction where I propose a definition of hieropraxis, and reasons for its decline in Europe. Then, I emphasize the need to look upon ancient drama from a non-European viewpoint. Next, I take up the problem of dating the *NŚ*, followed by a chapter which briefly explores the socio-cultural parallels between Greek and Indian dramatic themes. The first part is concluded with a chapter setting out the historical evolution of both the theatrical traditions from dance.

The second part, which makes for the bulk of the book offers a detailed analysis of all the conceptual tools, mechanical apparatus, the visual, the aural and the spatial elements together with a critical evaluation of the rival mimetic concepts. I begin with a chapter on a reassessment of the basic concepts of the two theories. I give here a scheme under which the rival concepts are juxtaposed for comparison and contrast. All the concepts are classified under three broad divisions: theatrical space, aural and visual content, and the dramatic genres. Then begins a detailed comparison. To start with, a chapter is given to an examination of the concepts of ***mimesis*** and *anukaraṇa*. It is argued that the Greek theorists, Plato and Aristotle are preoccupied with gauging art in terms of the worldly objects and experiences, whereas the Indian approach attempts to create, almost entirely, an artistic universe independent of the one we live in. This is followed by a chapter on the media of imitation, where the unification of the different channels of discourse is shown to be a concept that is common to both Aristotle and Bharata Muni. Then follows a chapter on performance space where it is argued that in both the theatres space was divided into areas meant predominantly for speech activity, dance motions and musical expressions. From here, I move on to a chapter dealing with visual content where Greek stage gestures, dance and choreology are contrasted with the Indian *abhinaya* and its theory. It is pointed out that in the ancient theatre, gesture was an independent language, neither subservient to the verbal nor just an amplification of the verbal intent, but a complimentary device that created its own area of signification.

In the chapter "Aural Content" the relationship between the spoken and the sung words in theatre is examined in detail. It is shown that rhythm was accepted as the common basis for speech, metre and song in both traditions. This chapter includes a juxtaposition of Greek musical theory with the Indian musical system called *Gāndharva*. This part of the book concludes with a chapter on dramatic genres and play-structure, in which the basis of genre classification as practiced by ancient societies is also stated. The rival concepts of ***muthos*** and *itivṛtta* are also dealt with.

The third part of the book gears the argument to a conclusion. It is held that the two dramatic theories, earlier defined as hieropraxic, adopting the technique of multi-chanelled discourse, aim at two objectives. One, that theatre is essentially the business of transforming reality, not of depicting it. Two, that theatre should provide a deep emotional arousal and a consequent psychological relief to the audience. Pre-occupied with transformation, hieropraxis avoids not only a portrayal of characters but also a depiction of social classes and the conflict of class interests as well. It does not aim to "reactualize on stage what has happened elsewhere" (Schechner 98), but creates a world of its own. Music, dance and gesture totally transform the objects of imitation. Bharata Muni has maintained that this transformation was either *lokadharmī* or *nāṭyadharmī*. Though there is no parallel concept stated in Aristotle, in actual practice the Greek theatre achieved a transformation which was no less embellished than the one on the Indian stage. For this reason, our present day categories that divide theatre into "folk," "classical," "realistic" or "commercial" cannot be applied to hieropraxis. In the concluding chapter, I consider the concept of two *dharmīs* in detail, explaining them as guidelines for theatrical transformation and then examine the purpose behind emotional arousal. ***Psuchagogia*** or emotional arousal as mentioned in Greek rhetorics and theatrical context, is reviewed and is confronted with the Indian theory of *bhāvavyañjanā*. The result of emotional arousal, namely katharsis, is also reviewed as a clinical, spiritual and aesthetic concept and is finally compared with the *rasa* concept as stated by Bharata Muni along with a critique of the four well known interpretations. A close scrutiny of these interpretations reveals some shortcomings and therefore, a fresh approach is proposed which is called *saṃyuktivāda*.

In this study, I have attempted to create a new matrix for comparative study based on an examination of specific structural elements. It is shown here, that even though the Greek and the Indian concepts may be similar in many respects, their practical applications are very different. For instance, depersonalization of the actor is a common concept but one theatre does it through mask while the other through facial painting and expression. On the whole, the two dramatic theories get better clarified, even as comparison reveals differences rather than similarities now and then. Differences help us to understand each system better than interpretations in a unicultural context do. For instance, in this study, the difference between the Greek and the European dramatic approaches has been emphasized by placing the Indian system side by side the both of them. Most often, the Greek and European systems are clubbed together and regarded as one tradition called "Western." On the contrary, I have tried to show the closeness between the two ancient systems and their distance from the European practices.

A word about the critical editions of the two basic texts that I have used. For my purpose only a general statement of the concepts was sufficient and there was no need for an analysis of the variant textual readings and differing translations. I have, therefore, relied only on one translation of the *Poetics,* that by Butcher, and have not referred to the translations of Else or Bywater. For the same reason, I have used only the critical edition of the *Nāṭyaśāstra* including *Abhinavabhāratī* published by the Oriental Institute, Baroda. I have thought it neither necessary nor very useful for the present purpose, to see the variant readings in Manmohan Ghose's edition, or in the antiquated *Kāvyamālā* edition. The Baroda edition is currently under revision and some of it is in the press, but it has not been possible for me to consult it.

For the exposition of the concepts and terms found in the *Nāṭyaśāstra,* I have extensively depended upon the *Abhinavabhāratī.* This is not out of any blind admiration for the great doyen of Indian scholarship, but because I do not choose to forget, as do so many of my contemporaries, that Abhinavagupta belonged to a tradition in which the *NŚ* was studied as an exclusive and serious academic pursuit. There were many schools for its study in the country and Abhinava had been trained to study it under one of the most illustrious teachers of his day. His word then, is not his alone but stands for a whole era of scholarship. It has the authenticity of knowledge handed down systematically (*sāmpradāyikī śikṣā*) through a traditional system of education.

I have tried to retain wherever possible, the original Sanskrit terms for the concepts stated in the *NŚ* and likewise the Greek terms used by Aristotle. Risking the odium of pedantry, I have done this to avoid confusion caused by translations. If we study classical concepts, we might as well cultivate the use of original terms. Therefore, terms like ***dianoia, ethos,*** *vibhāva, anubhāva* and many others have been retained. However, terms such as ***eleos, phobos, pathos,*** *karuṇa, bhayānaka, gīta,* etc., which do not lose too much in translation have been translated. All Sanskrit words are given in italics and the Greek words in bold italics.

All translations into English from the *Nāṭyaśāstra* and the *Abhinavabhāratī* are my own. I have quoted extensively from the *NŚ* (Baroda edition) but in translation. To give the original Sanskrit verses for all the quotations in end-notes would have taken up too much space. I have, therefore, provided only the most essential verses of the *NŚ* and crucial passages from the *Abhinavabhāratī* in Sanskrit.

I must express my deepest gratitude to Professor J. Birje Patil, for showing me the way to place this rather old-fashioned topic in the perspective of contemporary thinking on performing arts to highlight its present day utility. And no less, I have to thank Professor V.Y. Kantak, who was kind enough to spend many long hours in discussion. But for the constant vigil provided by him this book would not have taken its present shape. The key term, 'hieropraxis,' which I have used to denote sacred drama as a category in itself in the history of drama, was suggested to me by Professor A.N. Athanassakis, Chairman, Department of Greek Studies, University of Crete. In the end, I sincerely thank all those who, like Gaṇeśa Vighneśvara, encouraged me to complete this work either by creating obstructions or by removing them.

Bharat Gupt

Contents

Preface vii

Part I : ANCIENT DRAMA AS HIEROPRAXIS

1. INTRODUCTION 3

Ancient Drama as Hieropraxis
Unification of Speech, Gesture and Dance in Hieropraxis
Departure from Hieropraxis
Growth of European Drama
Poetics and *Nāṭyaśāstra* as Systems of Performance

2. THE DATE OF THE *NĀṬYAŚĀSTRA* 19

Antiquity of *Daśarūpakas*
Gandharvas and *Gāndharva*
Pre-epic Themes of Early Drama
The Prose Passages in the *NŚ*
The *NŚ* as a Compilation

3. INDO-EUROPEAN BELIEFS IN GREEK AND INDIAN DRAMA 41

Miasma-katharsis or *Śauca-aśauca*
Ancestor Worship and Burial Customs
Oracles and Curses

4. DRAMA AS FESTIVE RITUAL 63

Drama and Ritual
The Nucleus of Dance in Greek Theatre
Origin of Indian Drama
Indian Festive Setting

Part II : CONCEPTS AND TECHNIQUES

5. BASIC CONCEPTS OF ARISTOTLE AND BHARATA MUNI: A REASSESSMENT 85

6. THEORY OF IMITATION 93

Mimesis
The Concept of *Anukaraṇa*

7. MEDIUM OF IMITATION 103

Rhythm, Language and Harmony
Āṅgika Abhinaya
Verbal *Abhinaya*
Sāttvika Abhinaya
Āhārya Abhinaya
Unification or *Samānīkaraṇa*

8. COMPARISON OF GREEK AND INDIAN THEATRICAL SPACE 125

Hieropraxic Division of Space
Greek Performance Space
Indian Performance Space
Open Theatres

9. THE VISUAL CONTENT 145

Greek Gesture and Dance
Greek Choreology
Greek Dance Genres
Visual Content in Indian Drama

10. THE AURAL CONTENT 169

Lexis, Rhythm and Tone
Greek Musical System
The *Vāgabhinaya* Concept
Elements of *Pāṭhya*
Dhruvā Songs and *Gāndharva*

11. DRAMATIC GENRES AND PLAY STRUCTURES 203

The Serious and the Trivial
Daśarūpakas
The Four *Vṛttis*
Play Structures
Ethos and *Nāyakas*

Part III : TRANSFORMATION AND EMOTIONAL AROUSAL

12. TRANSFORMATION AND EMOTIONAL AROUSAL 233

Transformation of Reality
Lokadharmī and *Nāṭyadharmī*
Greek Theory of Emotional Arousal
Indian System of Emotional Arousal
Katharsis and Hedone
The *Rasa* Concept
Views of Lollaṭa, Śaṅkuka, Bhaṭṭanāyaka and Abhinavagupta
Saṃyuktivāda
Katharsis and Rasa
Epilogue

Bibliography 275

Index 287

Part I

ANCIENT DRAMA AS HIEROPRAXIS

1

Introduction

DRAMA of the ancient world, no matter of what region, should be seen as a category by itself. In some respects, it may have been a forerunner of modern drama, but still the two are not to be equated. Ancient drama had a distinctive make-up, the characteristics of which can be found in its practices in Greece, India and Egypt. It was primarily a communal and a sacred action which no later theatre could ever be. It was also not merely ritualistic and religious in spirit, as is often believed. On the contrary, it preserved very well the difference between theatre activity and religiuns rites. But, being sacred action performed on a festive occasion, ancient theatre came to acquire special characteristics and performance techniques which were quite different from modern theatre and are therefore, difficult to comprehend today. Let us consider those salient features of ancient drama which may have marked the great theatrical achievements of Greece and India and which Europe at a later date was unable to appreciate.

Ancient Drama as Hieropraxis

Ancient dramatic performances were localted within the wider activity of festivals (***hieromenia*** or *parva*), a time when a community set aside the constraints of normal existence to communicate intensely with itself, with its ancestors and its gods. In this location, even though it did not seek the same end as religion, drama was meant to please the gods as well as men. This gȧve it a purpose significantly different from that of European drama which was meant to please the audience only. Besides being sacred, this drama was also an action (***praxis***), committed to enact a ***muthos*** or an *itivṛtta.* It was not supposed to depict merely a state of mind as in *Hamlet.* Rather, it had to be a drama or deed (action), which traversed from one state of being *(avasthā)* to another, from fortune of one kind to that of the opposite kind. To highlight these two essential features of ancient drama, I have called it hieropraxis or sacred action. Later drama sidelined both the sacredness and the nature of action as conceived in ancient drama.

Unification of Speech, Gesture and Dance in Hieropraxis

Some of the characteristics of hieropraxic drama may be stated briefly. 1. Here, there was no primacy of the aural, particularly of the speech content, over the visual content. 2. The visual was never intended to be realistically representational but evolved instead as a sign language. 3. All gesture and body movement was highly embellished and codified and was mimetic of the cultural semiones and habitual gestures of the people it represented. These semiones were codified modes of actions and gestures which had well-known meanings in their cultural context. 4. A major part of the visual content of hieropraxis was dance. It was often included as an act of worship, besides being a dramatic representation. 5. The aural content was wide in range, modulating from speech to intricate song. 6. Simple speech was used in a limited way but stylised speech, declamation and song-dialogue were amply used. 7. The visual and the aural were combined into a unified whole to produce a theatrical reality which was not meant to relfect directly upon the world beyond theatre, but was designed to be absorbing in itself. It was also meant to produce an elevated state of feeling in the audience.

The theatrical practices of both ancient Greece and India were fine examples of hieropraxis, having all the characteristics noted above. The primary aim of this study is to show how the multi-channelled theatre was prescribed in the *Poetics* and the *Nāṭyaśāstra,* and how the two traditions practised it, each in its own way. But it is equally essential at the outset of this study to point out how and why the production techniques of hieropraxis were forgotten both in the West (Greece and Europe) and in India.

Departure from Hieropraxis

The Greco-Roman theatre declined rather rapidly. With the increasing influence of Christianity the art itself came to be looked upon as unholy. It was revived in Europe, by extricating it from the Christian theological bias centuries later in the Reniassance, but by then, it had undergone a major transformation. From a multi-channelled discourse, it changed into a word-centered performance. Even though it was imagined to be a restoration of the original Greek tradition, it used few of the methods that the Greeks had employed. Its lexicality, in fact, wiped out the very memory of the Greek methods. Largely the same story was repeated in India. During the British occupation of India, realist-naturalist-spoken-word centered theatre was ushered in as representative of all Western theatre, the Greek included. The European practice was so enthusiastically imitated on the urban stage that even classical Indian plays were produced in the naturalist mode. Unfortunately, the general public has ever since regarded them as a legitimate revival of Sanskrit theatre. Although the ancient Indian system of multi-channelled performance survives strongly in the traditional theatrical forms like Kuḍiyaṭṭam, Kathakali and *aṣṭapadī* dances such as Bharatanāṭyam, these forms have not been able to penetrate the urban theatre productions permanently. In brief, under the impact of post-Renaissance European theatre, the departure from ancient production techniques has been complete both in Europe and in urban India. It is, therefore, vital to understand how the European theatre itself came to evolve its techniques.

Growth of European Drama as Word-centered Performance

Whereas the ancients regarded theatre as a medium in which both the visual and the aural channels had an equal place, and in which the visual was endowed with a deep symbolic meaning, in Europe there developed a theatre in which the verbal content, particularly the spoken word, dominated all other channels. Other channels of communication were restricted in their scope and functions and were made to yield to dialogue. This constriction marks the major difference between the ancient and the post-Renaissance European performance techniques. Even a quick look at classical Indian or Greek drama would reveal that the actor's body, his costume and adornments, mask and body movements were of primary significance. Here, the spoken word was secondary. The actor's dress and his gestures operated under a wide system of signification, which I shall later elaborate upon. The spoken and the sung word and the musical accompaniment were subservient to gestures and body movements. This exemplifies the well known rules of performance in both Greek and Indian traditions. Such a well defined relationship between speech (song, as well) and gesture did not exist in European theatre. Contrary to what happened in ancient productions, in the European practice, speech succeeded in making gesture totally subservient. Thus the art of gestural expression dwindled from the Renaissance onwards, to the point where the actors' bodies, even the charming figures of heroines, were reduced to statuesque instruments meant only to spout dialogues. To draw the spectator's attention there was minimal gesture, and that too, was made realistic, common and banal. It was totally subjugated to the literal meaning of the uttered word. The ancient theorists, as I shall show later, considered gesture and not the spoken word to be the starting point of drama. In Europe, this situation obtained only till the survival of Morality plays. With the flowering of modern European languages, however, the status of the visual became devalued. The visual not only lost its symbolic power but was eventually made to represent merely the material reality of things. This story of ***opsis*** from the significantly codified to the insignificantly real (as Naturalism and Realism) is in itself a topic for an exclusive study. For now, I venture to give a few reasons for this change.

Christian Bias Against Transformation

Early Christian Fathers objected to the ribaldry and corruption pervading the Roman theatre. But in the denunciations made by Tertullian, Jerome, and Augustine and a host of later day theologians there was a deeper rejection of the very art of theatre which was thought to be antithetical to Christian theology. For the Christians, the hieropraxity of Roman theatre was nothing more than pagan worship. Participation in theatre amounted to blasphemy. "A man cannot be a Christian and an actor, because he is serving pagan gods, and the audience are his abettors" (Garton 37). Moreover, the epistemology propounded by Christians was contrary to the one upheld by Greeks and Romans which approved of persona and mask. As Napier puts it, "only direct epistemological incompatibility can account for the Church's persistent criticism of the stage"(11). Taking up a theatrical persona or wearing a mask is not merely a technique of acting. The technique rests upon the view that a given culture takes of personification, role-playing and the very concept of individual personality. In short, representation of personality on stage is effected in accordance with the accepted definition of what makes up a person. For the Christian, the world is motivated by only one force. There is no possibility of the Godhead commingling with the individual in any manner. Except perhaps in the case of mystics, whom Christianity has usually regarded as heretics, it is expected that the divine influence upon an individual shall make him devout and morally elevated, but any kind of enthusiasm or ecstasy is always suspect. For the Church, there can be no holy possession. On the contrary, possession is the way of the "arch-enemy." An individual, therefore, should never budge from his own persona, nor should he allow himself to be taken over by another personality.

For the Indo-European people the approach of personality was entirely different. "Often in polytheistic contexts, people and spirits are both necessary participants in the process of change. Greeks not only thought that they could have personal contact with the supernatural but that they could even, at least in principle, have offspring with them" (Napier 27). The Indian view was no different. Possession by the divine was not only viewed as normal by the Indo-European, but all possession was regarded with awe and was often welcomed. Transformation or change of the self was shown not as a change of intellectual position or opinion, but as brought under the impulsion of an external agency. This was represented on stage by the actor transforming into a mask with persona (as in Greek theatre), or the actor changing into a codified persona costume (*āhārya*, as on Indian stage). The mask not only eliminates the personal self of the actor, who happily surrenders to the force that the mask represents, it also penetrates the temporal world of the audience with the presence of a reality which is beyond time. Transformation through mask, costume or *āhārya* infuses the temporal with the eternal and for this reason has been regarded as a sacred activity. For the Greeks there was no acting without this transformation. As Jevons says:

> There was no acting without masks, and there were no masks without acting. To wear a mask was to act a part; and the idea that it was ever possible to act a part or to perform in a play without wearing a mask was one which never occurred to the mind of those responsible for the Greek style. (Jevons 1916b, 173-74 quoted in Napier 10)

I shall later on show, while discussing the concept of *āhāryābhinaya*, that things were no different for the Indian audience.

The Christian Church took a long time to suppress the tradition of mask and persona. But when it did, it left no room for its revival. In the period when Morality theatre was dying out, it became clear that "mask focuses on its role as evil disguise" (Napier 11). Its association with anything good, let alone holy and spiritual, had come to an end. This Christian bias resulted in desemiotizing the visual content in theatre. It was assisted by another upcoming philosophy, that of scientific materialism, which defined reality in objective terms and which geared the concept of mimesis towards versimilitude. However, this philosophical stance did not have its heyday till the nineteenth century. In fact, it was the Christian world-view, that had been working all along to reduce the visual in theatre to a non-sign status. After the relegation of mask and codified cosume to disguise and deception, theatre as a venue of morally instructive entertainment closed its doors on masks. Their use in private parties, "masks" or "masque" was, again, to facilitate deception. The Christian participants did not aim at becoming the faces they wore. It was an interplay between the self and the mask, a hide and seek game; it was in no way a transformation.

Christian hostility to transformation and its visual representation pushed European drama towards logocentricity. Gradually the nature of the verbal content became very different from the classical one. The verbal was no longer, as it had been in classical times, chained to the uniform use of rhythm, to a unified pulsation of words, song and body movement. It was now a mere expression of conversational dialogue, in which the rhythm of daily speech took over. The association between the measured word and the rythmic visual was broken by conversational rhythm. The visual, already desemiotized with the discarding of mask and other symbolic gestures weakened in its significative power, and shrank even more as a medium of communication in theatre.

Elimination of Dance and Music

Reduction of visual codification and increase in conversational speech left less and less room for dance and music in drama. For the Greeks, as for many other ancient peoples, dance was not only a popular part of most social events, but was, in fact, a mode of worship. When a dance form was transferred from a purely ritual setting to theatre, as it happened when dithyramb grew into the tragic chorus, the dance form continued to retain its gestural language. This language constituted a major part of the performance text. But European theatre had no rituals to draw upon, as Christianity had long eliminated or supressed dance rituals. Besides, one should remember that in Europe there seems to have been no tradition of mimetic dance, or any thing that might compare even remotely with Greek ***phoroi*** and ***cheironomia***. The elimination of dance from acting and theatre was therefore, an easy affair. Along with dance, there was also the casualty of its most natural ally, music. As a result in Elizabethan plays music came to be used mostly as an interlude. No part of the dialogue had a musical base, say as in the ***parakataloge*** of the Greek plays.[1] Here, all dialogue was only a shade removed from the conversational rhythm, at best declaimed not even intoned.

Rise of Portraiture

Within the broad sweep of Humanistic philosophy, the emphasis on individual identity changed the concept of characterization in drama. For the Greeks the essential thing in a dramatic character was ***ethos***, that is, the ability to make a choice. "Character (***ethos***) is that which reveals moral purpose, showing what kind of things a man chooses or avoids" (*Poetics VII, 17*). Ancient drama was not interested in personality projection. It looked for ***ethos.*** In contrast, European dramatists, while keeping a character's capacity to choose, invested a character with so much personal idiosyncracy that the actual act of making a choice was often lost sight of. Sometimes the projection of the many facets of a personality, and the attempt to create a unique character overlooked the basic requirement of ***ethos***. Hamlet is so mysterious and complex that he need not choose. Here the inability to choose is presented as an ***ethos***. For the ancients such a character is no character at all for they perceived little value in deft portraiture.

Portraiture calls for an expansion of the verbal medium because individual complexities are best brought out by dialogue and description. Visual imagery tends to depersonalize. Codified costume works best for types, embodying the commonly acknowledged tendencies of human nature which may often be represented by mythic figures. But, when drama is preoccupied with the creation of individually distinct personalities and when psychological realism demands deeper exploration of the particularities of human nature, the burden on the verbal channel in theatre is maximized.

Social Reformism

In comparison with ancient theatre, modern European theatre has a propagandist inclination. It has taken upon itself the burden of promoting upcoming theories of social change. As these changes have been faster and more pervasive during the life span of this theatre, it could not have avoided relfecting them. Although, issues like war and the consequent plight of women were taken up as early as Aristophanes, the dramatist was not specially interested in offering logically worked out solutions to contemporary problems. He was content to reflect the turmoil that he saw. European theatre, on the contrary, has always taken up a moralistic stance and has shown a greater concern for the ethical than for the metaphysical or the epistemological problems. From the late nineteenth century onwards, social reform came to be heavily propagated through theatre. Till the fifties, quite often the playwright posed as a master thinker with the players as his mouthpieces. As Leonard Pronko puts it, "We ponder the questions of the hour as they are presented to us by philosopher-sociologist- politician-playwright and we consider frivolous and shabby every play that does not give us food for thought" (179). The drama of Ibsen, Shaw and Brecht was the high point of this trend. Needless to say that verbal discourse was the only medium that could have fulfilled the requirement of discursive exposition which had to be delivered through theatre.

I have dwelt upon the reasons for the preponderance of verbal discourse in European theatre in order to contrast it with the ancient practice of unified discourse. My purpose has been to set apart the technique of European theatre and prevent the understanding of the systems of Greek and Indian antiquity from getting vitiated by the European habit of mind. However, the main purpose of this study is to compare and contrast the two ancient systems themselves. Hence the manner in which this needs to be done.

The Poetics and the Nāṭyaśāstra as Systems of Performance

It will be more fruitful to compare the two works as two systems of performance rather than as two sets of dramatic theory meant for certain dramatic genres. For many years literary criticism has tended to view drama as printed text and not what it actually is, a performance script. By giving priority to the written play over its theatrical realization, we seem to assume that the written play contains within itself all that is brought out in the performance. The written text and the performed text are often taken as synonymous. It is presumed that dramatic theories have also evolved more to guide the writing of plays and not so much for producing them. For this reason our understanding of dramatic theories has shaped in terms of what is seen on the printed page and not what is seen and heard as the phenomenon of performance. It is not surprising, therefore, that dramatic criticsm, when it deals with the ancient theories of Aristotle and Bharata Muni, is mostly preoccupied with analysing and defining, and then, contrasting the genres of tragedy and comedy with *nāṭaka, prakaraṇa* and *bhāṇa*, etc.

Dramatic criticism has regarded dramatic traditions as nothing more than growths of literary genres and has been content to define their excellence and their artistic beauty, in literary terms, that is, as prose and poetry in the mode of dramatic narration. Furthermore, it has postulated the creation of these genres as the prime purpose of the total effort of theatrical activity. For such criticism, the aim of Greek drama was to evolve a faultless tragedy like *Oedipus Rex* and of Sanskrit drama to create a perfect *nāṭaka* like *Abhijñānaśākuntalam*. At the time of undertaking a comparative study, this sort of criticism has usually complained that the genres of Europe or Greece are not found in Asia. For instance, many pages of sterile ponderings have been spent on the question, why there is no tragedy in Indian drama. It is often asked that if Europe, and even America could imbibe tragedy from Greece, then why did not India do so from Europe? By way of answering such questions, many equally futile pages have been filled in arguing either that tragedy is present in a concealed manner in Sanskrit drama or that for several vital philosophical reasons tragedy was not possible in India. This line of comparison can lead only to dead ends. In my view, it is sensible to concede that literary genres are unique to each culture because of different historical experiences. It seems more pertinent to see the common ground, if any, behind these genres and to investigate how in ancient times, theatre in different lands was used to produce these genres. One may ask, was there any similarity between the techniques and elements of production in the two traditions? And also what was the difference in ways in which the Greeks and the Indians handled dramatic production, whether it be of tragedy on one side, and the *nāṭaka* on the other? Today, a comparison of performance modes is likely to be more illuminative than a comparison of literary genres. To begin with, this shall help us to reconstruct ancient productions and later to see the literary texts in a new light. More than anything else this exercise may help us to indicate the possible lines of theatre development in the future.

Having set out on this comparative enterprise, it is necessary that I take stock of the material to be compared. There is the corpus of plays extant in Greek and Sanskrit. For the purpose of simplicity I will limit myself to the so called classical periods: Greek drama of fifth century B.C. and the Sanskrit plays upto fifth century A.D. Here, one needs to bear in mind that only a small portion of the total output has come down to us.[2] Besides the plays, there are general references to the art of theatre in both Greek and Sanskrit literatures, but very little can be gathered from these regarding the exact nature of performances. However, the archaeological evidence is slightly more rewarding. In the case of Greece, theatre-ruins and pottery are valuable source material; in the case of India, there is only sculpture to help us reconstruct dance. There is little to help us reconstruct drama as performance.

The ancient works of dramaturgy are our chief sources of information other than the plays themselves. And here, we have only one text on each side, namely, *Peri Poietikes* of Aristotle and *Nāṭyaśāstram* ascribed to Bharata Muni. Whatever material, literary or archaeological, that happens to shed light on the ancient performing modes, has to be related to these texts, as they alone are the two extant works written specifically to record and explain the art of their times. As no other work survives it has become customary to concede that Aristotle is representative of all ancient Greek opinion and Bharata Muni, that of the Indian side. A comparison of the theories of the *Poetics* and the *Nāṭyaśāstra*, seen in the light of the extant plays, is nearly synonymous with a comparison of Greek and Indian performance theories.

It may be noted that in their magnitude and content the *Poetics* and the *Nāṭyaśāstra* are diagonally different. The most important difference which has remained hitherto unnoticed is, that the *Poetics* was written well after the best had been achieved in classical Greek theatre, whereas the *Nāṭyaśāstra* was known much before the extant plays came to be written. Plays on the basis of which the concepts of the *NŚ* were formulated were lost very early. As a result, the *Poetics* while stating the general features of tragedy and partly of comedy, also provides a stance on literary criticism and an evaluation of works within its purview. It presents *Oedipus Rex* as the ideal tragedy. The *NŚ*, on the contrary, avoids all references to plays; its method is not empirical but enunciatory. It is primarily concerned with formulating principles of performance and not with examining examples of literary excellence. There is another major difference of approach between the *Poetics* and the *NŚ*. Whereas Aristotle has taken up the whole subject of poetics and dealt with theatre as one part of poetics, Bharata Muni has taken up theatre (*nāṭya*) and dealt with poetry, literary forms and music as part of *nāṭya*. Therefore, in the *Poetics* it was logical for Aristotle to distinguish a non-dramatic form like the epic from tragedy, while for Bharata Muni there was no need of this kind. He need not have distinguished the *daśarūpakas* (the ten dramatic genres) from the *Purāṇas* (epics) as his work was not on poetical theory but on drama. Let alone the *Purāṇas,* Bharata Muni has not paid attention to any literary genre prevalent outside of theatre. Nonetheless, as theatre includes the art of poetry, dance and music, his formulations on the nature of these arts have acquired the status of primary enunciations *(āptavākya)* in the Indian tradition.

Regarding the problems of date and authorship, they exist in the case of the *NŚ* only. In the case of the *Poetics* matters of chronology are more or less settled. But scholars are divided on the date of the composition or compilation and the authorship of the *NŚ*. They place it variously within the wide span of seventh century B.C. to fifth century A.D. I have argued that the text of the *NŚ* was in existence when the *Rāmāyaṇa* was being composed by Vālmīki (Gupt 63-76). This means that *NŚ* was in circulation around the fifth century B.C., if not earlier. In other words, its basic concepts on dance and drama were prevalent in India a long time before Aristotle's *Poetics* was recorded in 355-335 B.C.

On the subject of a possible influence of one text over the other, there is little that can be said conclusively. Scholars who assign a late date of composition for the *NŚ*, such as second century A.D. onwards, have suggested that the *Poetics* might have arrived in India with Alexander or with later Greek satraps, and could have influenced the formulation of the *NŚ* ideas. This theory can hardly hold ground. If there was such a direct borrowing at all, it would have left not one but many tell-tale marks. Other than ***mimesis,*** from which Bharata Muni could have derived his *anukaraṇa*, there seems to be no other trace of the ideas of the *Poetics* on the *NŚ*. Regarding the possibility of an influence of the *NŚ* on the *Poetics*, even if earlier dates of the *NŚ* composition are authenticated, it is again no more than a mere speculation to say that *anukaraṇa* led to ***mimesis***. It is true that contacts between India and Greece were quite considerable before Alexander, and extensive cultural exchanges had taken place between the two countries (through the part of western India occupied by the Persians). The invasion of Gāndhāra by Cyrus I (circa 525 B.C.), and its Persian occupation till Alexander's invasion facilitated many exchanges. But there is no evidence to suggest that Indian ideas on drama had travelled to Greece, as it happened undoubtedly in the area of medicine.[3] In any case, Aristotle's definition of ***mimesis*** was in reaction to Plato's definition who had denigrated ***mimesis*** in art from his peculiarly elevated metaphysical and ethical standpoints. Some people have, perhaps rightly, seen a striking similarity between Platonic and Upanishadic Idealism, but nowhere in the Indian tradition has the status of art and art medium been suspected of leading us away from truth. The Indian *anukaraṇa* and the Greek ***mimesis,*** therefore, have entirely different origins. For these and many other reasons, I would prefer to regard the *Poetics* and the *Nāṭyaśāstra* as independently conceived works. They have common features which are not a result of exchanges, but stem from the fact that both were written for a common aim, that of sacred drama. It is also possible that the two works are not so far removed from each other historically as has been hitherto presumed. In the next chapter, I shall examime the *NŚ* to see if it can be brought historically closer to the *Poetics*.

Notes

1. "***Parakataloge*** is the term applied to all sequences in between speech and song. I assume that it mostly implied a chant with many syllables on one note, or a very primitive tune of only a very few notes. But it seems that it may well have covered the entire range

between speech and song, from something very near speech but against a musical accompaniment, to something almost song . . . It was used for nearly every employment of ***anapaests***." Leo Aylen, *The Greek Theätre* (London : Fourleigh Dickinson UP, 1985) 104-05. What Aylen has suggested may sound something similar to Vedic chants.

2. "The fifth century alone should have seen the production at the Great Dionysia of 900 tragedies, 300 satyr plays, 400 comedies, together with an uncertain number at Lynaea from 442 B.C. onwards, and that of this vast output only 32 tragedies, one satyr play, and none of the comedies survive in a more or less complete state." J.A. Davidson and Stanford, *From Archiolochus to Pindar* (New York: Macmillan, 1968) 2. M. Ghosh has observed that 550 titles of various kinds of Sanskrit plays are known to us mainly from literary references. Out of this only about 90 plays are known to have survived. *Contributions to the History of the Hindu Drama* (Calcutta:Firma, K.L. Mukhopadhyaya, 1958) 11.

3. J. Filliozat has suggested that between Indian and Greek medicine, there are some very particular and precise similarities not easy to ascribe to chance. Therefore some exchange through the Persian court-physicians can be safely presumed. By examining the *Hippocratic Manuals* and Plato's *Timeus,* Filliozat has come to the conclusion that in Greek medicine the theory of four humours is derived from the medicinal doctrine of Āyurveda. He also argues that in its basic form this doctrine had come to be formulated as early as the *Atharvaveda*, and by the time of *Śatapatha Brāhmaṇa* and the much later *Kātyāyana Sūtra* (circa 7th cent. B.C.) it had been well codified. *The Classicial Doctrine of Indian Medicine* (Delhi : Munshiram Manoharlal, 1964).

2

The Date of the Nāṭyaśāstra

TO give an exact date, is impossible not only for the *NŚ*[1] but for any work of Indian antiquity. The best one can do is to examine the contents of the *NŚ* in relation to the *Purāṇas* and *Smṛtis* and other important works, and to see if the *NŚ* can be placed before or after them. I shall try to do this mainly on the basis of developments in music, dance and theatre as they are described in different works.

The Sanskrit of the NŚ

M.M. Ghose speculated that the *NŚ* contains a good deal of *ārṣa* Sanskrit (archaic and pre-Pāṇini).[2] Bharata Muni, then, perhaps wrote soon after Pāṇini, when the injuctions of the newly formulated grammar system were not yet pervasive in their influence. Ghose also lists 22 words which are not used in classical Sanskrit and are not even found in lexicons. They are simply peculiar to the *NŚ*. He similarly identifies 13 words that do occur in lexicons but have hardly been used. The Sanskrit of the *NŚ* is, indeed, quite unshadowed by classical usage in the sense that it is less indebted to the formalized structures of classcial Sanskrit and retains a distinct freshness and simplicity.

All the same, the stage of development of the grammar can never be a sure clue to the age of a work, particularly if the work has been later expanded. The archaic usage and pre-Pāṇini remnants in the *NŚ* only confirm that its first writer was a close successor of Pāṇini, and that he was relying upon works which were, perhaps, of greater antiquity than Pāṇinī himself. These could be the writings of Nārada and Tumburu. We should now turn to the contents of the *NŚ*, to find some clues to its date.

The Antiquity of Daśarūpakas

Looking at the entire corpus of the extant Sanskrit plays, we notice a hiatus between the time of their composition and the compilation of the *NŚ*. The *NŚ* defines ten kinds of plays which are basically either romances or action dramas. However, by the time of Bhāsa, or even as early as Aśvaghoṣa, the action scripts like *samavakāra, ḍima, īhāmṛga* and *vyāyoga* had declined in popularity. The major figures in the ranks of Sanskrit dramatists as known today, never tried their hand at these forms. By the second century B.C. half the forms classified in the *NŚ* were either dead or dying. It is of course highly unreasonable to believe that some of these forms were only fanciful classifications by Bharata Muni who had no actual examples before him. Here, we must not forget that the first play produced by Bharata Muni himself was a *samavakāra,* written on the theme of the churning of the ocean. These action plays portraying the prime mythic theme of ocean-churning (*samudramanthana*) are decidedly lost. One reason for their disappearance could be that their scripts were improvised and were not of any great literary excellence. Still, it remains to be noted that if these plays went out of fashion because of a change in the taste of the audience, such a change would have occurred not in a generation or two but over a few centuries.[3] This again is a pointer to the existence of Bharata Muni long before Aśvaghoṣa and later dramatists.

Musical Instruments in the NŚ

Musical instruments that figure in the *NŚ* are obviously those of a pre-Christian era. In the *NŚ* there are no zithers but only harps. It is doubtful if the lute was known to Bharata Muni. The primary *vīṇā* of this period was a bow-like instrument with gut strings. Such harps go back to 3000 B.C. Egypt (called ***bint***), but they disappear in India in A.D. 300 as sculptural evidence would have us believe. The reliefs of the Kuṣāṇa period depict besides harps, some lutes (something similar looking to the modern sarod) which are totally unknown to the *NŚ*. The text (*NŚ 29*) describes only the fingering of harps. It has not a word on techniques required for producing notes by sliding fingers on strings or frets. The lute, which is a sister to the zither and is structured on the same principle (as found in the Mathura sculptures) seems to be generations ahead of the bow-like *vīṇā, vipañcī* and *citrā*[4] described in the *NŚ*.

Gandharvas and Gāndharva

The present day word for music is *saṅgīta* which does not seem to be of great antiquity. Though it occurs as early as Vālmīki (*Rāmāyaṇa, Kiś. 28/36-37*) but the passage containing this word is a later interpolation. By the Christian era, *saṅgīta* had come to denote popular musical activity, but the term used for standard classcial music was still *gāndharva*. The *NŚ* throughout has one word for the art of music and that is *gāndharva*. The *NŚ*, therefore, belongs to a period when *gīta*, so much used in *NŚ*, had not yet become *saṅgīta* (singing together).[5]

Gāndharva as an activity or a practice of the beings called *Gandharvas* was known to the epics, the *Smṛtis*, *Brāhmaṇas* and the *Vedas*.[6] But it did not always mean music. It was only as late as the epic period, that '*Gandharvas*' and their *gāndharva* came to be associated with the art of singing and playing upon instruments.

Going into the history of the *Gandharvas*, we find that in the *Brāhmaṇas*[7] they are depicted as handsome male supernatural beings that consort with their female partners, the *Apsarās*.[8] They symbolise fertility and eros.[9] However, they were still not associated with dance or music. On the contrary, the *Śatapatha Brāhmaṇa* tells a story that *Vāk* was wooed by both the gods and a *Gandharva* called Viśvāvasu. The *Gandharva* recited the *Vedas* to enchant *Vāk* by his knowledge. The gods on the other hand played upon the harp and succeeded in enticing her.

The stories of the *Brāhmaṇas* are an amplification of the earlier stories found in the *Ṛgveda*[10] The *mantras* describe how for the sake of humanity, Indra vanquished the *Gandharva* (here also spoken of in the singular) and obtained *soma* from him. The *Vedas,* too, knew of *Gandharvas* as the guardians of *soma.* But in the Vedic story the *Gandharva* is given nothing in return for *soma.*

In the Vedic *Saṃhitās,* the *Gandharva* only appears as an individual. He is not human but heavenly, and has air, sky or holy waters as his habitat. He is once called Viśvāvasu and another time Vāyukeśa. He has varied yet interrelated functions, such as guarding *soma,* being a physician and in one case giving birth to the first pair of humans, Yama and Yamī.[11] He is credited with having a special power over women whom he has a right to possess.[12] For this reason *Gandharvas* are invoked in marriage ceremonies[13] and being endowed with mystical powers are considered to be involved in ecstacy and other abnormal mental states. A parallel with Greek daimons of trees, waters and valleys is obvious.

Post-*Saṃhitā* literature makes a class (*jāti*) out of the *Gandharvas.* They are shown as subject to *Varuṇa,* and their consorts, the *Apsarās* are governed by *Soma.* They are invoked in gambling with dice,[14] and they are also to be feared as possessing the ability to harm. Gradually they were put in the category of *Rākṣasas, Kimiḍinīs* and *Piśācas.* However, two *Brāhmaṇas* still speak of them as revealers of the *Veda* to *Vāk* and preceptors of the *Ṛṣis.*[15]

From all this, it is obvious that in the Vedic and the Brāhmaṇic times, the *Gandharvas* had no connection with music. It is the epic age that attributed this art to them. Why should this have happened? It seems that the *Gandharvas,* as spoken of in *Saṃhitās* and later literature, had derived their name from a geographical people, the *Gāndhāras,* as was the case with the *kinnars.* Most likely they belonged to Afghanistan (which still has a township called Kāndhāra). It is also possible that originally the *Gāndhāras* may have belonged to the region of the Caspian sea and in ancestory were related to the people whom the Greeks called Centaurs, (***kentauros, kenthargos***). The association of an ancestory derived from the horse is common to both the *Gandharvas* and the Centaurs.[16]

If a relationship between the *Gāndhāras* and the *Gandharvas* is accepted, then it is possible to propose a hypothesis that the epic age conferred upon the *Gandharvas* the new attribute of musical knowledge because it was perhaps at this time that the *Gāndhāras* raised the art of music to a great height. This region of the subcontinent at the time had become the locus of a great confluence of the musical traditions of the East and the Mediterranean.[17] The very art, thus, came to be known by the name of the region and was so called by it even in the heartland of India. This name, *gāndharva,* continued to be used for music for centuries to come. In the *Vāyu Purāṇa* one of the nine divisions of *Bhāratavarṣa* is called *Gāndharva.*[18]

Bharata Muni and his *Nāṭyaśāstra,* therefore, seem to belong to a period in which the art of music had newly acquired the name of *gāndharva,* a name which was present in the Vedic *Saṃhitās* and even the *Brāhmaṇas* but with no musical connotations.[19] The Vedic terms for song and singing are entirely different. There the term *gāthā* is used for song, so is *gāyatra,* and for singing the word is *gāthin.* The reciters of Sāman chants are called *sāmagā. Gāyana* for singing or singer is to be found only as late as Pāṇini.[20]

Pre-epic Themes of Early Drama

Indian drama, was not dependent upon Vālmīki's text for its maturity but had long before come into its own through the enactment of many other stories like *Lakṣmīsvayaṃvara* and *Amṛtamanthana.* Although, today in the popular Indian theatre the episodes of *Rāmāyaṇa* and *Bhāgavat* are the most depended upon, they need not have been the only source material for early dramatic enactments. Besides stories like that of Urvaśī and Purūravas, a paradigm of romance, the *sura-asura* conflict had been a good source of episodes for action plays. Those who have argued for a post-epic appearance of Indian theatre were labouring under a basic prejudice, a common belief of their times, that the first element of theatre is dialogue. Sustained dialogue, they thought, can ensue only from a well-formulated story, which should not only belong to public memory, but should have also taken the shape of written literature. Drama, thus, for all those who have been raised on the modern European masterpieces, is the staging of an epic or a popular story. It is not, therefore, surprising that Keith presumes that the development of Indian drama started taking shape only after the Kṛṣṇa legend had been well formulated and the '*śobhanikās*' as mentioned by Patañjali had begun their performances.

The NŚ and the Rāmāyaṇa

Although references to drama and other performing arts in the *Rāmāyaṇa* of Vālmīki have been noted by scholars, there has been little effort at finding out the possible relationship between these references and the *NŚ*. From my study of most of the terms related to music, dance and drama in the *Rāmāyaṇa* (and it must be admitted that there are more terms for music than for drama), I have come to the conclusion that the text of Vālmīki as it stands today shows a clear awareness of a *śāstra* of music and that this *śāstra* was most likely that of Bharata Muni. Vālmīki has used many words like *samāja, gāndharva, gīta* and *vīṇā* which even a lay person would use while talking of a musical event. But in addition, Vālmīki has used so many musical terms, such as, *śruti, sthāna, mūrcchanā, jāti, sammūrcchita, aṅgahāra* and *ātodya,* and while using them he shows an awareness of their definitions as given in the present day version of the *NŚ*.[21]

From this it is not wrong to conclude that Vālmīki did know of Bharata Muni. It may be conceded that some of these verses which contain *nāṭya* terms might be later interpolations, as this epic too like the *Mahābhārata,* grew with the passage of time. All the same there is no reason to suppose that all these references definitely belong to the interpolated sections. In any case, even if it is conceded that the verses showing the influence of the *NŚ* are a part of later additions, the compilations of the *NŚ* was perhaps being done almost at the same time when Vālmīki was writing the *Rāmāyaṇa*. This is again the same era in which the *Gandharva* had been recognised as a musician and the predecessors of Bharata Muni like Tumburu and Nārada, well known by tradition to be of *gāndharvajāti*, had come to be recognized as great musicians.

The NŚ and the Mahābhārata

The *Mahābhārata* is considered to be of a later period than the *Rāmāyaṇa*. The story of Rāma has been referred to in its verses. '*Rāmopākhyāna*,' a summary of the *Rāmāyaṇa*, as found in the *Mahābhārata* is no longer considered by scholars to be a later interpolation. Thus, the references to the performing arts and to music in the epic are likely to occur more extensively. As the epic itself is bigger, meandering and receptive to additions, it is all the more difficult to say which of its portions are the oldest and which are of a much later period. The *Anuśāsana Parva* of the *Mahābhārata* contains a definition of *svara* (defining it as *iṣṭa, aniṣṭa, saṃhata* and *pravibhāgavān*) which seems an elaboration of the *vādī, saṃvādī* concept of *svara* as given in the *NŚ*, but the terms used in the verses of the epic are not found anywhere else. An exhaustive study of the *Mahābhārata* providing useful clues for research on the *NŚ* still remains to be undertaken.

The Prose Passages in the NŚ

Much has been made of the few extremely brief and widely interspersed prose passages in the *Nāṭyaśāstra*. These and some scattered lines of prose have been given the status of *sūtras*. It has been claimed that these passages are a proof of the material that pre-dates the verses, it being a natural presumption that prose of the *sūtra* period preceded the style of writing in verse. But a keen probe into the context of all these passages in prose does not show them to be of a different school of thought or style which might suggest the authorship of a predecessor of Bharata Muni such as Śilālin or Kṛśāṣva.

Let us see where and how the prose comes in. But before going into a chapterwise examination of the occurrence of prose in the *NŚ*, it must be stated that the language of this prose is not in any way similar to the famous *sūtra* works of any era. In the actual *sūtras* the language is purposefully terse, concise and brief. The *sūtra* literature depended upon a line of traditional teachers for decoding its meaning and imparting instruction to students. The prose of the *NŚ* has no such structure. On the contrary, it is not condensed, it tends to expand and illustrate.

Out of the 36 chapters only 10 contain prose passages. In terms of the total text, they seem to be hidden in a jungle of verses, as they are so puny. In chapters eight, thirteen, fourteen, and thirty-three, the prose passage in each chapter is of no more than thirty words and in the seventeenth it is hardly notable. Thus, it is only in five chapters that they are sizeable enough to be influential. It is on the basis of these chapters that any conclusion regarding the nature of the prose can be drawn. Out of these five chapters, the prose of the chapters twenty-nine and thirteen can neither be called prose nor poetry, as it is just a notation of strokes for drums. Effectively, we are left with the chapters six and seven, which deal with the subject of *rasa* and *bhāva* and the twenty-eighth chapter which lays down the scales and notes of ancient music.

From the sixth to the seventeenth chapter the prose passages are followed by verses which are called '*anuvaṃśya*' (preserved by tradition). Along with the passages, these verses are also thought to support a case for the existence of pre-Bharata material that is supposed to have been incorporated in the *NŚ*. Whereas the verses so named may be granted to be of an earlier period there is no saying that the prose is not that of Bharata Muni. The 'traditional' verses very often either repeat what is said in prose, or add little. This only goes to show that the verses existed at the time of compilation, and the prose was written by Bharata Muni to make some things clear which may not have been so explicit in the verses. Although, it was not impossible to convey the content of the prose in verse, it is obvious that wherever prose was more conducive to precision and unambiguity, prose has been chosen unhesitatingly. That seems to be the only discernable reason for this choice. If it had been only a matter of incorporating older texts, then, many other passages would have found their way into the corpus without any justification.

The *anuvaṃśya* verses disappear from the eighteenth chapter onwards, though verses not called *anuvaṃśya* perform the same task. Similarly, in the musical sections, dependence on prose seems a wiser course and on some occasions the only one. For instance, the *śruti*-demonstration experiment would have lost much of its coherence in verse as it did when Śārṅgadeva repeated it in his *Saṅgītaratnākara*. To conclude, then, the prose is not genuine *sūtra* literature and the *NŚ* should thus not be dated on the basis of it. The prose could be of Bharata Muni, or drawn from works extant in Bharata Muni's time. But its presence in the *NŚ* is not a case of random interpolation but of thoughtful selection by Bharata Muni. That it serves a purpose can be seen by analysing its content in relation to the preceding and succeeding verses. Those who argue that Abhinava has called the *NŚ*, '*Bharatasūtra*' should allow for the fact that he has done so to indicate its structural coherence rather than using '*sūtra*' in its technical sense.

The NŚ as antedating Kauṭilya, Vātsyāyana and Amarakośa

Kālidāsa's awareness of the *NŚ* and his recapitulation of the contents of its first seven chapters in *Mālavikāgnimitram*, is well known.[22] In any case the poet, despite the controversy about his era is chronologically too late to show any proximity to Bharata Muni. By his time the *rasa* doctrine had acquired an orthodoxy. A work which does show some proximity to the *NŚ*, however is the *Arthaśāstra* of Bṛhaspati.

The *NŚ* refers to it,[23] and uses *'dvāstha'* (courtier) and *'kumārādhikṛta'* (warden of princes), which are pre-Kauṭilyan words. The *NŚ* nowhere mentions the *Arthaśāstra* of Kauṭilya, which was written as a successor to Bṛhaspati's work. The words given in the *NŚ* become *'dauvarika'* and *'kūmārādhyakṣa'* in Kauṭilya, and have since been included in all lexicons.

Similarly, the *NŚ* does talk of a *'kāmatantra.'*[24] But what is referred to are not of the famous *sūtras* of Vātsyāyana. It hardly needs to be added that while dealing with feminine psychology and sexual relations (*strīpuṃsopacāra*) the *NŚ* presents a world which has heard nothing of Vātsyāyana's classification. Bharata Muni follows a system of classifying women into 22 kinds named after *deva, dānava,* and *gāndharva* and animals like *vānara, mīna, makara,* etc. The classification seems to be more of a fanciful kind, not so much meant to illustrate the nature of sexual activity, but more to describe general feminine behaviour for the purpose of dramatization.

Although, the *Amarakośa* is a very late work of about fourth century A.D., we are constrained to comment upon its possible relation to the *NŚ* as some have argued for placing Bharata Muni later than it. It has been said that as the *Amarakośa* in its section on music does not mention terms like *'mūrcchanā'* and *'mārjanā'*, there was presumably no *NŚ* extant before it. Such an argument is misleading. Besides these terms, the lexicon does not mention a hundred other terms which a vast repository of music and drama like the *NŚ* is replete with. But the *Amarakośa* clearly mentions the eight *rasas* as laid down by Bharata Muni. It also follows Bharata's classification of instruments into *tata, avanaddha, suśira* and *ghana*. By the time of the *Amarakośa, 'bharata'* had become an occupational name for the stage people. The dictionary, therefore, took shape centuries after Bharata Muni.

Similarly, the influence of Bharata Muni's doctrine had shaped words like *'rasika'* which was used for the actor by Patañjali (*Yog. 5.2.95*).

The NŚ as a Compilation

As early as Abhinavagupta it was believed that the surviving text of the *NŚ* was not from the pen of a single Bharata, but that it was a coalition rendered by Bharata Muni by combining the separate works of three schools: *Brahmamata, Sadāśivamata* and *Bharatamata.* The progenitor of the last school is perhaps the same as Vṛddha Bharata, that is, Bharata senior. This was the view held by a '*nāstika*' teacher (probably Jain) contemporary to Abhinavagupta.[25]

To add to this is the comment of Śāradātanaya that the earlier compilation of the *NŚ* consisted of twelve thousand verses and that Bharata Muni did the job of reducing it to six thousand more relevant and essential verses.

Thus, Śāradātanaya in his *Bhāvaprakāśana*[26] merely echoes the widely held traditional belief that by no means could Bharata Muni be regarded as the first to produce a work on dramaturgy. The hundred sons of Bharata Muni as named in the *NŚ* are believed by some to be his contemporaries if not predecessors. But they are more likely to be his successors and not 'elders' (*gurujana*), for no follower of Bharata Muni, however devoted, would go against traditional respectfulness towards 'elder' dramatologists and demote them to the status of the sons of his mentor (*sampradāyaguru*). Dattila, Kohala, Vātsya and Śāṇḍilya are thus successors of Bharata Muni who had little distinctive contribution of their own to add to the work of Bharata Muni and were therefore absorbed into his family. Such a fate did not befall Tumburu, Nārada, Svāti or Nāndikeśvara, who according to all sources have been unquestionably held to be seniors to Bharata Muni. For Abhinavagupta, Tumburu and Nāndikeśvara are the same person.

Now whether 'Bharata' was a historical *ācārya*, or a term which denoted a school called 'Bharata', or merely a compiler with great acumen, is not easy to decide. However, it is a fact that since circa fifth century B.C. no famous work on drama has been in existence other than that of Bharata Muni. The *Aṣṭādhyāyī* of Pāṇini (4/3/29, 110-11) mentions the '*naṭasūtra*' of Śilālin and Kṛśāśva, but no later work repeats this reference. The non-mention of Bharata Muni by Pāṇini should again not be taken to indicate his non existence at that time. Undoubtedly, Bharata Muni has called the *naṭas* as *'śilālin'* and the *Śatapatha Brāhmaṇa (13/5/13)* names them so. The *Āpastamba Sūtra (6/4/7)* also talks of a *'Śilālin Brāhmaṇa.'* These facts, however, merely confirm the name of śilālin as a predessor of Bharata Muni. They do not prove that his contribution was greater than that of Bharata Muni.

Bharata Muni, a Person not a 'Tradition'

Even if there has been a profession of *bharatas* as the lexicons and Śāradātanaya would have us believe, there are still weighty reasons to believe in a Muni who preceded these *bharatas* and *naṭas*. This Muni, by achieving eminence in the field of *nāṭya*, gave the professionals of theatre the nomenclature of *'bharatas.'* The ruling class of *kṣatriyas* who were known as *bharatas,* and who gave the region of North Western India the name of *Bhāratavarṣa,* were not likely to allow any of their clan, even in *'āpaddharma'* (in times of social disorder) to take up the profession of *naṭas*. The stage-life seemed to have become taboo for a *dvija* (a twice-born person). The *kṣatriya bharatas* would not have taken to what even a *vaiśya* disliked and still retained their geneological nomenclature in the new profession of stage-work. The possibility of *'bharata'* having been coined etymologically with reference to its connotation is also slim. The word contains little that can be related to any characteristic (*lakṣaṇa*) of *nāṭya*. The injunction, *'nāṭyavedamimaṃ yasmāt bharata iti'* or *'veṣaṃ vayaḥ karma ceṣṭā bibhrat, iti bharata'* (the one who has received the *nāṭyaveda* and taught it or one who wears the form, age, manners and actions of others, is called *bharata*), is a fanciful etymology (*vyutpatti*) given by later commentators like Śāradātanaya. Such imaginative etymologies are a delightful pastime that the Sanskrit grammarians never miss a chance to indulge.[27] It is not in the word *bharata* that any clue to its association with theatre or performing arts is to be found, but in the simple fact that the first great compiler or the *śāstra* of theatre happened to be carrying the name of Bharata, and thus in the course of time the actors, directors etc. came to be known as *bharatas*, after him. That this happened soon after Bharata Muni, is evidenced by the obviously interpolated passage in the *NŚ (36:35)* which calls the actors *bharatas* because they followed the *śāstra* of Bharata Muni. As the *Bharataśāstra* was their *Veda* (the book of their profession and knowledge), they were called the '*manasputrāḥ*' (mentally conceived sons) of Bharata Muni.

However, it may be noted that *bharata* as a term for a performer has hardly been used in any poem, or prose passage in Sanskrit or even a medieval Indian language. It seems that while following the meaning of *bharata* as given in the *NŚ* and lexicons, Śāradātanaya never looked for its verification in actual practice. If he had anything to rely on at all it was the *NŚ* (*36:35*) itself.[28]

The balance of probability, therefore, is that around 450 B.C. there lived an individual who was not a great dancer or actor (*naṭa*, being the word for both dancer and actor) nor simply an *ācārya* (master scholar and teacher), but a profound thinker who collected all the available material related to performance and gave it coherence and structure related to the ethos of stage-skills. It was Bharata, later on designated as '*muni*' who raised the art of performance to the level of an ecstatic experience that has been well defined by the mataphor of '*rasa*.' There is no labouring the point that material on theatre craft existed before Bharata Muni in the form of some *sūtras*, perhaps of Śilālin origin, and perhaps also in the shape of *kārikās* composed by earlier innovators like Tumburu, Taṇḍu, Svāti and Nāndikeśvara. There was also the contribution of a host of others like Nārada and Viśvāvasu who are a part of the legendary names in the early history of Indian *nāṭya*, but none of this material, no work by any of them, is extant today. It was Bharata Muni who gave all this material a unity and magnitude. It was for this achievement that Bharata was very early called a '*muni*', and '*āpta*' and a '*lakṣyacakṣuḥ*'. (Thinkers who have no predecessors with recorded views, are called '*āpta*'. Those thinkers who can envision a given *lakṣya,* an art or a science, in all its totality are called '*lakṣyacakṣuḥ.*' They are contrasted with most of us who are able to comprehend only a few aspects (*lakṣaṇa*) of a given subject and are therefore called '*lakṣaṇacakṣuḥ*').

To recognise the personality of Bharata Muni is not to deny that passages have been interpolated in the *Śāstra* since his time, and that mutilations and losses have also not occurred. The case of the *NŚ* of Bharata Muni is typical of the way in which all Indian *sāstras* were compiled. A great mind like Pāṇini, Vātsyāyana, Manu or Kauṭilya reviewed a particular branch of learning, gave it shape and coherence, reconciled the differences of opinion but still left room for later additions. However, Bharata Muni is the most distinguished among all compilers (*śāstrapraṇetāḥ*). Whereas Pāṇini had grammarians soon after him, Bharata Muni had nobody to attempt a successive work for another millennium till Mataṅga. Besides, none of the later writer ever succeeded in achieving the scope and unity of his vision. Śārṅgadeva, Pārṣvadeva, Śāradātanaya and many others have copiously drawn upon him, even if, at times, it meant not reconciling his concepts with the changed practices of their times. The presence of a Bharata in the *NŚ* was clearly recognised by Abhinavagupta who simply called him '*muni*'.

Later Growth of the NŚ

An attempt to give a philosophical and cosmological significance to *nāṭya* began with Bharata Muni and was continued by his successors like Dattila, Kohala, Saindhava, Vātsya, and others, known as the 'hundred sons of Bharata' (*śataputrāḥ)* listed in the *NŚ*. Most of these names from the list of hundred are not mentioned in the later texts related to drama. And therefore, it is difficult to say if the list is authentic. On the other hand some well known names like Dattila and Kohala have been regarded as predecessors of Bharata Muni by some modern scholars. It is said that they had been demoted to the status of Bharata's sons, and this distortion was committed to elevate Bharata Muni. But as we have earlier said this sort of act goes against all traditional norms. A small piece attributed to Dattila is extant and his views have been mentioned by Abhinava and later medieval commentators. But not a word from any other 'son' survives. In view of this, it is not rash to presume that most of the 'hundred sons' were engaged in the task of preserving and teaching the *NŚ* as compiled by Bharata Muni. Perhaps it was in their time that the text might have acquired some of the passages that seem rather later interpolations.

To my mind the text of the *NŚ* ceased to acquire anything new very early. By the second century A.D. it had become in many respects antiquated. Out of its ten genres (*daśarūpakas*) only three or four were being practised by playwrights. Most of the heroic genres had gone out of vogue; all the well known dramatists did not try their hand at *ḍima*, *samavakāra* or *īhāmṛga*. Theatre seems to have declined in its mass appeal as is witnessed by the disappearance of action drama. The distinction between a practical performance script and a script written more with literary niceties in mind seems to have crept in. As a result, plays with literary value were preserved even when they had outlived their immediate potential as performance. No wonder that now we have only a tiny fraction of the total number of plays that saw the light of theatre. The case is identical with those hundreds of Greek plays that were performed but were never preserved.

By the fifth century A.D. the living theatre of Bharata Muni's tradition virtually vanished from India. The job of the *nāṭyācārya* was taken over by the *vyākhyākāra*. The practioner of the art was substituted by the critic. And this new tribe of commentators did not have the living art to witness, but only the revered book to study and explicate.

Since the fifth century B.C., when Bharata Muni compiled it, the structure of the *NŚ* has remained intact. Changes in lines, loss of passages, repetitions have entered but they have not clouded its natural effulgence and meaning. Hardly any major contradictions have crept in nor has any jarring doctrine shown its face. Similarly, there have been no alterations or emendations to its original purpose. Thus the great stature of Bharata Muni as recognized in tradition, is no exaggeration.

I have attempted to establish that Bharata Muni was the unquestionable force of both compiler and writer (how much of what, who can know?) of the *NŚ*; also that the *NŚ* was put together about the same time as the great Indian epics. This brings the *NŚ* in a historical proximity to the *Poetics*. Both the *NŚ* and the *Poetics* are thus placed in a common era, that of sixth to third century B.C. in which the intellectual gains of the 'axial age,' as Jaspers called it, were consolidated (Schwartz 1). The best Greek drama flourished in this period and so must have the Indian, even though the play scripts of the period are not extant. Let us now turn to see the general climate of social beliefs and culture patterns, both Greek and Indian, of the life of that period out of which the two theatrical traditions and their canons of performance took birth.

Notes

1. Editions of *NŚ*: An extensive account of the printed editions is given by S.P. Sharma, *Nāṭyaśāstra* (Varanasi : Chowkhamba, 1978) 25-26.
2. The Sanskrit of the *NŚ*: a detailed discussion of pre-Pāṇini Sanskrit in the *NŚ*, showing archaic usages and laxity in *sandhi* rules etc., is given by M.M. Ghosh in his Introduction to his translation of the *NŚ* (Calcutta: Manisha Granthalaya, 1952).
3. *Samavakāra:* The change of taste could be caused by a change in audience. It seems that in the early stages, theatre in India, was for all social classes; it was practised at public festivals and for days together to please a mixed audience. But the later day drama from Bhāsa onwards, it seems, was patronized more by the royalty and the upper classes. In any case, the surviving plays, which were patronized by the upper classes, are the ones which are entirely the works of playwrights. These sophisticated literary scripts had a greater chance of survival than the improvised scripts

of action plays. However, all action plays, that is, *samavakāras, ḍimas* and *īhāmṛgas* need not have been totally improvised by actors. Some texts of literary excellence must have been composed which are now lost.

4. *Vīṇās* of Bharata Muni's period: My observations are based upon the *vīṇās* depicted in sculptured panels of Sātavāhana period (second century B.C.) to be seen at Sānchī and at other specimens of sculptured panels displayed in the collection of Mathura and Delhi museums. These sculptures depict instruments which match very well with the descriptions of *vīṇās* and drums as given in the *NŚ*. As there is very little documentation of ancient instruments as depicted in sculpture, no published work can be cited. One may, however, see the cover jacket of Ācārya Bṛhaspati's *Nāṭyaśāstra*, Chapter 28 (New Delhi : Brahaspati Publications, 1986).
5. *Saṅgītasahāyanī* is used by Kālidāsa in *Mālavikāgnimitram (V. 2)*. It denotes vocal accompaniment.
6. *Gāndharva* is mentioned as a form of marriage in *Aśvalāyana Gṛhasūtra (1.6.5.)*, in *Manusmṛti*, and in *Yājñavalkyasmṛti* too. Likewise in the earlier texts *Ṛgveda (X.80.6)*, *Śatapatha Brāhmaṇa* and in *Mahābhārata (III. 8421)* and *(XIII.5103)*.
7. *Gāndharva* and his relation to speech : *Aitreya Brāhmaṇa (1.27)* and *Śatapatha Brāhmaṇa (III.2.4.7)*.
8. *Śatapatha Brāhmaṇa (IX.4.1.2)*.
9. "*Gandharvas* and *Apsarās* love pleasing smell and form. Therefore, one wants pleasant odour and beauty in coitus." *Śatapatha Brāhmaṇa* (IX.4.1.4).
10. Indra's victory over the *Gandharva*, *Ṛgveda (VIII.1.11 and 77)*.
11. Viśvavasu is the name of a *Gandharva* in *Ṛgveda (X.85.21- 22)*. *Gandharvas* as inhabitants of sky, air and water are mentioned in *Ṛgveda (1.2.14)*; *(VIII.77.5)*; *(IX.85.12* and *86* and *36)* and *(X.10.4)*, also in *Atharva Veda (II.2.3.)*. Also as guardian of *Soma* in *Ṛgveda (IX.*

83.4 and *85* and *12)* and as parent of Yama and Yamī *Ṛgveda (X.10.4)*.

12. *Gandharva* as possessor of women in *Ṛgveda (X.85.21* and *22; 40* and *41)*.
13. They are invoked in marriage ceremonies; *Atharvaveda (XIV.2.35* and *36)*.
14. They are invoked by dice : *Atharvaveda (VIII.109.5)*.
15. *Gandharvas* are shown as preceptors of *Ṛṣīs: Śatapatha Brāhmaṇa (XI)*.
16. *Gandharva* as horse in *Mahābhārata* (*III.11762*) (*II.1043*); it could be corelated to the Centaurs on the basis of the Indian story of *Gandharvī* who is the daughter of Surabhi and the mother of the race of horses. The story is referred to in *Mahābhārata (I.2631f)* and in *Rāmāyaṇa (III.20.28f)*.
17. *Gandharvas* as a tribe : *Rāmāyaṇa (VII.100.10f)* and Varāhamihira's *Bṛhadsaṃhitā (XIV.31)*.
18. *Gāndharva* as an area of *Bhāratavarṣa* : *Vāyupurāṇa (II.3.7)*.
19. In the Vedic literature there is no evidence that music, except as part of *yajña*, was a means of earning spiritual merit.
20. *Gāthā : Ṛgveda (I.67-68)* and *(IX.11.14); Gāthin : Ṛgveda (I.7.1); Gāyanas : Aṣṭādhyāyī (III.1.147)*
21. References to dance and music in the *Rāmāyaṇa: Tantrīlaya (Bāl.2.18); sarvaśrutimanoharam (Bal.4.27); sthānamūrcchanākovidau (Bāl. 4.20); jāti (Bāl. 4.8); samāja (Ayo. 51.23); śrutiśīla (Ayo.65.2); samāja (Ayo.91.49), saṅgīta (Kiṣ. 28.36); sammūrcchita (Kiṣ.30:50), ātodya (Sund.10.49); mūrcchayitvā (Ut.93.14)* and *kalāmātrā (Ut.94.7)* These references are taken from the Gita Press, Gorakhpur edition of the *Rāmāyaṇa*.
22. *Devānāmidamāmananti munayaḥ kāntaṃ kratuṃ cākṣuṣam Rudreṇedamumākṛtavyatikare svāṅge vibhaktaṃ driśyate Nāṭyaṃ bhinnarucerjanasya bahudhāpyekaṃ samārādhanam.* The first line recapitulates the '*krīḍanīyakam*' of Bharata Muni but it is a '*kratum*' (ritual) which is meant to please visually. '*Munayaḥ*' is the plural form of '*muni*'

used so to show greater respect. It refers to Bharata Muni. The second line describes *tāṇḍava* and *lāsya* which were created by Śiva and Umā. The last two lines imply that *nāṭya* which consists of many *rasas,* is able to please men and women of all dispositions.

23. The *Arthaśāstra* of Bṛhaspati : "*Sarvaśāstrārthasampannāḥ kumārādhikṛtastathā bṛhaspatimatādeṣāṃ guṇāścābhikāṅkṣayet.*" *NŚ* (*24:88*).

24. "*Kāmatantra,*" *NŚ* (*22*; lines *151*, *192* and *202*) also (*23:77*). Besides, a '*vaiśikaśāstra*' is mentioned in the *NŚ* (*6*: prose, *309*). It is difficult to ascertain if '*Kāmatantra*' and '*Vaiśikaśāstra*' are two names of the same book.

25. The view of *Nāstikadhuryāḥ*. Since very early times doubts have been raised about the authenticity of the introductory story in which Bharata Muni is questioned by other *munis* about the origin, purpose, parts, length and contents of the *NŚ*. As is evident from the *Abhinavabhāratī*, there has been an opinion that the *NŚ* consisted of parts not all of which were written by Bharata Muni. Some have held that the introductory story was added to the *NŚ* later on by a disciple. Abhinava rejects these ideas. For him :

    Taccāsat. Ekasya granthasyānekavaktṛvacanasandarbhamayatve pramāṇābhāvāt. Svaparavyavahāreṇa pūrvapakṣottarapakṣādīnāṃ śrutismṛtivyākaraṇatarkādīśāstreṣvekaviracit eṣvapi darśanāt.

    Etena sadāśivabrahmabharatamatatrayavivecanena brahmamatasāratāpratipādanāya matatrayīsārāsāravivecanaṃ tadgranthakhaṇḍaprakṣepeṇa vihitamidaṃ śāstraṃ na tu munī viracitamiti yadāhurnāstikadhuryopādhyāyāstatpratyuktam.

    "It is not true because there is no evidence that the views of many people are to be found in this one book (i.e. the *NŚ*). Anyway, we see that in *śruti, smṛti, vyākaraṇa* and *śāstras* of logic etc., one writer presents his views and also those of his opponents (for the sake of developing the argument).

    In this way, I have also contradicted the *nāstika* teacher

who holds that this work (*NŚ*) was not written by Bharata Muni but that for the purpose of upholding the *Brahmamata,* the manuals of *Śadāśiva, Bharata* and *Brahma* schools have been put together to make this *śāstra* so that there could be an analysis of the views of the three schools and as a result of this comparison the *Brhamamata* could be upheld." *(NŚ Ab, 1 : 9)* In modern times we tend to overlook the fact that the narrative device of talking about oneself as a third person was used by many writers of antiquity. In the same way, in the *Mahābhārata,* Vyāsa narrates as a third person the incident between him and Brahmā and the help given to him by Gaṇeśa. So it is nothing new that Bharata Muni himself narrates how he was questioned by the *munis* and what he said in reply.

26. *Evaṃ dvādaśasāhasraiḥślokairekaṃ tadardhataḥ/Saḍbhiḥ ślokasahasrairyo nāṭyavedasya saṅgrahaḥ/Bharatenamitasteṣāṃ prakhyāto bharatāhvayaḥ. Bhāvaprākaśana* (Bombay : N. Sagar Press, 1937) 287.

27. *Sudhāvyākhyā* of *Amarakośa* by Bhānūjī, son of Bhaṭṭojī Dīkṣita. He defines, *'svāṅgaṃ vibharti iti bharataḥ.'* He is followed by *Śabdakalpadruma* and *Vācaspatya-bṛhadabhidhānaḥ.*

28. The professional performer in ancient India was reduced to śūdrahood by the epic age. The story in *NŚ (36:35)* seems to be an aetiological myth about this phenomenon. It narrates how the sons of Bharata Muni parodied the sages in their plays. The sages cursed them with śūdrahood. In the *Brāhmaṇas,* the *vīṇā* players who participate in the *Aśvamedha* are *brāhamins* and *kṣatriyas.* There seems to be no chance of their being other than *dvija.* The *Śatapatha Brāhmaṇa (13.1.5.2.)* declares that *vīṇā* playing must be done by caste persons to revitalize their castehood. In the ritual playing at *Aśvamedha,* only religious efficacy was desired, but in the later times entertainment was as much of a motive. In the epic and later times the professional performer's social status (caste) did not

allow him to go for vedic knowledge. However, in the hierarchy of theatre people there existed an uppermost caste of *nāṭyācāryas*. These, in addition to their higher learning, were likely to be brahmins and the keepers of the books of the trade. Perhaps, in spite of their association with the śūdra actor they kept distance from him in matters of food, living and marriage. Such an hierarchical arrangement is not improbable and exists even today among the architecture people of Gujarat. These traditional temple makers are called Sompurās.

3

Indo-European Beliefs in Greek and Indian Drama

IT has been customary to think of the Greek achievement in science and arts as the intellectual base upon which the later edifice of Western European learning has been raised. The Greeks have been primarily proclaimed as the progenitors of Western philosophy, rationalism, naturalistic investigation and scientific logic. Their literature has been the model for all later writing in the West. However, while this approach succeeds in providing an ancestory to European thought, it eclipses the totality of the Greek experience. It pays less than adequate attention to those aspects of the Greek way of life which did not directly contribute to European culture of the two millenniums after Christ. Greek ways and beliefs which either ceased to be followed with the advent of Christianity, or which were lost into the folk traditions, were not noticed by the official European historians. Nor did they properly reckon with the Oriental constituent of Greek culture which was a major reality.

The Greeks, as early as the Pelasgians, have been regarded as a people of Indo-European stock, the parent race of which is said to have originated somewhere in Central Asia. The evidence for this belief has no archaeological foundation. It is primarily linguistic. However, even if it is presumed that there was a parent or an ur-language for the large number of languages classified as Indo-European, there is no reason to believe that there was a single race to which this language belonged. We have, then, to presume that the diverse speakers of the so called Indo-European languages, who shared many linguistic structures, must have also shared many other thought structures and habits as well, to sustain their linguistic similarities. Looking at the ancient Greeks and the Indians, we find that their languages, rituals, divinities and a host of other cultural habits reveal many such similarities. These cultural similarities, rather their cult-related habits of everyday lives provide a base for dramatic mimesis in their theatres.

Miasma-katharsis or Śauca-aśauca

There is no feature of the Indo-European culture more distinctive than its preoccupation with pollution and purity. Cultural historians and anthropologists have very often considered it as a peg to hang upon an immense variety of rituals, whether of the late Hellenic period or of the *smṛti* age in India. But no keen observer can overlook the fact that the later-day rituals of purity-pollution are only an elaboration of the earlier rituals based on the very primitive experience of loss and restoration of vitality.

The earliest of Greek ***muthoi*** preserve elements that repeat the motifs found in *Vedas*. From the Vedic verses it is clear that ***miasma*** was a later version of impotence. The duality of vitality and impotence (not always sexual) pervades every human event and condition, whether social or private. In the case of gods, vitality is endless though not eternal. In fact, that is their basic vitue (*sattva*), the element of godhood. The gods possess endless vitality because they eat ambrosia or drink *soma*. For mortals, as there is no nectar, there is only prayer to the gods to grant vitality. They can only partake the remains of oblations to bring them vitality as a divine gift. Receiving this gift was never a private affair but always ritualistic and public. That *soma* was a vine is certain, though its modern form still remains to be identified. Ambrosia again is still a mystery and the guess of Robert Graves that it was the mushroom, amanita muscaria, is as plausable as any other.[1] Ambrosia was reserved for gods and the food as such was not to be taken by any mortal. So was the *soma* drink, which in the later epic age becomes '*amṛta*'. The drink of *amṛta* is not only a giver of immortality, it is a panacea and provides unebbing power. No wonder, then, that the ***muthos*** of *amṛtamanthana* has been a primary story in all epic literature in India.

The Gift of Vitality

For mortals this vitality was not available in essence, but it could be gained in its earthly manifestation as physical prowess or martial success. It could be obtained as a gift in the form of psychic intervention. To the Indo-European man the world was inhabited by many unseen but all the same subtly present beings ranging from the supremely divine to the most inferior tree spirits. These he frequently invoked to influence his daily life. He preferred to live a life governed by external agencies, the externality of which in later religions became internalized in the form of introspective meditation or personal prayer. This externality of beings was not remote but always at hand and could be tuned into any time. When the communication did take place the recipient was said to have been impelled by the gift of the spirit invoked. Thus the typical Vedic prayer to *Savitā* to inspire the self (*dhiyo yo naḥ pracodayāt*) or the Homeric ***ate***, a madness that visited man. So is ***menos***, a sudden upsurge that rejuvinated the heroes in the *Iliad*. Not only the influence of higher beings but that of inferior beings also worked the same way. The ***daimons*** possessed humans and so did their counterparts the *gandharvas* (*gandharva-grahīta* being the phrase for a possessed person). In the later stages of religious thought, power was visualised as taking birth from within, as in the Yoga system of Patañjali, but the notion of invoking and inviting divine grace was never totally repudiated. In the Greek culture pattern introspective withdrawal is very nearly absent but prayer or sleep is sufficient to invite divine intervention.

As Dodds explains :

> Another psychic intervention which is common in Homer is ***menos***, the communication of power from god to man. This ***menos*** is not primarily physical strength; nor is it a permanent organ of mental life, like ***thumos*** or ***noos***. It is like ***ate*** a state of mind. When a man feels ***menos*** in his chest, or thrusting up pungently into his nostrils, he is conscious of mysterious excess of energy, the life in him is strong, and he is filled with a new confidence and eagerness.[2]

It is not only this gift of power to defend oneself or to do a great task that is received from without, but so is a confusion or imbalance in normal thinking said to be caused by an external agency. Again to quote Dodds:

> There are a number of passages in Homer in which unwise and unaccountable conduct is attributed to ***ate***, or described by the cognate verb ***aasasthai***, without explicit reference to divine intervention. But ***ate*** in Homer is not a personal agent; nor does the word ever, at any rate in the *Iliad*, mean objective disaster, as it so commonly does in tragedy.[3]

Making a very useful distinction between mental insanity and a visitation Dodds clarifies :

> Practically always, ***ate*** is a state of mind, a temporary clouding or bewildering of the normal consciouness. It is, in fact, a partial or temporary insanity; and, like all insanity, it is ascribed, not to physiological or psychological causes, but to an external daemonic agency. It is by no means a synonym for or a result of, wickedness. Nor is it the punishment for guilty rashness.[4]

In other words, all abnormal emotional states have their source in unseen (*adṛṣṭa*) but very tangible forces. This gift of power can be in forms other than that of inspiration to the individual. It can be a gift of off-spring as were the sons of Kuntī, or a gift of weapons as to Paraśurāma or Arjuna. The ***muthos*** of divine origin of weapons whether of Achilles, or of Rāma, or a host of other heroes, is certainly more than an aetiological expansion of the fact that good weapons were scarce in ancient times and therefore they were so highly prized that they comprised of the most precious part of the legacy of a family or a line of fighters. Weapons which had been endowed with divine efficacy, by virtue of their godly origin were consecrated in India with the use of *mantras* (*mantrapūta*, literally meaning purified with *mantras*). They were not necessarily better than the usual ones in make but only in 'potency' which was a part of the cultural belief.[5]

A converse to the belief that power and vitality purify, is, that their loss is the primary ***miasma***.. When there is a decline in the natural force, the element or the *satva* of a person, human or divine, the state of impurity begins. Lunar or solar eclipse is the most obvious example of cosmic impurity. In the Indian ***muthos*** of eclipse, the Sun and the Moon were overpowered by Rāhu till Viṣṇu came to free them. All eclipses are a repetition of the first eclipsing of the powers of the Sun and the Moon.

From this it follows that any loss of limb in the body is also impurity. The lame, deformed or misshapen would thus be kept away at the time of an auspicious ceremony. Just as an eclipse is a temporary loss in the cosmic body (*brahmāṇḍa* or the bigger egg), disease or menstruation is a loss in the human body (*piṇḍa*). From physical loss there is one small step to loss of status, wealth, good name (***timee***) or vow. Whatever is essential or elemental to individual existence or public esteem or particular or general health, if lost or even eclipsed, leads to pollution. This ***miasma*** can strike a people or a family and pass on from one generation to another. The children of a succeeding generation may have to pay for the ***miasma,*** that is for impurities, incurred by their forefathers as it happened in the house of Atreus or the line of Sagara.

Where ***miasma*** is not incurred but inherited the penalty is no less severe on that account. And the individual has no choice but to accept his situation and attempt to free himself or herself at any cost. In fact, Antigone lived with pollution which was caused by her father's action and did not rebel against the situation or think of herself as different from her family. The misfortune was her portion ***(moira)***, just as it was of Orestes, or just as it was the duty of Janmejaya to avenge himself over the serpent Takṣaka. The tragic situation of Orestes or Antigone does not arise out of any error (***koros, hamartia*** or ***hubris***) on their part. On the contrary it was their ***moira*** to inherit the pollution. Just as ***menos*** or inspiration is from without, so is ***miasma***. The early Indo-European strain of thought gives too little choice to the individual. Overcome with the prospect of killing his kith and kin, Arjuna was asked by his mentor to take up arms as he was a caste warrior for whom not to fight would have meant lasting infamy. For Arjuna, then, as for Achilles, the demands of ***timee*** are supreme. Public esteem again forces Rāma to desert Sītā. Tragedy or reversal of fortune (***peripeteia***), is not to be attribued to any logic, human or divine, nor to any cosmic justice. That the human condition may be related to some sort of cosmic justice is only a wish stated by Aeschylus and other tragedians. In practice, as a Greek axiom they accept the visitation of pollution to be as arbitrary as the flow of wind or the eruption of a volcano. It was only in the later classical period in Greece, and in the *Smṛti* period of Indian cultural development, that ideas on individual choice, responsibility and interpretation of *dharma* or ***moira*** came to be formulated. The concept of pollution and its cure also came to be questioned. Doubts were expressed if sacrifical blood could wash away impurity. Heraklitos and other Ionian philosophers raised such doubts which may have contributed to the decline of earlier ritual. In India, similar doubts were raised by the Buddhist and Jain thinkers who enouraged the decline of sacrificial immolation in Vedic *yajñas*.

However, ***miasma,*** its ***katharsis,*** and the concept of tragedy belong to an age when individual responsibility had not been socially accepted. Tragedy, thus, only selects that situation of fortune reversal, that visitation of ***miasma,*** in which there can be a concentration upon ***pathos.*** It intensifies ***pathos*** in a state of the helpless innocence of the hapless protagonist. This kind of tragedy is very different from the tragedy of the Christian era, where ***hubris*** and ***koros*** lead a great man to his downfall. In the Greek situation, ***miasma*** generally leads to purification. The tragic predicament is not as pessimistic as has been supposed by scholars for a long time. After the eclipse there must come the full phase. Living through ***miasma*** one attains purity. Orestes is eventually freed of his pollution and the trilogy ends in reconciliation. So does the sacrifice of Janmejaya in the *Mahābhārata*. The enactment of the pollution phase, and ritual mimesis of suffering, results in ***katharsis***. Therefore, tragedy was made part of the total ritual of the annual festivals. Keeping this in mind, it may be argued that the ***katharsis*** that Aristotle talks about was not for the individual spectator alone but for the city as a whole. For the purpose of "ritual promoting or magically seeking salvation an element of death and sorrow was isolated, placed centrally and submitted for all time to reflection and contemplation." (Adrados 322).

Katharsis, then, is also not merely getting rid of the impurity. It is more than a therapeutic restoration; it is a new inflow of vitality. It ends in serene well-wishing and in an awareness that the impurity is gone. This feeling is evident in the last play of the only trilogy that is known to us today, namely *Oresteia*. The note on which the single plays end is different. The bulk of tragedies that have survived and have come to determine our idea of tragedy are antithetical to *Oresteia*. They amplify the note of agony and continuing horror, the feeling that ***miasma*** is permanent and can never be removed. But this note should not determine our over-all view of tragedy and its function (***ergos***). It was actually a trilogy with an appended satyr play that formed the total cycle of ***miasma*** and ***katharsis***; it represented a complete structure of this high and noble form of drama which while touching briefly upon low (***phaule***) subjects, amplified the grave theme of man's eclipse and renewal.

Ancestor Worship and Burial Customs

There is no society in history which has not believed in a continuation of existence after death. Some form of the self, the nature of which is described variously, is believed to exist; the idea of total extinction has had little acceptance. Funeral rites, therefore, have been rites of passage which prepare the dead for a journey to their new destination. A variety in these rites has been caused by the diversity of beliefs held about the nature of the new home of the soul. This home has been mostly envisaged as a permanent one, except in India where the idea of reincarnation gained stability in post-Vedic times. In Greece, the belief in reincarnation had a transitory currency with Pythagoras and his followers. As a corollary to the belief in after-life, there is always the desire to communicate with the departed. It has been thought that they can protect, bless, curse or help the living to perform some of the social functions which they did while they were alive. Thus, the duty of the living towards the dead has been envisaged as a regular affair. The ritual of their propitiation has been a daily obligation in some cultures. In some, it is to be held on marked days like the ***Anthesteria***, in some to be observed on personal dates like the *śrāddha* in *pitṛpakṣa.*[6]

In the lives of Indo-Europeans the presence of ancestors was a continuing reality. The physical body was looked upon as one manifestation of being. The non-corporeal manifestation of being called the ***eidolon*** or *sūkṣmaśarīra,* continued to exist even after death. For the ancients, the ancestors possessed the same quality as the gods, namely of being free of clocktime and earthly space. Like the gods they were invoked to assist, bless or interfere in the daily affairs of men. They were endowed with semi-godhood which offerred protection and promoted cohesion in the family, ***phratria, genos*** or *gotra.*[7] As compared with the human relationship with divinity the relationship between the individual and the *pitṛs* was more intimate and emotionally stronger as it was a conversion of a once very worldly attachment into an other-wordly bond. In ancient drama this feeling for ancestors was more extensively depicted than the relationship between man and the Divine.

In Greek plays, burial rituals and worship at tombs become a part of the dramatic action itself. Such instances are rare in Indian plays. Libations of water by Yudhiṣṭhira to the supposedly dead brothers in *Veṇīsaṃhāra* is an exception. In the Greek tragic ***muthoi***, the frequency of thanatological ritual on stage is accounted for by the culture pattern of desecration and prevention of burial. It was not simply the war vendetta which enouraged desecration of the dead, but a faith that prevention of the rites of passage shall weaken the opponent and his successors.[8] On the contrary, in India, funeral rites (*antyeṣṭi*) are still considered to be too sacred to be disturbed. The dying man is regarded as beyond the pale of animosity and there is a culture pattern of seeking his advice. Bhīṣma's death sermon in the *Mahābhārata* epitomises this norm. When depicted in drama this pattern also promotes a peacefulness, diminishing the pangs of horror. It was under this spirit that the dying hero of Bhāsa's *Urubhaṅgam* is made to give up his life-long hatred for the Pāṇḍavas. On the other hand in the Greek tragic world, horror is intensified by the victor's demand for ransom for the desecrated body of the vanquished. The fury of the desecrater is portrayed as a mark of his heroic wrath and the plaint of the relatives of the dead as a sign of their filial and pitiful obligation. The burial customs thus intensify the tragic conflict in one case while in the other they resolve it into a contemplative repentance.

As an extension of ancestor worship in India, there also evolved the doctrine of *Pitṛṛṇa*. To be free of the debt of ancestors the individual was called upon to beget and raise a son who shall take over the task of providing libations for the family line.

Protection to the Supplicant

According to Greek tribal law, punishment or vengeance (***prorresis***) was to be wreaked on the murderer by the victim's family.[9] It was not the duty of the State as in modern times. In such a situation, it was natural for the guilty to flee his home and seek refuge in extended or permanent exile. The population of exiles in ancient Greece used to be in considerable numbers. Fugitives sought the protection of distant families or of powerful rivals of the victim's house. Normally a third family would not interfere in the process of vengeance and would not thwart the attempts of the victim's family in capturing the murderer. But in the case of an offending relative they would intervene to settle a ransom or bloodprice. Or in the case of very minor crimes, temporary refuge was provided to enable further escape. This was done even in the case of an offender who had incurred great wrath or pollution. Moreover, in Greece and India alike, it was the bounden duty of a reputable person to grant refuge to one who had surrendered or had been unjustly threatened or victimised.[10] In Greece, if the supplicant had sought refuge at a temple, then he became as inviolable as the temple itself. If he were to be turned away, the community may incur the wrath of the deity. As the Supplices say to Pelasgus, "Do what you will/Thy house remains to pay/Find in thy children/Justice is equal/Mark the Justice of Zeus" (*Supplices,* lines 193-96). Some of the well known instances of supplicants seeking successful refuge are daughters of Danaus before Pelasgus, King of Argos; Iphigenia and Hekabe before Achilles;[11] and Odysseus pleading before Hekabe in Troy.[12] In the Indian lore, the classic example is of Sugrīva and Vibhīṣaṇa[13] winning the protection of Rāma. Both the supplicants are exiles who were unfairly banished. A lesser known instance from dramatic literature is that of Śakāra in *Mṛcchakaṭikam* saving his life by becoming a supplicant of Cārudatta. Śakāra need not have been granted protection as he did not deserve it according to any norm. He ought to have been refused, but Cārudatta true to his magnanimity and the moral obligation of granting refuge to a supplicant (*śaraṇāgata*), spared his life.

In contrast with the Greek classical codes, reasons for exile in India were usually political. Here, punishment for homicide was executed by the State, except during the course of a war where vengeance was sought by kith and kin. In case, where shedding of blood caused pollution as in matricide or brāminicide, there was in addition to the penal sentence, a system of purificatory rites to remove *aśauca*. There was, however, the case of the embryo-killer Aśvatthāmā who could not be purged by any rite because of the curse that Kṛṣṇa laid on him.

The Greek method of removing ***miasma*** or *aśauca* consisted of seeking forgiveness at the shrines of divination such as Delphos. But the main practice was to worship Zeus Katharsios,[14] in which the offender was washed with the blood of a consecrated pig. The Greek ***miasma*** removal was a public affair unlike the Indian set of rites like *Cāndrāyaṇa* which were austerities to be practiced by the individual privately.

The Power of Oath

In cultures where writing was far removed from the lives of men, a pledge spoken in the presence of witnesses was as binding as is a promise in writing today. In grave matters the pledge came to be registered in the communal memory and the community waited for the promisory to fulfil his pledge or pay the price that he had himself set for his failure. To swear or to make an oath in trial was much more complicated in ancient societies than it is today. "Oaths and ordeals are two sets of trials accepted by Dharmaśāstra writers" (Pendse 186). To break a vow was not only to lose self-esteem but also to defame the family and its ancestory. In the Greek world, an oath-breaker incurred pollution which he had to get rid of like any other impurity. There was punishment for it even after death. A broken oath was sometimes personified as a pursuing spirit similar to the Erynes.[15] The Indians had no such spirit to be afraid of, but for them loss of esteem and accumulated merit (*puṇya*) was a mortal dread. For the Indo-European, the oath defined his commitment to his fellow beings, which was expected to be enforced by divine agency. In drama, the oath becomes a dominating culture pattern which is used as a device governing the plot.

The instances of vows made by tragic and other heroes are too many to be recounted. Some of the most distinctive examples are the oath of Oedipus to banish from Thebes the killer of Laius; of Herakles to go and seize from Death his friend's wife, Alcestis; of Hippolytus not to give away the secret of Phaedra's love proposal; the vow of Bhīma to dress Draupadī's hair with Duhśāsana's blood; of Arjuna's to kill Jayadratha; of Karṇa's to kill no other Pāṇḍava than Arjuna (*Veṇīsaṃhāra* and *Karṇabhāra*). For keeping the oath the hero has to pay a heavy price. Oedipus is discovered to be a great sinner, even when he escapes the ignominy of being an oath-breaker. Herakles's is a success story, as he is able to keep his oath with no unfortunate results. Hippolytus like Oedipus is taken to his tragic end by his own oath. He is unable to tell his father how his mother proposed to him and thus fails to plead his case. Similar is the plight of Karṇa who gave away the divine armour to keep his word, knowing full well that his charity would result in his death. In the Indo-European situation the world may be lost, but the well-kept word brings everlasting glory. One who loses his life for the sake of his oath has a higher place than one who victoriously fulfils his vow and earns the best of both the worlds.

Oracles and Curses

Divination for the Indo-European was not an effort to decipher future events for the sake of useful knowledge; it was sheer communication with the extra-terrestrial beings who were believed to inhabit the universe as surely and permanently as do the humans. Hence, it was not the calculation of man which was sought to be perfected, but the will of the divine that had to be consulted. The culture pattern here has lesser faith in individual choices; it has a greater trust in discovering what the divine has in store for one. Just as the choice of an individual is influenced by the opinions of his family members and friends today, similarly, for the ancients, the extended family of the supernatural beings, ancestors, sages and prophets had to be conferred with. The oldest method of divination was prophecy by interpreting bird movements. The etymologies of words 'augury' and '*śakuna*' testify this. Other than this, a host of other methods such as throw of dice, weather signs, observation of entrails and vitals of the sacrificed animal (found in Homer and *Yajurveda*), and astralogomancy were widely practised. However, the Greek oracula (***menteia, khresteria***) and the Indian *devavāṇī (siddhavāṇī* or *ākāśavāṇī*) are to be found in maximum vogue in drama. Perhaps in life, too, they were the most popular methods.

In the dramatic structure of a given play an oracular announcement or a *siddhavāṇī* is synchronically present. Like the oath, all action is geared towards it. Its fulfilment in itself does not matter, but the feeling that every event is directly or circuituously leading towards its fulfilment, is what matters most. Whereas an oath fell within the area of human effort *(puruṣārtha* or ***aretee***), a prophecy was supernatural. It was *daiva*, ***dike***, or ***moira***. The purpose of nearly every ***muthos*** was to show the interplay between individual virtue and divine intervention. The result could be tragic or happy.

The oracular tends to dominate the Greek dramatic scene with a force which has no equal in any other drama. This is more true of tragedy, perhaps because the confrontation of the human with the Olympian is what makes up tragedy. The Greek commedies or the satyr plays do not have the terrorizing figures of hoary prophets as these comedies are an exercise in scoffing at the divine, which is depicted as weak and tardy. In the Indian dramatic universe, there is as much intervention of the divine through prophecies or curses as in the Greek plays, though the confrontation here between the human and the divine does not result in tragic ***sparagmos***. To sum up, the human and the divine are constantly juxtaposed in both the theatres even if one theatre chooses to show the horrific form of the divine, while the other depicts its finally conciliatory nature.

There is no need to cite examples of mantic pronouncement from the Greek plays, as there is hardly a play in which an oracle is not announced either through a soothsayer, or a message is not received from the shrine of ***mantike.*** If none of this, a god himself or herself may appear to make a pronouncement, as does Aphrodite in *Hippolytus* and Appollo in *Alcestis.* Sometimes the hero narrates how he is pursuing a course of action under an oracular command as does Oresetes in *Choephori* and in *Iphegenia at Tauris.* In the Indian plays, *daivavāṇī* or *śāpa* is usually not uttered during the course of the play. Of course, there are famous instances of Durvāsā's curse upon Śakuntalā and Cārudatta's upon Pālaka, both pronounced and effected during the plays; so is the Rāma of *Uttararāmacaritam (Act II)* instructed by "bodiless voice" (*'aśarīriṇīvāk'*) to kill the erring Śambūka. However, in most cases the prophecy to be fulfilled in the play is reported to have been made long before the events depicted.[16]

Some Other Common Beliefs

These behaviour patterns of Indo-European life mimetized in Greek and Indian drama, are sustained and enforced by certain beliefs of cosmological signification. These belief are: the parole of the Universal Egg, multitheism (*bahudevatva,* godmingling, ***theokrasis***), perception of five elements as extension of the five senses, notion of time as a cycle of four ages, and metapsychosis. Whereas behaviour patterns such as oath-taking and others give shape to modes of action in drama, these beliefs about the universe define the identity of the individual. The Great Egg does not have a beginning in the same sense as Darwin's first cell. It was not created at a given point of time. The beginning is taking place again and again, after every cycle, or in other words it is taking place all the time. And so is a man or woman (*'piṇḍa'*) eclipsed and renewed, polluted and purified constantly. In this belief-system no being comes to an end; death is not the end of existence; the shades of the departed either inhabit Hades or reincarnate. There is extinction only when there is an end to time. This 'end' or *pralaya* is no end but a suspended animation, a waiting for rebirth.

In some Ṛgvedic hyms, Sky and Earth are looked upon as the first parents; in some other verses the Golden Embryo (*hiraṇyagarbha*) is thought to be floating on primeval waters (*Ṛgveda 10.121.1*). By the age of the *Brāhmaṇas*, 'non being became being; the latter changed into an egg, which after a year by splitting in two became Heaven and Earth; whatever was produced is the sun, which is Brahma" (*Chāndogya Upaniṣad V. 19*).[17] The idea is repeated in the Pelasgian ***muthos*** where Eurynome laid the Egg out of which came the Universe.[18] The Homeric and the Orphic creation ***muthoi*** also mention that black-winged Night was courted by Wind and thus laid a silver Egg from which the Universe was hatched.[19]

From the Great Egg vision of Universe, which accepts the basic sexuality of creation, unlike the Judaic ***muthos*** of genesis which introduces sexuality as an outcome of original sin, we turn to Indo-Greek polytheism. It is not our purpose to trace the common ancestory of Indian and Greek gods, whether through philological methods or through mythographic analysis. For the study of drama, we are content to note that fire sacrifice or *yajña* was the main mode of worship and that in both the pantheons, the divinities do not fall into any hierarchy. There was, of course, Zeus as the supreme force among Olympians, but that mattered little to the ordinary worshipper who had to turn to the appropriate divinity as required by the nature of his plaint. Even Zeus was viewed in many forms. For the Indians the Supreme was a trinity and in Vedic lore the very question of supremacy among gods did not arise. The hostility of the Greek gods towards ardent devotees of rival gods is well known. In the Indian ***muthoi*** similar jealousies are not uncommon. Here, if the worship of a god did not rouse the ire of another, the devotees of different gods were often pitted against one another and each received help from his patron deity (*iṣṭadeva*). Gods were like super heroes patronizing inferior human supplicants. They answered the call of whosoever invoked them. A deity did not wait to measure the merits or demerits of a devotee, justice in the end was not to be meted out by him but by the all seeing Zeus, or by ***dike*** itself, or by the law of *karma.*

In the classical Greek era, and in India long before the Upaniṣadic times, the universe was thought to be made up of five elements; earth, water, fire, air and ether (***aither***) or *ākāśa.* The genesis of this idea was undoubtedly in India from where it travelled to Greece through Persia as a corollary to the doctrine of Ayurveda.[20] In Greece, it exercised the minds of all early Ionian thinkers who tried to discover the primary element out of the five. Without going into details we may mention here that this division into five elements is a method of relating the human body to the cosmic body or egg. The later Indian doctrine of "*yat piṇḍe tat brahmāṇḍe*" (that which is present in the body is also there in the Universe), though stated a little later, had been conceived in the *Puruṣasūkta* of *Ṛgveda Saṃhitā.* The five elements are a division of the Universal material made by the measure of the five senses of smell, taste, sight, touch and hearing. It is through the five senses that the individual *(piṇḍa)* perceives the Universe and it is of these five elements that the body is made of. This equation between the microcosm and the macrocosm came to be established during this time and it held its sway in the European world till Copernicus and Newton replaced it with the notions of modern physics. In the cosmology of five elements, man is not a fragmented creature but a part of the whole; he is in essence and value the same as the Universe.

The Greek belief in the five ages of history was stated only by Hesiod and even though the notion of declining history continued to be entertained widely, Hesoid's demarcation of it into five ages soon lost currency. This belief again was an import from India where it was clearly expressed in the *Aitreya Brāhmaṇa (VII.14)* and later elaborated in the *Mahābhārata* and various other *Smṛti* works. The cycle of four *yugas, manvantaras* and *kalpas* is the most pervasive statement about the universal eclipse and renewal. It was surely as a corollary to this thinking that the belief in reincarnation came to be formulated. If nothing comes to an end, why should it be so for the individual self? The *Upaniṣads* and the *Brāhmaṇa* literature give full evidence of this belief formulated into the concept of *yugas* and reincarnation. It had been a common belief in Egypt, too. Egyptian palingenesis, however, emphasized the migration of the soul into animal and bird forms rather than rebirth into the human, whereas in India all possibilities were accepted.

It should be noted that all these beliefs which heavily influenced the lives of average Greeks and Indians, are projections of a universe that is certainly not anthropocentric. In this universe, Man is created, empowered and destroyed by forces greater than him. These forces are acknowledged as greater than Man and communication with them is regarded as necessary for human well-being. The days on which communication with Divinity or ancestors is attempted in a communal manner are marked as festivals or ***hieromenia***. When drama was enacted on such sacred days, not only did the dramatic ***muthoi*** reflect the non-anthropocentric universe by reiterating these beliefs of the community, the theatrical act itself became a part of the bigger ritual of festival worship.

Notes

1. Though no reasons are given, Graves's view is stated explicity in his *The Greek Myths,* Vol. I (London: Penguin, 1955), 9-10.
2. ***Menos*** and such other divine inspirations are analysed by E.R. Dodds in his *The Greeks and the Irrational* (Berkeley: Univ. of California Press, 1951), 10.
3. By the age of the great playwrights the Greek view of ***ate*** had changed substantially. Now ***ate*** was no more regarded as a happy visitation.
4. To the modern mind the cause of a fit of passion is always internal, at the most arising from the subconscious. The individual must own responsibility for all the acts done in such a fit.
5. In the second volume of his work Grave summarizes

the Greek belief in the divinity of Heracles's weapons. "It has been said that Heracles when he set forth on his labours, Hermes gave him a sword, Apollo a bow and smooth shafted arrows, feathered with eagle feathers; Hephaestos a golden breast plate; and Athene a robe... The gift of Poseidon was a team of horses; that of Zeus, a magnificient and unbreakable shield" (102). In the same way, the Indian belief in supernatural weapons is reflected in many plays. In *Uttararāmacaritam (Act I),* while going through the picture gallery Rāma shows Sītā how the painter had depicted the divine *'jambhṛka'* arrows. Sītā worships them and with the blessings of Rāma her sons are given the weapons in inheritance. The lines from Bhavabhūti are as follows:

> Rāma : *Vandasva devi, divyāstrāṇi.*
> *Brahmādayo brahmahitāya taptvā*
> *Paraḥ sahasraṃ śaradāṃ tapāṃsi*
> *Etānyadarśaṅguravaḥ purāṇaḥ*
> *Svānyeva tejāṃsi tapomayāni.*
> Sītā: *Ṇamo edāṇam (namo etabhyaḥ).*
> Rāma: *Sarvathā edānīṃ tvatprasūtimupasthāsyanti.*
> Sītā: *Aṇugahīdahmi (anugrahītāsmi).*

6. Daily offerings to *Pitṛs; Yājñavalkya Smṛti (Gṛhasthakarma, 102).* They are called *svadhā:*

> *Balikarmasvadhāhomasvādhyāyātithisatkriyāḥ*
> *Bhūtapitramarabrahmamanuṣyāṇāṃ mahāmakhāḥ.*
> Explaining this, the famous *Mitākṣarī* commentary says:
> *Balikarma bhūtayajñaḥ, svadhāpitṛyajñaḥ, homo devyajñāḥ, svādhyāyo brahmayajñaḥ, atithisatkriyā manuṣyayajñaḥ. Ete pañcamahāyajñā aharhaḥ kartavyā nityatvat.*

7. *Pitṛs* as protectors: *Yājñavalkya Smṛti (Srāddhaprakaraṇa 270).*

> *Vasurudrādisutāḥ pitaraḥ śrāddhadevatāḥ/Prīṇayanti manusyāṇāṃ pitṛśrāddheṇa tarpitāḥ/Āyuḥ prajāṃ dhanaṃ vidyā svargaṃ mokṣaṃsukhāni ca/Prayacchati tathā rājyaṃ prītā nṛṇāṃpitāmahāḥ.*

8. Prevention of Burial: "Heracles next vanquished Pyrachmus, king of Euboeans, an ally of Minyans, when he marched against Thebes; and created terror throughout Greece by ordering his body to be torn in two by colts and exposed unburied besides the river Heracleius" (Graves 2) 100.

   Desecration of the corpse to weaken the opponent's spirit: "The power of the dead man was so formidable, his desire for reprisals so certain, that the murderer, whenever he could, tried at least to escape his direct intervention so as to have to answer only to his living avengers. He would, therefore, strive to render him powerless by mutilating his corpse. He would cut off the latter's extremities, the feet, ears and nose, pass a cord through them and fasten the whole to the victim's neck by attaching the cord under the armpits. Deprived in this way, of his sensory organs and means of movements, the victim was rendered inoffensive." Emile Mireaux, *Daily Life in Times of Homer,* trans. from French by Iris Sells (London: George Allen and Unwin, 1959), 173.

9. For details see Mireaux (177). An example is given on the banishment of homicider: "Amphitryon vented his annoyance by throwing a club at one of the cows which had strayed from the heard; it struck her horns, rebounded, and killed Electryon. There upon Amphitryon was banished from Argolis by his uncle Sthenelus... Amphitryon, accompanied by Alceme fled to Thebes, where king Creon purified him and gave his sister Perimede in marriage" (Graves Vol. 2, 85).

10. *Yājñavalkya Smṛti, (Rājadhārma, 326).* Supplicant (*tavāhaṃvādin*)

    Tavāhaṃvadinaṃ klībaṃ nirhetiṃparasaṅgatam/Nahanyādvinivṛttaṃ ca yuddhaprekṣaṇakādikam.

11. Promise of Achilles:

    No, by the foster-son of Ocean's waves,
    Nereus, the sire of Thetis who bare me,
    King Agemmenon shall not touch they child—

Iphigenia at Aulis, Trans. *A.S. Way* (Harvard: Loeb Classical Library) 948-50.

12. Reference to Odysseus's supplication to Hekabe in Troy:

> Hekabe: I saved thee--saved thee--send thee forth the land.
> Odysseus: Ay, thanks to thee, I see the sun's light now. *Hekabe (249-50)*

However, true to his foxy character Odysseus was too mean to accept Hekabe as his supplicant and to return the favour that she had done to him when he was in her power.

13. The supplication of Vibhīṣaṇa as in *Mahāvīracaritam* of Bhavabhūti (Act V):

> Rāma: *Vatsa, brūhi kiṃ sandiśayatāmevaṃvādinaḥ priyasuhṛdo laṅkeśvarasya mahārājavibhīṣaṇasya.*
> Lakṣmaṇa: *Yadā laṅkeśvaraḥ priyasuhṛdityuktamāryeṇa tatkimavaśiṣyate sandeśasya?*
> Rāma: *Yathāḥ saumitriḥ.*
> Śramaṇaḥ: *Anugrahītāsmi.*

14. Worship of Zeus Katharsios: "The usual piacular victim was a young pig, which was held over the head of the guilty, as we see Apollo holding it over Orestes in a vase painting that represents his purification. And the blood of the slaughtered animal was then poured over his hands, with invocation to Zeus Katharsios. In some accounts bathing in water of a river or the sea appears to have been a necessary part of the ceremony." L.R. Farnell, *Cults of the Greek States,* Vol. 1 (Oxford: 1896) 69.

15. Oath Personified: "The strength of this belief in the religious character of the oath is shown by passages in Homer which speak of the punishment of oath-breaker after death, and by the lines of Hesiod's *Theogony* where the oath is already personified as a child of the lower world, born to be 'the scourge of men'; while in Sophocles he is spoken of as all seeing child of Zeus" (Farnell 70).

16. Of the horrible curses in Greek drama some glaring examples are: Tiresias's curse upon Oedipus; Theseus's upon his son Hippolytus; Polymestor's upon Hekabe that she shall drown in the sea and become a dog before she submerges and that shall Kassandra and Agememnon shall be killed.
17. Also in *Śatapatha Brāhmaṇa:* "In the beginning it was all water. They the waters wished to be reproduced. They fermented and got heated with devotion. At this point a golden egg came into being which floated on waters for a whole year. In a year's time a man, a Prājāpatī was produced therefrom. He broke open this golden egg" (XI.1.6.1.)
18. Graves gives a short account in his *Greek Mythology* (Vol. 2, 18).
19. See on page 30 of *Greek Mythology* Vol. 1, a summary of the myth as found in various sources.
20. Says J. Filliozat, "That is why there are between Indian and Greek medicines, so very particular and precise similarities which are not easy to ascribe to chance." *The Classical Doctrine of Indian Medicine* (Delhi: Munshiram Manohar Lal, 1964). Åyurveda, which can be traced back to as early as *Atharva Saṃhitā* recognizes air, fire and water as three elements that make up the human body, (*vāta, pitta* and *kapha*). The Greek medicine followed the same and recognized the three as the elements of the human body. This is evident from Hippocratic manuals and other great similarities given in detail by Filliozat. The Greek medicine taken up by Arabs was brought back into India where it still survives as a sister system to Ayurveda and is known as *'Unānī'* (Greek) medicine.

4

Drama as Festive Ritual

MODERN theatre-goers cannot conceive of a theatrical performance scheduled according to certain dates marked as sacred in the calender. But such was the compulsion in ancient times that festivals could be held on certain auspicious days only. Much has been written on the rhythms of these days, their links with the seasonal and astronomical cycles. Whatever the logic, the purpose behind these fixations was always unambiguously to celebrate the visitation of something greater than Man. Theatre was an integral part of this event. It was a substructure of the macro-structure of the feast itself. It took the shape it did because it was enacted as one essential ceremony in a chain of many ceremonies.

In Europe festive drama proper died with the Morality Plays. Drama of sacred action or hieropraxis as we have called it, was a thing of the past even in the Elizabethan times. Since then, spectators have crowded into play-houses largely for entertainment which the purists have always condemned as morally detrimental and the connoisseurs have credited with aesthetic education. Theatre going has become voluntary not obligatory, and the value of theatre itself has become debatable. But such a debate would have been irrelevant to a Greek and other ancient theatre visitors for whom participation was either obligatory or a near compulsion under the sway of festive euphoria. Theatre had to be attended in the same manner as many other festive rituals had to be enacted. There was no need for evaluation of theatrical activity in isolation from the necessity of the festival itself. Such a need for evaluation arose mainly for the Europeans who wished to be reassured that dramatic entertainment was not a waste of time. Drama had to be preserved from not merely falling into vulgarity and cheapness, but was also to be saved from the Church for whom the very act of ***mimesis*** or impersonation was an ontological sin.

In Europe, the grounds for delinking drama from the sacred were many. The link between theatre and the sacred was rediscovered when the modern anthropological studies introduced the European public to theatrical activities of Asia and Africa. Europeans, then renewed their interest in festive theatre. They started looking for the origin of their own theatre in ritual. This led to the emergence of many theories from Frazer ownwards about the ritual origin, not only of drama, but of myth, poetry and all other performance. This need to theorize about the transition from ritual to dramatic entertainment was a Euro-American imperative. It was the urge of a desacralized culture, of a non-festive society, that first created the dichotomy between ritual and entertainment and later attempted to explain it. For a festive society such as of India, where this dichotomy has not yet come into existence, such an enquiry is futile. For example, the question whether the *Rāmāyaṇa* enactment is worship or entertainment is absurd to the north Indian players and the audience who hold it annually in October. Scores of other dance-dramas with religious stories are still performed in India on holy days and the participants do not think of them as just drama or sanctified ceremony. For them they are not distinct. Entertainment is combined with worship. Even for the performer, the individual actor, director or drummer, the ultimate aim "is not to 'earn his living' by his participation in the sacred play of Hinduism, but to reach that total absorption in his *sacer ludus* that does not last temporarily—as in ordinary play—but eternally (*mokṣa*)" (Kersenboom-Story xvii).

Drama and Ritual

This is not to assert that there is no difference between

ritual proper, say a sacrifice made in a temple or a market-place, and the enactment of a play with a sacrificial episode such as in *Iphigenia at Aulis*. Ritual worship by an individual is an enactment with the specific purpose of seeking fulfilment of a wish. It may be done by the individual, or the community as a whole. But the prime purpose of a ritual act is to seek a benediction. In case a ritual is not a prayer, it may be enacted for the recognition of a social contract or for a pledge such as marriage. In every case it is always a well-declared demand. But in drama, the purpose of enactment changes from demand to pleasure. A ritual is performed to purge a city, to get rid of a plague, to seek the death of an enemy, to sanctify an alliance, but a dramatic enactment is done only to please and perhaps to instruct. How does, then, ancient drama differ from the modern secular one, if both are performed to entertain? It differs in a very vital way. The ancient theatre sought to please both gods and men at the same time, whereas secular drama fulfils human needs only. To please divinities and humans simultaneously was quite in harmony with the very nature of a festival in which the sacred and the profane came together. As noted by many, the feast is a twilight time, a "liminal state," when an abnormal visitation takes place, when the profane time changes into sacred time.[1]

Sacred drama could thus be called ritual, only so far as it serves the purpose inherent in the nature of every celebration, that is to please a divinity. Ample statements to this effect may be found in Indian texts and the records of the presence of Dionysus's ***eidolon*** in Greek theatre indicates the same purpose.

We may also add in passing that another important feature common to both ritual and drama, is ***mimesis***. Both enact what is not present in reality but is posited to be present through a sign, ***agalma, eidolon*** or a dramatis persona. But again we must distinguish between ritual and drama by recognizing their different ends. One is prayer, the other is pleasure. One is essentially a rite of passage, from the point of not having to having, from being here to there, whereas the other may be called a rite of message, from person to persons or from the artist to audience. Attempts to place ritual, myth and drama in a chain of evolutionary growth are not a representation of actual history but a result of the Darwinian mind-set. We need not look upon them as one leading to another. They all have co-existed and shall continue to do so. With change of purpose, one form changes into the other. Many rituals grow into entertainments when the purpose of their performance is altered. For example, the Garbā dances of Gujarat, were performed till the last decade on a specific religious occasion, but they are now being danced as a form of secular celebration. Many rituals were originally entertainments which became converted into ritualistic repetitions for maintenance of tradition. The swing festival, known in North India as '*teej*,' now done ritually, was an entertainment of the rainy season. It may also be added that the ends of ritual, ***muthos*** and drama are not entirely exclusive, but as we have said, they often coincide or overlap. This realization will make it easier to understand why certain rituals change into drama whereas others remain religious acts.

The Nucleus of Dance in Greek Theatre

Looking at the visual and aural media of ancient theatre, we find that dance was the nucleus around which the superstructure of the performance script had grown. For tragedy, Aristotle has observed that it had grown out of dithyramb, a two-step dance. Likewise, the ***phallika*** was not far from dancing. Similarly, in the Indian theatre, dance was no less cardinal. In the history of Greek drama it is not difficult to trace how the ritual dance of worship, whether of ancestors, of Dionysus, or of both, transformed itself into the classical plays. Even those who question Aristotle's theory of the growth of tragedy from dithyramb on grounds of the absence of the mimetic, agonic and threnodic elements in dithyramb (Adrados 1-3), believe that dance formation provided a stable nucleus of development. F. Adrados, who has put forward the hypothesis that the

komos was the primary structure from which the dramatic structure of both tragedy and comedy developed, credits dance with the potentiality of dramatic growth. He explains:

> Every dramatic ritual is always based on dance. The passion and agon are simple variants of it, while the individual characters, with varying mimesis are an emanation. It is at the same time liturgy and amusement and efficacious action for warding-off evil and promoting fertility, war or the chase. In the ritual even without mask the human being is transformed, in communion with the life of animals or gods or of his ancestors, who are incarnate or in different symbols. (Adrados 231)

As early as Homer the recitation of the godly deeds by a bard was combined with dancing (*Odyssey VIII.266-78*). Here Demodocus sings of the love tale of Ares and Aphrodite, while the dancers gather around him. However, it is not clear from Homer's account whether the dance was to illustrate the deeds in the song. But we do know that as early as Homer there was a form of dancing which illustrated song and was called ***huporkhema***. The element of ***mimesis*** being already present in this way in dance, its introduction into theatre need not have waited for the arrival of dramatists like Thespis and Arion. It also seems logical that ***huporkhema*** as dance was already an established combination of mimesis and ***muthos***. If the Phacian dancers were mimetic of Demodocus's song, then we already have at this stage the essential elements of a later dramatic performance script. What needed to be added was the epirrhematic dialogue, which by its very late addition cannot be said to be of nuclear importance. We may even go on to assert further that as dialogue gained more and more importance, the dance content shriveled and this took theatre further away from sacredness. We may say that as a rule, greater the dance content of a performance script, the closer is its affinity to visual symbolism and ritual sanctity. The history of Greek drama illustrates this hypothesis better than any other theatre history. In early periods of Greek theatre, dance and its formations were the chief reasons for dividing the performance space into a large orchestra for chorus and a small platform for the actors (***hupokrites)***, as drama retained its ritualistic nature. Marking out a large space for dance was one way of affirming its dominance. On the other hand, ancient Indian theatre also used dance in a major way, but it did not mark out a large area for dance as it did not employ group dancing. Here the single dancer-actor was used to achieve the same end, that is foregrounding dance through an elaborate code of body and hand gestures.

Audience Participation

For sacred drama, deep participation by the viewers must be an ensured thing. For the Greeks it was done by the highly emotive musical orchestra around which the audience gathered. That this sort of gathering facilitates a more intense participation than the one allowed by the apron or proscenium stage, is a theory which has gathered considerable force these days. In my opinion, physical proximity or making the whole environment a performance space does not by itself ensure intensity of audience response. Proximity alone does not move the audience; communicability does more to enthrall them. Nor should it be thought that sitting in a ritual circle changes the status of the audience from theatre spectators to ritual doers. In a ritual there are no spectators but only a varying degree of doers. It is doubtful if the ancient audience thought of themselves as modern entertainees, yet they were well aware of the distinction between the player and the watcher which seems to be blurred for modern proponents of environmental theatre and audience participation. Ancient playgoing was a festive rite alright but one participated in it as only as a spectator. The kind of circle that was formed by the Greek audience was a remnant of the seating meant for the choral lyrics from which the dramatic forms had emerged.

There were numerous other valid reasons for the Greek to feel like a strong participator in the overall phenomenon of theatre events. There were, of course, foreigners who came from long distances, the dignitaries who were part of the show, prisoners who had a reprieve from confinement, but the average citizen often had something at stake, the chance of his tribal ***choregos*** winning the prize. May be a child or a relative of his was a member of the chorus. In addition to all this the citizen was doing the same thing which the whole hierarchy of the city was doing and the god Dionysus himself was doing. The presence of Dionysus in the Athenian theatre had many implications. This god was here in the audience just as he or other gods were often to appear among the actors. Dionysus on one side stood as an ***eidolon,*** the divine specatator, and on the other as a divine dramatis persona. This godly visitation makes the festive spot a sacred space and the festive time a holy moment. Even today in the Rām Līlā at Rām Nagar (Benaras) the gods (*devatās*) are enacted as watching the Līlā. The divine presence reinforces the liminality of festivals, which consists of an intermingling of the routine and the ecstatic, of the humdrum and the miraculous.

Another activity which greatly promoted audience participation was a preview of the plays held one day before the beginning of the Dionysian festival. This so called ***pro-agon,*** reported to have been held on the eighth day of ***Elaphabolion,*** called upon the playwrights to mount a temporary platform along with their actors and enunciate the subject of their plays. It is thought that at this moment the actors did not wear any masks. This sort of informal meeting with the performers must have raised many expectations among the more urbane spectators (Pickard-Cambridge 67).

Origin of Indian Drama

The situation of Indian dramatic performances in festive setting is more complicated. The history of theatrical shows is not so well documented here as in Greece. There is no mention even in the *NŚ* about a precedental performance genre from which theatre could be said to have developed. There are, of course, many speculations by scholars about what could have possibly led to the creation of *daśarūpakas*, the ten genres of early drama. For the Orientalists of late nineteenth and early twenthieth centuries, dialogue was the most essential element in drama. They were influenced by the prejudices of European realistic theatre. These scholars, therefore, ransacked Sanskrit literature for the earliest examples of dialogue and found them in the *Saṃhitās* of the *Ṛgveda*. Hence developed the theory of Vedic dialogues as precursors of Indian drama. As some examples of mime have been referred to in earlier Sanskrit texts, it was thought by one set of Sanskritists that some sort of puppetry was the precedental form of Indian theatre. Similarly, a group of scholars emphasised the secrets that the etymology of the word '*sūtradhāra*' may hold. This prologue speaker and director, it was argued, was originally a string manipulator of the puppets who retained the earlier nomenclature even when he became the play manager. It was overlooked by the proponents of this theory that he may have been called *sūtradhāra* (thread-bearer) because like all architects he carried a thread to measure the land for the theatre building which was constructed anew each time a performance session was held. Besides, the master director is called *ācārya* in the *NŚ*, and he was most likely not the same as the *śutradhāra*. Apart from these speculations on the origin, there was the view that Indian drama could not have come to its own without the availability of the highly developed ***muthoi*** structure of the *Rāmāyaṇa* and the *Mahābhārata*. This view, mainly championed by Keith, postulated that drama came into being when the narrators (*vyāsas*) of these ***muthoi*** began gesticulating while narrating the epics.

The *Nāṭyaśāstra,* too, has a story about the birth of drama which like all ***muthoi*** of origin needs to be decoded. According to the *NŚ*, the gods pleaded with Brahmā to create drama so that the knowledge of the *Vedas* became accessible to all castes. Brahmā gratified them by extracting words out of *Ṛk*, song out of *Sāma, abhinaya* out of *Yajus* and *rasa* out of *Atharva Veda* and combined them with ***muthoi*** or *itihāsa* to complete the Fifth Veda, called *Nāṭyaveda*. (*NŚ1:11-19*). Now this story is what has been called an aetiological myth, i.e., an invention to comment upon something which is already in existence and not a myth which proposes to trace the history of a thing's origin. The *nātya*-origin story (*nāṭyotpatti*) only relates the four essential elements of theatre (*pāṭhya, gāna, abhinaya* and *rasa*) to the Vedic ritual and establishes the sanctity and efficacy of *nāṭya* as the Fifth Veda. It demonstrates that being born of the same elements as the other four vedas, the Fifth Veda has the power to confer the same knowledge. Here, while we may accept the efficacy of the Fifth Veda, we cannot conclude that the actual text of *Ṛk* (whether or not in the form of dialogues), the modes of Sāman chants (of various *śākhās*), the actual movements and stances of the *adhvaryu* priests at Vedic sacrifices, and the theory behind the herbal preparations of Ayurvedic medicine, all these, actually led to the creation of dialogue, music, *abhinaya* and *rasa* theory respectively, as found in the *NŚ*. The *naṭyotpatti* story only implies that these above stated four channels are also a way to knowledge. They provide the same highest kind of knowlege which is available to the high caste initiates who study for the four *Vedas*. Thus, to look for the historical origins of theatre in the *Vedas* is to mistake the matter for the spirit, the form for the substance.

At the same time it cannot be denied that there must have been modes of performance using words, music and *abhinaya* in the Vedic age. And there must have existed some well defined relationship between modes of performance and the Vedic sacrificial ritual. Regarding this relationship it may be pointed out that the Vedic ritual practice isolated, even ossified, at a very early period in history. It was resistant to change because the '*vedavyavahāra*' or the Vedic ritual was made to keep a distinct identity and was not allowed to be polluted by '*lokavyavahāra*' or the ever changing practices of ordinary rituals. For this reason, setting of the Vedic *mantras* to secular musical scales and styles has always been forbidden. *Mantras* are chanted or sung only in the manner handed down by tradition. It must have been the same for early secular applications of *abhinaya*. They must have been different, distinct and distant from the Vedic movements of *adhvaryu.* The secular *abhinaya* and music had its own independent development and became the groundwork for the four-channelled *abhinaya* of the *NŚ*.

From all this we can only conclude that the origins of Indian drama are totally lost in hoary antiquity and the earliest records of performance modes available to us are the *daśarūpakas* as described in the *NŚ* itself. Obviously, the forms by the time of the *NŚ* were mature and well in vogue to acquire an exhalted position, else drama could not have dared to claim for itself the status of the Fifth Veda. At the same time, as is recorded in the *NŚ* too, it suffered a temporary loss of reputation and invited strict censure, otherwise such brave attempts to restore it to its hallowed position could not have been made.

We have argued that in the case of Greek drama, dance was the nucleus of every dramatic genre and was most expressive of the festive spirit. Was there, then, a comparable function of dance in the making of Indian theatre? It can be said without hesitation that it was so. But the manner in which dance came to be used was very different. It was very much a major part of the total structure of performance, though not in so obvious a way as in the Greek plays. There every dramatic mode whether tragic, comic or satyric was woven around a choric centre which contained a large dance group. In Indian theatre, *abhinaya* and *itivṛtta* (like ***mimesis*** and ***muthos***) combined with *nṛtta,* but there was no presence of large groups. Here the dancer/actor was more often than not, solitary. He or she was joined by other dancers for short intervals, but even the pure dance-work was done by a single person. An actor's body work, even while performing the *abhinaya* was dance based, especially when called upon to adopt the *kaiśikī vṛtti.* In fact, it is important to note that in performance terminology the words for acting (*nāṭya*) and dancing (*nṛtta* or *nṛtya*) often overlap. Transition from one to the other only requires a slight change of intent. *Nṛtta* has been defined as mere movement of the body (*'nṛttaṃ tu gātra vikṣepamātraṃ tu'*)[2] and *nāṭya* as movement with meaning (*'arthabhāvakam' NŚ 4:232*). Drama is mostly *nāṭya,* but it is not fanciful to suggest that *nāṭya* came into being from *nṛtta*, and that an account of this accretion can be traced to the text of the *NŚ* itself.

The initial productions of Bharata Muni, as the legend of the origin of drama says, were devoid of *kaiśikī vṛtti* or the erotic mode requiring plenty of dance and embellished movements. Such productions, while good enough for the heavenly audience of rarefied taste, would not have been entirely palatable to the earthly spectators. Anticipating this Brahmā suggested that Bharata Muni should evolve *kaiśikī* productions and for this provided him with *apsarās* who could perform various *karaṇas* and *aṅgahāras*. These embellished body postures had been created by Śiva through mediative rememberance. When Brahmā and the Muni paid a visit to Śiva, they were told that Śiva had 'remembered' (*smṛtam*) *nṛtta* with all its *karaṇas* and *aṅgahāras* while dancing at twilight. Thus we see that dance is without origin; it is primeval. As Abhinavagupta says, Śiva did not create dance, he only remembered it ("*mayā api idaṃ smṛtaṃ nṛttaṃ*"); 'remembered,' shows that *nṛtta* existed earlier only to be recalled; that it is without origin ('*smṛtaṃ iti anāditvaṃ darśayati*' *NŚ 4:13*). On Śiva's behest, Taṇḍu taught Bharata Muni all the *karaṇas* and their derivatives asking him to use them with thoroughness ('*samyaka prayujyatāṃ*'4:11), particularly in *vardhamāna* and *āsārita* songs of *pūrvaraṅga*.

The *piṇḍībandhas* and the *āsārita* songs were sung right after the *yavanikā* (curtain?) was cast aside and during the course of singing, pure dance consisting of worshipful poses called *piṇḍībandhas* was performed. A question is raised in the *Nāṭyaśāstra* as to why pure dance or *nṛtta* should be employed here, when *nṛtta* is devoid of *abhinaya*. In answer, it is said that *nṛtta* is employed as it is essential, auspicious and worshipful (*NŚ 21: 262-74*). The devotional rituality of dance was brought out by the *piṇḍībandhas* which were descriptive of the attributes of various gods and goddesses (that is, of their vehicles, standing postures, weapons and symbols). '*Piṇḍī*,' explains Abhinavagupta, is the physicality of form ('*piṇḍī ādhāra aṅgādi saṅghātaḥ*,' *Ab. NŚ 4: 254*) and, therefore, those gesture of dance (*karaṇas and aṅgahāras*) which make up (*'badhyate'*) the form of the divinities are called *piṇḍībandhas* (*"ābaddhyate, sampādyate, punar anena iti piṇḍībandhaḥ. Ante ca bhagavata eva vyaktarūpasya piṇḍībandho bhaviṣyati" Ab. NŚ 4:254-59)*. From this it is clear that the dance postures or the semiotic codes called *aṅgahāras* have been used from the earliest times as dramatic signs representing dieties. That Śiva 'remembered' them reinforces this hypothesis. That the function of *nṛtta* is purely religious for the sake of unseen benefit (*adṛṣṭa*), is quite obvious. For this reason *piṇḍībandhas* are to be used in the *pūrvaraṅga*. Abhinvagupta makes the point by noting:

> Whichever god is invoked, it is essential to placate him or her through dance. One should indicate his weapons, vehicle, deeds and temper, through gestures. For instance, while acting out the stanza *'pādāgrasthitayā...'* (of *Ratnāvalī*) if the posture (*karaṇa*) called *'talapuṣpapuṭa'* is performed then it results in the propitiation of Devī. By performing the posture of placing a hand on the forehead (the *karaṇa* called *nistaṃbhitam*, no. 64) one pleases Śiva. Holding of hand as in *nikuṭṭita karaṇa* or posture, indicates the trident. The *karaṇa 'garuḍaplutaka'* signifies the speed and shape of an eagle; *'gaṅgāvataraṇa'* stands for the *piṇḍī* called *'dhārā'*...(*"Etaduktaṃ bhavati... yā kācit devatā iti ucyate tasyāḥ paścānnṛtena paritoṣaṇaṃ kāryam. Tanmadhye ca tadīyāyudhavāhanakarmabhāvābhya (dya) nukārī aṅgaprayogo vidheyaḥ. Ata eva "pādāgrasthitayā" (Ratnāvalī 1:1) ityatra talapuṣpapuṭakaraṇena karmaṇā viśeṣasūcakena bhagavatyāḥ paritoṣaṇaṃ sampādyate. 'Tilake ca karaḥ sthāpya' ityabhinayena bhagavataḥ paritoṣaḥ. 'Nikuṭṭitau yadā hastau' ityanena triśūlākṛtiryā kāyasampattiḥ. Garuḍaplutakena tārkṣyākāragatisūcanaṃ, gaṅgāvatareṇa dhārāpiṇḍī,..." (NŚ Ab. 4:257)*.

The truth behind this story from the *NŚ* therefore, is that *nṛtta* which was initally performed for worship, was later transformed into a medium of dramatic mimesis. The creation of the mimetic gestures, that is of the *karaṇas* and *aṅgahāras*, first took place in dancing. What was earlier merely throwing about of limbs (*'nṛttaṃ tu aṅgavikṣepa mātram,' Saṅgīta Ratnākara, Nartana Adhyāya 7:27*) was invested with a deeper significance. From here began the codification of the language of *abhinaya*. This later developed into an intricate semiology of Indian dance which also became the basic language of theatrical communication. It was employed not only for embellishment as in *kaiśikī vṛtti* but for all other *vṛttis* as well. The four dramatic *vṛttis* used various kinds of postures and hand movements much in the same manner as in dancing. In fact, the use of intricate gestures was part of all acting throughout the history of Indian theatre, not only for performing erotic themes in *nāṭyadharmī* mode of production, but for the expression of heroic, frightful and all other emotions to be done in the *lokadharmī* mode, too. The manner in which dance is used for *anukaraṇa* or dramatic creation shall be dealt with in the relevant place while elaborating upon *āṅgika abhinaya.*

Indian Festive Setting

Was Indian drama performed only on festive occasion like the Greek drama? It must be admitted that the records of performances in India are not so detailed as they are on the Greek side. Also, even though Indian drama was basically festive, it did not remain under such severe restrictions as were imposed upon Greek theatre. The Greek performances were limited to major festivals as there are no accounts of private or nonfestive performances. It seems that dramatic genres performed by roving troups were either not much in vogue in Greece or have gone unrecorded. But in India, other than the private performances of well-known dramatic genres, a host of popular enactments like *ḍombikā, rāsaka, hallīsaka* and many others have always been held on the occasion of family celebrations. Moreover, the number of public festivals in India has always been staggeringly large.[3] Unlike two or three dramatic festivals of ***Lenaia, Katagrous*** or rural ***Dionysia*** in the month of ***Poseidon*** (December), or of ***Dionysus Eleuthereus*** in ***Elaphebolion*** (March) which were all the occasions in Greece, in India, the occasions were unlimited and varied. Here, not only the State but also the temples and families sponsored feasts which would include dramatic performances. In fact, '*samāja*' (performance) was a regular feature of any festival (*utsava*) and most wealthy cities took pride in being Ayodhyā-like which is fondly remembered by Bharata as 'full of festive performances' ('*samājotsavaśālinī*,' *Vālmīkiya Rāmayaṇa, Ayodhyākāṇḍa* 51:23). The first ever production of a play, according to the story in the *NŚ*, was undertaken by Bharata Muni on Brahmā's orders. The play called '*Amṛtamanthana*' was performed on the occasion of the 'banner festival of Indra,' which was described as the most appropriate time for a play, (*mahānayaṃ prayogasya samaya pratyupasthitaḥ/Ayaṃ dhvajamahaḥ mahendrasya pravartate*,' *NŚ 1:54*). Similarly, the temples held their own festivals on the days sacred to their deities and drama was part of the fare. All the three famous plays of Bhavabhūti were performed during the annual car-ambulation (*rathayātrā*) festival of some famous Śiva temple of his times, where people from many parts of India participated ('*sannipatitaśca bhagavataḥ kālapriyanāthasya yātrāprasaṅgena nānādigantavastavyojanāḥ*,' *Mālatīmādhavam*).

Community Involvement

Having noted how dramatic performances were held mainly on festivals, let us also examine the nature of community involvement in these performances. One thing may be stated right in the beginning. Unlike the Greek theatre which consisted of sufficient amateur participants, the Indian performers, except for some dancers who performed portions of *pūrvaraṅga*, were all professionals designated as '*naṭa*,' '*śailūṣa*,' etc., by caste. About the Hellenic productions we know that dramatists, who were themselves respectable citizens, trained men and boys of good birth to make up the chorus. Only the actors were a class apart named as ***tragadoi*** or ***commodoi***, and as professionals they travelled from place to place. Like them, all the performers of the Indian stage were a caste apart, and these along with the musicians had been relegated to the *śūdra* (not untouchable) category at a fairly early period in history. Whether Bharata Muni himself was a *śūdra* or not, is a question I have discussed elsewhere.[4] But these performers, also known by the caste appellation of '*bharatas*,' were always on the move and were thus temporary, though regular, visitors to a performance location. Similar to the Greek playwright-director, their director also had a high social status and belonged to an upper caste. This master-director (*nāṭyācārya*) was supposed to consecrate the theatre-house with *mantras* which could not be taught to a *śūdra (NŚ 3:2.82,* etc.).

Inferring from the second and third chapters of the *NŚ*, it can safely be said that very often a king or a local chieftain engaged a company and sponsored the performances of drama in the same spirit as he did a Vedic *yajña.* He performed the role of the *yajamāna* with a responsibility and thoroughness which was same as in a sacrifice. Needless to say that his being at the helm of affairs would also involve whole hierarchy under him. We shall give below a brief summary of the manner in which the theatre-house was constructed and consecrated to indicate the indispensable participation of the whole community which had invited the performers.

For the construction of a play-house an appropriate spot was chosen and after astrological consultations the area was purified with Vedic incantations. Foundations of the building were laid to the blowing of conches and trumpets, while all inauspicious, stigmatic and mendicant people were kept away. Many sacrifices of food and flowers were offered to the ten directions. Brahmins were fed sumptuously and at a later auspicious hour the walls were raised. This was followed by the placing of wooden pillars by the *nāṭyācārya,* who had been fasting for three days. The four pillars were named after the four castes and were decorated in white, red, yellow and blue colours with the distribution of foods of the same colours to the members of the four castes. Each *varṇa* was given the food of his caste colour, for instance, white milk-rice for the Bṛahmins and so on. Gold, copper, silver and iron were respectively placed in the foundations of these pillars. The pillars were then raised with great care and any mishap in the process was thought to be indicative of a social misfortune. Vedic chants and din of instruments filled the air while the four pillars, and many more were raised. After this the architects raised the various other parts of the theatre-house. And then began a week long consecration of the whole building.

For seven days cows were kept inside the theatre and brahmins carried out a *japa.* The *nāṭyācārya* fasted again for three days and then spinkled the area with holy waters. He then dressed himself in new wear and performed the ceremony of inviting the various gods and goddesses to come and take their stations located in the different parts of the building. He sought their help and protection, prayed for the well-being of the king/sponsor, defeat of enemies and other obstacles, welfare of cows and brahmins and the flourishing of drama. Elaborate worship with offerings of cereals, milk, meats and others foods were made to all the deities according to prescriptions. After this, all the musical instruments were given new covers and worshipped with flowers, incese and lights. The *jarjara* pole was offered rich oblations. The king-sponsor and the dancing girls were also worshipped with music, *mantras,* sweets and show of lights. They were praised for high birth and fine accomplishments. (This seems to suggest that dancers were perhaps non-professionals from upper classes who were given a place on the stage for ritualistic potency.) The king was then blessed by the *nāṭyācārya* wishing the success of performance. A pitcher was then ritually smashed by the *nāṭyācārya,* symbolically crushing all obstacles. And finally, the theatre was made to resound with the din of war cries, calls, and shouts, the sound of conches, drums and trumpets. Duels were enacted and any one hurt at this moment signalled a good omen. It is stated that this *raṅgapūjana* or theatre-house worship is most auspicious for the sponsor, the young, children and the aged of the 'city and the countryside' (*'purasya janapadasya ca' NŚ 3:94*). Any slackness in this brings great misfortune.

The above account amply illustrates the extensive and deep involvement of all the sections of the audience population whether of a city or a village. It must not be forgotten that in those days it was customary to make a new theatre-house for each performance cycle. The construction was in wood and was obviously dismantled once it had served its purpose. It was, like a sacrificial alter, made for one event and for the sole purpose of *nāṭya,* a divine offering.

Notes

1. Using the Latin 'limen' (threshold), Victor Turner in his *Ritual Process* (Ithaca: Cornell UP, 1969), has developed the term liminality to denote the state of marginality of experience.This occurs when a person is passing from one status to another, as in the rites of passage or when one is living outside the social structure as a beggar, clown or hermit, etc. On a festive occasion under the slackening of social constraints and diffusion of roles, a greater degree of liminality prevails and the permanently liminal people take the lead in celebrations. Liminality also creates the conditions necessary for 'communitas,' (a deeply shared experience by small and large groups which is a value and an end in itself). As Turner says, "I would argue that it is in liminality that communitas emerges, if not as spontaneous expression of socialbility, at least in a cultural normative form." *Drama, Fields and Metaphors* (Ithaca: Cornell UP, 1974) 232. This liminality as Turner has also admitted, is vital to drama, religion, arts and culture. For the audience of a dramatic performance, the constraints of the daily consciousness of self versus others are slackened or even obliterated if the absorption is intense, the normal world is set aside from which there is a passage to the worlds of theatric reality. In theatre, a myth/***muthos*** is created and its sacred world is actualised in a non-temporal time frame. As Mircea Eliade has put it, "This mythic or sacred time is qualitatively different from profane time, from the continuous and irre-

versible time of our everyday, de-sacralized existence. In narrating a myth, one reactualises, in some sort, the sacred time in which the events narrated took place. (This, moreover, is why the myths, in traditional societies, are not to be told however, or whenever one likes; they can be recited during sacred seasons, in the bush and at night, or around the fire after or before the rituals, etc). In a word, the myth is supposed to happen—if one may say so—in a non-temporal time, in an instant without duration, as certain mystics and philosophers conceived of eternity." Mircea Eliade, *Images and Symbols* (New York: Sheed and Ward, 1952) 57.

2. The *NŚ* has not made the triple distinction between *nāṭya, nṛtya* and *nṛtta,* something which became the norm in medieval times. For the *NŚ*, there is only *nāṭya* and *nṛtta. Nṛtta* is not defined at length, but it is implied that it was not required to convey the meaning of a song, nor any other specific message. (*'na gītārthasambaddhaṃ na cāpyarthasyabhāvakam' NŚ 4: 262)*. That is, it is defnined as a movement of limbs without role acting or without the gestural rendering of a story. But all the same, it conveys some sense and in that respect it may be called *'abhinaya'* of that sense, as it (*nṛtta*) is certainly not meaningless or futile. The thirteenth century A.D. work, *Saṅgītaratnākara* and its successive works have defined *nṛtta* along the same lines. "It is the throwing about of limbs and is without any *abhinaya* but it uses the same movements of the body which are prescribed for *āṅgika (abhinaya.)* (*'gātravikṣepamātraṃ tu sarvābhinayavarjitam /āṅgikokta-prakāreṇa nṛttaṃ nṛttavido viduḥ' Saṅgītaratnākara Nartana Adhyāya 7:27)*. As in the *NŚ*, so in *S.R.*, *nṛtta* is acknolweged to be of two sorts, *tāṇḍava* (masculine, harsh) and *lāsya* (feminine, soft). In addition, some more classifications of *nṛtta* are made: *viṣam* ('rope walking,' the acrobatic kind), *vikaṭa* ('fierce looking' as in the form called *peraṇī'*), and *laghu* (with little use

of *aṅgahāras* as in rural feminine dances). Now, in addition to *nāṭya* and *nṛtta*, the medieval authors thought it necessary to classify dance also as '*nṛtya*' "that which express the emotions through *abhinaya* of the body is called *nṛtya* and which the experts of *nṛtya* also call by the name *mārga*." ('*Āṅgikābhinayaireva bhāvāneva vyanakti yat/ tannṛtyaṃ mārgaśabdena prasiddhaṃ nṛtyavedinām.*" *S.R. ibid. 26*). How does this differ from *nāṭya*? Kallinātha has suggested that *nṛtya* does not involve *āhārya abhinaya*, that is, the dancer need not dress up as a dramatic character. From this we can infer that when a single dancer enacts an emotional state—it has to be of some person though not of a dramatis persona--and uses the movements of *abhinaya* to express that state, the dance can be called *nṛtya*. As the *karaṇas* and *aṅgahāras* of Bharata Muni's tradition seemed to have been used in the medieval *nṛtya*, the form was also given the nomenclature of *mārga*. All the ancient music and dance forms which survived in the practice of the day were given the general category of *mārga* or *mārgī* by medieval pundits. The category of *nṛtya* as made in medieval times was redundant for Bharata Muni as for him nothing could be non-emotional (*bhāvahīna*) nor without *abhinaya* (incommunicable). He distinguished *nṛtta* from *nāṭya* because in *nṛtta* specific ideas were not meant to be communicated through dance codes.

3. Vātsyāyan's *Kāmasūtra (1-4:27-28)* gives a list of festivals that were celebrated with great fervour in the cities and in which the '*nāgarika*' was supposed to take active part. Moti Chandra has amplified on it thus, "Among these feasts *yakṣarātri* (now known as *divālī*), *kaumudī jāgara* (*kārtika pūrṇimā*), *suvasantaka* (*vasantapañcamī*) were proper city fests. The wider celebrations were *sahakārabhañjikā* held at the time of picking mangoes; *abhyūṣakhādikā* when fresh gram was eaten; *bisakhādikā* when the fresh lotus stalks were cooked; *navarātrikā* when the new year celebrations were held by playing

with spring leaves; *udakakṣveṛika'* was time for sprinkling people with coloured water; on *pāñcālānuyāṇa* people mimicked each other, *kaśālmalī* was the day for making ornaments of *'semala'* flowers; on *yavacathurthī*, that is the fourth of *sukla vaiśākha* young men spinkled barley powder on each other. *Alolacaturthī* on the third day of *śrāvaṇa śuklā* was time for swinging; on *madanotsava* the god of love was worshipped and *damanabhañjikā* was celebrated by offering flower-ornaments; *holikā* as of now; *aśokottaṃsikā* was the time for wearing ornaments of *aśoka* flowers; *puṣpacayanikā* was the day for making head-gears from mango *'mañjarī.'* *Ikṣubhañjikā* was for eating fresh sugar-care; on *kadambayuddha* folks pelted others with *kadamba* flowers." Moti Chandra, Foreword, *Caturbhāṇī*, by Vararuci and others, edited and trans. into Hindi, Moti Chandra and Vasudeva S. Aggrawal (Bombay: Hindi Grantha Ratnakara Karyalaya, 1959) 58. For more details and some important clues to the nature festive activities see *'jayamaṅgalā'* commentary. Vātsyāyana Muni, *Kāmasūtra* with Jayamaṅgalā commentary of Yasodhara, 3rd ed. with Hindi commentary by Devadatta Sastri, Kashi Sanskrit Granthamala 29 (Varanasi: Chaukhamba Sanskrit Sansthana, 1982). These celebrations were mostly seasonal new-corn feasts and there is no indisputable evidence that dramatic performances were held on all of them. Some of the references (Devadatta Sastri 147-9) to these holidays in *Purāṇas* indicate inclusion of dance, music and drama, something without which no festival was complete.

4. I have discussed this issue at length in my article, "Vālmīki's *Rāmāyaṇa* and the *Nāṭyaśāstra*," *Sangeet Natak*, Journal of Sangeet Natak Academy, 81-82 (July-Dec. 86): 63-76.

Part II

CONCEPTS AND TECHNIQUES

5

Basic Concepts of Aristotle and Bharata Muni: A Reassessment

THE contents of both the *Poetics* and the *Nāṭyaśāstra* are not so abstruse as to evade recapitulation, nor is it an insurmountable task to see how the various aspects of general dramatic elements have received the attention of the two great theorists. But to juxtapose the two theories, one requires to have a method and a purpose in mind. I take up the elements of performance, such as spaces, visuality, aurality, etc., and see what each has to say about them. I have earlier laboured the point that both theorists are exerting to capture the reality of a drama which is above all sacred action or hieropraxis. Its theory has to be very different from that of secular theatre. And for this reason Aristotle and Bharata Muni were both preoccupied with production techniques which facilitated an abundance of dance and music to create an unsplinitered unity in the visual and aural. But in spite of this commonness of purpose, the distinctiveness of the Greek and Indian experience of life as a whole, must have found some expression in the dramatic theory of each culture and it should be part of our task to point that out. I shall, therefore, also look at those features of Aristotle's and Bharata Muni's theories that set them apart and indicate the distinctive quality of their vision.

The dramatic theory in the *Poetics* can be said to consist of four principles of ancient classificatory system. First, the concept of ***mimesis***, which is common to all fine arts; secondly, the treatment of various genres of poetry, namely epic, tragedy and comedy; thirdly, the division of tragedy, but by implication of all performance modes into six elements, ***muthos, ethos, dianoia, lexis, melopoiia,*** and ***opsis***; and fourthly, the cryptic statement about ***katharsis*** upheld by western critical tradition as a principle of Aristotelian aesthetics.

In the *Nāṭyaśāstra*, there is a verse in its sixth chapter which can be quoted as Bharata Muni's own summary of his dramatic theory. "The combination called *nāṭya* is a mixture of *rasas, bhāvas, abhinayas, dharmīs, vṛttis, pravṛttis, siddhi, svaras,* instruments, song and theatre-house."[1] Here, *svaras*, song and instruments could be reduced to a single comprehensive element of musical application called *gāndharva*. The concept of *anukaraṇa* which has been stated elsewhere in the *NŚ* should be taken as covered by *abhinayas* which are a media for *anukaraṇa*. Before going on to a detailed comparison and analysis of these terms vis-a-vis Greek poetics, let me briefly comment upon them. *Rasa* is well known as a doctrine central to the Indian aesthetic theory; it is synonymous with the pleasure that is felt in watching drama; *bhāva* is not to be taken simply as emotion, but as a psychological theory about the nature of emotions which are classified as dominant (*sthāyī*) and subsidiary (*sañcārī*); *abhinaya* may be taken as acting in common parlance, but for Bharata Muni it represents the whole gamut of visual and aural semiotics, stated in meticulous detail. The two *dharmīs, loka* and *nāṭya,* are a theory about the nature of transformation in theatre, which may be simple or embellished; *vṛttis* stand for a division of dramatic enactments on the basis of four major emotional modes, the erotic (*kaiśikī*), the robust (*ārabhaṭī*), the argumentative (*bhāratī*) and the heroic (*sāttvatī*). *Pravṛttīs* are defined as the input of the regional styles in a production, something essential and unavoidable in a vast and variegated country. *Siddhi* means success of a play with the cosmic audience. By defining *siddhi* as worldly and divine, Bharata Muni has indicated the necessity of pleasing both men and gods. *Svara,* instrument and song cover all the literary and musical content of a performance text. *Raṅga*, is the theatre-house.

In making a comparison let us first consider the subjects that both Aristotle and Bharata Muni have treated, and then, take up subjects that only one of them has dealt with. Being a work of much larger size the *NŚ* takes up very nearly all the topics dealt with in the *Poetics*, although it treats them in a way suited to its own contextuality. In addition to these it propounds some cardinal concepts which are peculiar to the Indian theory. The comparable concepts of the two theorists can be paired as follows : ***Mimesis*** and *anukaraṇa* or *abhinaya*; objects of imitation and *vṛttis* (i.e., tragedy and comedy compared with *daśarūpakas*); ***muthos*** analysis and *itivṛtta;* ***ethos*** and *nāyaka-nāyikās;* ***lexis*** and *vākyābhinaya*. Concepts that do not compare are *siddhi, dharmīs, pravṛttis*, details of *gāndharva, vibhāva, anubhāva, sthāyī* and *sañcārī*. Similarly, Aristotle's ***dianoia*** has no comparable concept in the *NŚ*, although enunciations of noble thoughts and generalizations about life, maxims and proverbs are abundant in Sanskrit plays. In the forthcoming pages we shall deal with all the above enumerated concepts, placing them in one chapter or the other. Here, their location and the reasons for placing them so are indicated.

The subject of ***mimesis*** can be considered in two ways, as a principle and as a practice. As a principle ***mimesis*** is a kind of human urge that creates drama and is endowed with aesthetic values. As a practice, ***mimesis*** is a way of handling theatrical devices to reflect the principle. I have dealt with the principle and the practice in separate places. The purpose of ***mimesis*** and *anukaraṇa* and their aesthetic values will be considered in the chapter called, "Theory of Imitation." Then I shall take up the unsplintered channels of rhythm, language and harmony and compare them to the fourfold *abhinaya* in the chapter "Media of Imitation."

Aristotle deals with men of high and low ***ethos*** as objects of ***mimesis***. Poets who liked graver themes wrote tragedies and the lovers of lowliness (***phaule***) produced comedies. The high and low objects form a basis for Greek dramatic genres. For Bharata Muni, the basis is different. It is stated in terms of fourfold psychosomatic behaviour patterns called *vṛttis*. The ten dramatic genres or *daśarūpakas* are based on these patterns discussed in the chapter "Dramatic Genres and Play Structures."

Muthos, which was called the soul of tragedy by Aristotle, and which was interpreted by Europe as a licence to create intricate secular stories with detailed portraiture, has a near synonym in *itivṛtta* of the *NŚ* which favours fabulous capsulation. In the chapter "Dramatic Genres and Play Structures" a detailed comparison is offered. As for ***ethos,*** Aristotle refers only to the tragic hero; comic heroes would have found a place in his treatise on comedy. Bharata Muni has described a whole range of characters for the *daśarūpakas*, as we will see later. ***Lexis*** or *vākyābhinaya,* or the diction content is normally treated as an analysis of the figures of speech, but in drama it is part of the total content of the aural channel, which is one of the two primary media that make up the performance as play (*krīḍanīyakam*). For Bharata Muni, a play is defined as a poem in action which is seen and heard (*'dṛṣyaṃ śrāvyaṃ ca yad bhavet' NŚ 1:11*). In a hieropraxic creation, all sound, speech, song and instruments are interlaced. The kind of splintering between the spoken and the sung which occurs in discursive theatre does not exist here. For this reason I have thought it appropriate that ***lexis*** and *vākyābhinaya* be treated along with ***melopoiia*** and its counterpart *gāndharva,* in a single chapter entitled "The Aural Content."

It has been repeatedly pointed out that ***opsis*** has not only the last but the least place in the Aristotelian scheme. Although ***opsis*** should be taken to mean everything visual, such as the formation of choric dancers, their costume and movements, their gestures and ***chieronomia,*** and all this of the actors too, it seems that Aristotle limited the sense of the word to stage scenery only. But whatever be the definition of Aristotle, the total ***opsis*** or the wealth of visuality was immense in Greek theatre. Any study in this area should not underestimate its richness and function on account of Aristotle's negligence. We shall, therefore, include in ***opsis*** the totality of Greek visuality and compare it with the parallel concept of *āṅgika* (by body), *sāttvika* (subtle physicality) and *āhārya* (decoration of the actor's body and play area) *abhinaya* as stated in the *NŚ*. Just as speech and song form a unity in the aural channel, similarly gait and dance are subpatterns of the total kinesics of theatre. Dance, for this reason, is taken as part of visual to be treated in the "Visual Content." The *āṅgika abhinaya* with all its *karaṇas*, *aṅgahāras*, *nṛttahastas* etc., has been expounded in unbelievable detail by Bharata Muni. Without going into the particulars, I shall consider the theory behind the methodology of encoded gestures and their function in drama. As Aristotle has not written at length on the subject of gestures, and the references made to it by other classical authors like Athenaeus and Lucian in the context of dance is too sketchy, the system of Bharata Muni is the only one which can give us an insight into the gestures of ancient theatre. In the *NŚ*, gestures are treated not only as poses of the body in different emotional states, but also as an independent language neither subservient to the verbal nor just an amplification of the verbal intent, but as a complimentary device that creates an area of signification which would not be possible without this language of gestures. I shall try to establish that in the system of Bharata Muni, still so dynamically prevalent in India, a sign is not a '*liṅga*' or '*saṅketa*', that is a closed signifier, but an open category capable of varying signification (*NŚ Ab. 1:119*). The methodology of *abhinaya* thus, is not a mimesis of things but of *bhāvas* which are ever changing in significance.

The *Poetics* being generally silent on theatrical details, accounts of acting styles and differences between the Athenian, Peloponnesian or Ionian productions can only be inferred from the textual context. As Bharata Muni has provided ample details on this aspect of Indian theatre, *dharmīs* and *pravṛttis*, I shall consider them also. I shall also include another feature of Bharata Muni's dramatic theory, *gāndharva* or the art of music as applied to drama. Here the relationship between musical colour and the dramatic emotions can be seen as existing within the pervasive concept of *rasa*. Lastly, in the same chapter I shall deal with

Aristotle's comments on ***dianoia*** and see how it appears to be related to the art of rhetoric which was a major performance mode in Greek social life. Bharata Muni does not isolate enunciation of noble thoughts, philosophical musings etc., as an element of drama, even though Sanskrit plays are full of such exhortations.

The uniquely Naṭyaśāstric division of emotions into *sthāyī* and *vyabhicārī* and the division of the theatrical medium into *vibhāva* and *anubhāva*, shall be examined in "Transformation and Emotional Arousal." As we have seen Aristotle has classified the modes of ***mimesis,*** but he has not created categories like those of Bharata Muni who has divided all media of *anukaraṇa* into *vibhāva* and *anubhāva*. The actor and his surroundings are called *vibhāvas* and all his action, including speech and song, as *anubhāva*. The advantage of creating these categories is that all channels of communication are condensed into these two. *Vibhāva* and *anubhāva* could also be called signifiers, but different from other signifiers as they are only theatrical, or by extension, only art signifiers. As compared to a scientific or philosophical terminology, they are different in another sense also. They are meant to convey a primarily emotional content or a *bhāva*, further classified as *sthāyī* or *vyabhicārī*. The emotional content or significance is neither devoid of nor divorced from the anlaytical, but its signification is largely in terms of feeling. *Vibhāva* and *anubhāva* then, signify *bhāvas* and in doing so they not only lead to meaning (*artha*) but also to aesthetic pleasure or *rasa* which other non-art signifiers are incapable of creating. In fact, creation of *rasa* is essential for signification of meaning because in theatre or art, without *rasa* there can be no meaning *('na hi rasāt ṛte kaścit arthaḥ pravartate' NŚ 6:32)*. In the chapter on *vibhāva-anubhāva*, we shall also conduct an examination of the *rasa* concept and the four famous classical interpretations by Lollaṭa, etc., along with a view of my own called *saṃyuktivāda*.

Although, Aristotle has talked about the "proper pleasure (***oekeia hedone***) of tragedy", it is axiomatically accepted that this ***hedone*** is felt within the fold of ***katharsis*** which is a general mental state that tragedy must bring about (where?

in the play as Else suggests, or in the audience as Butcher says?). ***Katharsis***, then has been accepted as the end of tragedy, and by implication of all drama. The last chapter, a comparison of ***katharsis*** with *rasa*, should thus be a befitting conclusion to this study.

Note

1. *Rasā bhāvā hyabhinayāḥ dharmī vṛttipravṛttayaḥ*
   Siddhiḥ svarāstathātodyaṃ gānaṃ raṅgaśca saṅgrahaḥ.
   (*NŚ 6:10*)

   The verse was noted as a cardinal one at a very early period in the age of commentary writing on the *NŚ*. Abhinava mentions that according to the school of Kohala, this verse implies that *nāṭya* consists of eleven parts. Some believed that Kohala inserted this verse and it does not come from Bharata Muni. Followers of Udbhaṭa postulated that the order of enunciation from *rasa* to *raṅga* was an inversion of the earlier order. But the school of Bhaṭṭalollaṭa held that this was pointless talk, the verse was authentic and it upheld the principles of Bharata Muni. It seems that the controversy erupted, when the status of *rasa* and *bhāva* as possible constituents of *nāṭya*, began to be questioned. The commentators tended to uphold them as the telos of *nāṭya*. Abhinava, himself perfected this enterprise by declaring *rasa* alone as the very end of drama: in fact, he made *rasa* synonymous with *nāṭya*. However, Bharata Muni's approach was different, it was holistic, for him *rasa* is an ingredient, and like other ingredients, combines to result in 'pleasure' or '*harṣa*.'

   The verse quoted above belongs to a chapter which starts with some saints questioning Bharata Muni on the nature of summarising, that is '*saṅgraha*' and '*alpasūtra*' making. Knowledge, says the Muni, is unlimited and therefore its summarising is essential for putting it down in books. He, then, tells us in brief how *nāṭya* consists of *rasa, bhāva,* etc. He gives this verse as a '*saṅgraha*' and explicates it by additional

17 verses (15-31), enumerating the subconstituents of each of the eleven elements, i.e., *rasas* are eight, *bhāvas* are forty-one in all, *abhinayas* are of four kinds and so on.

6

Theory of Imitation

A SIMILARITY that seems to be the most obvious one, between the theories of Aristotle and Bharata Muni, is that of ***mimesis*** and *anukaraṇa*.. Both the terms have been translated into English as 'imitation' and, therefore, the finer differences between the two concepts have been overlooked. At the same time there is an area of meaning which is common to both, and that, too, has not been properly recognized. This has led to the speculation that the Indians may have borrowed it from the Greeks: and in the recent decade some have argued that it could have been vice-versa. At the very outset of the book, I have said that there seems to be no possible evidence to speculate one way or the other and that ***mimesis*** and *anukaraṇa* shoud be looked upon as ideas of independent origin. There was a clear thinking in Greece upon ***mimesis,*** which primarily meant 'making' of one sort or another. This is well recorded in Plato. Plato gave a whole metaphysical and epistemological perspective to ***mimesis,*** enlarging its sense from 'making' by human hands to making by universal force. Yet, ***mimesis*** always retained the sense of not only 'making,' but of making a copy of some original which was never totally independent of the model. The Indian concepts of *anukaraṇa,* on the other hand, even though the word literally means 'following after' or 'copying,' has projected the result of *anukaraṇa* or *anukṛti,* as an independent creation free of the model. In Bharata Muni's dramaturgy, *nāṭya* is a new creation not a shadow, it is a parallel and a free world, full of its own significance, even though it is unreal (*alaukika*).

In the Platonic theory, all art (***techne***) has been taken to mean some kind of manipulation close to craft. In the *Sophist*, Plato has divided ***techne*** into acquisitive, productive and creative categories of which the last brings into existence things not existing before. However, the highest, art, in the scheme of Plato is not music or poetry, but statecraft, which is compared to the making of a tragedy in the *Laws* (817B) and to sculpture in the *Republic* (420C). All production, in a general way, is ***mimesis***. As Beardsley puts it, there was not only the term ***mimesis*** but others also which were close to it in meaning.

> As we shall see, it is important to Plato that the arts are imitative in some sense in which the other crafts are not: but to get our bearings on this important but elusive concept (or cluster of concepts), it is best to begin by considering the broadest use to which Plato puts it. For in this sense it is the heart of Plato's whole philosophy. There is not only the term ***mimesis***, but three others that are often used in something approaching synonymity with, and even in apposition with ***mimesis, mithexix*** (participation), ***homoiosis***, (likeness) and ***paraplesia*** (likeness). The relation marked by these terms—the relation between an image (*eidolon*) and its archetype—is noted everywhere. Not only are objects imitated by pictures of them, but the essences of things are imitated by names (*Cratylus 423-24*), reality by thought, eternity by time (*Timaeus 38b*). The musician imitates divine harmony, the good man imitates the virtues, the wise legislator imitates the Form of the God in constructing his state, the god (or the demiourgos) imitates the Forms in making of the world of the mixed. Theatetus speaks, judiciously, then, in the *Sophist* (234b trans. Cornford), when he remarks that the term "covers a very large variety." (33-34)

Thus, imitation is not only production, it is following something which the imitator must set before himself. For every kind of activity there must be an Ideal to be followed, and every Ideal or Form must have its Super-Form. But to avoid this endless regression, Plato postulated that there a primary Form, which was the essential nature of every object or thought, it was immutable and complete and could not be embodied in anything of the world. Worldly objects are ***eidola*** of the Ideal Forms and pictures or poetic descriptions, are, in turn, ***eidola*** of the objects. ***Mimesis***, then always falls short of the original. "If the image were perfect—expressing in every point the entire reality of its object—it would no longer be an image, but an example of the same thing" (*Cratylus 432* trans. Jowett, qtd. Beardsley 35). Because it leaves out important qualities, it is a lower order of reality than the archetype. In Plato's metaphysics this is the general presumption. The wordly knife falls short of the Ideal knife; time of eternity and government of Justice. Platonic ***mimesis*** and thus all art, remains a turning away from Truth.

Plato also postulates that sometimes ***mimesis*** is an accurate reproduction of the original, with all the properties to produce a genuine likeness (***eikon***), at other times ***mimesis*** may be a semblance (***phantasma***). ***Phantasma*** is false representation and poets and painters are adept at doing this. "Hence their low status in *Phaedrus*. When the newly arrived souls, having beheld true being, sink into various degrees of forgetfulness, and are placed on nine levels, Socrates says, "to the sixth (class) that of a poet, or other imitative artist shall be fittingly given" (Beardsley 38). The arts are viewed by this worshipper of knowledge as seducers from truth. As a way of knowledge the arts are certainly not commendable. They also undermine morality. Plays like *Medea* appeal to the baser part of our soul and that "stimulates and strengthens an element which threatens to undermine reason" (*Republic 605b*). To sum up, Plato sees little good in art, and it is doubtful if he would have liked to transfer the ***katharsis*** that he saw in Corybantes to a comparative phenomenon in art.

With Aristotle the concept of ***mimesis*** undergoes a major transformation. It retains the condition of being a copy of a model, but the Platonic denigration is reversed. This reversal is based on a metaphysical revision. The permanent reality is not transcedental in Aristotle's opinion. As Beardsley goes on to explain its implication:

> When the universals are thought of as transcedental forms, they are remote from the works of the etcher or draftsman, but when they are thought of, Aristotle's way, as existing only in substances, then the draftsman, who abstracts and reproduces in another medium certain dog universals, is not doing something poles apart from, say, the taxonomist, who is abstracting and connecting other dog universals. (Beardsley 58)

In Aristotle's view, art, as all imitation leads to knowledge. The pleasure that ***mimesis*** provides is on account of knowledge that is acquired through ***mimesis***, even though this knowledge is of particulars:

> And since learning and admiring are pleasant, all things connected with them must also be pleasant; for instance, a work of imitation, such as painting, sculpture, poetry, and all that is well imitated, even if the object of imitation is not pleasant; for it is not this that causes pleasure or the reverse, but the inference that the imitation and the object imitated are identical, so that the result is that we learn something. (*Rhetoric I,* xi, 1371 b; trans. Freese qtd. by Beardsley 57)

Besides, possessing didactic capacity ***mimesis*** is defined as a pleasurable likeness. Later on, we shall see that the Indian theorist Śaṅkuka also argued the same—that *anukaraṇa* was a unique likeness (*vilakṣaṇa pratīti*). Aristotle defines the pleasure giving quality of ***mimesis*** in the *Poetics,* as follows:

> First, the instinct of imitation is implanted in man from childhood, one difference between him and other animals being that he is the most imitative of living creatures, and through imitation learns his earliest lessons; and no less universal is the pleasure

> felt in things imitated. ...Thus the reason why men enjoy seeing a likeness is, that in contemplating it they find themselves learning or inferring, and saying perhaps, 'Ah, that is he.' ... Imitation, then, is one instinct of our nature. (*Poetics IV.1-6*)

As a corollary it follws that the artist is no dissembler or liar, but on the contrary, is one who leads to Truth. However, Aristotle seems to have limited his vision when it comes to enumerating the objects of imitation. In Plato, all creation was ***mimesis*** of Forms, which were transcendental. It has been customary to think that for Aristotle, the Form or ***eidos*** exists, not as transcendental but as within Nature or objects and that Nature itself, tends to attain it. Art helps Nature in this endeavour. This interpretation of Aristotle's metaphysics has been based upon his oft-quoted saying, "art imitates Nature ("***he tekhne mimeitai ten phusin***" *Physics ii.2 194a 21*) and, at times useful arts even supply its deficiencies and that "the artist may imitate things as they ought to be" (*Poetics* xxxv: 1). Amplifying from this Butcher had concluded:

> If we expand Aristotle's idea in the light of his own system, fine art eliminates what is transient and particular and reveals the permanent and essential features of the original. It discovers 'form' (***eidos***) towards which an object tends, the result which nature strives to attain. (150)

There is little in the writings of Aristotle that can explicitly sustain such a conclusion. This discovery of ***eidos*** in objects tends to make Aristotle into a shadow of Plato. Aristotle admits that there is something permanent and enduring in art, but that something could be called ***eidos***, is beyond substantiation from Aristotle's writings. Similarly, the dictum, "art imitates nature," has given rise to many interpretations over the centuries. It has been argued that the inner principle of Nature is what art imitates. "But if we follow out his thought, his (Aristotle's) reply would appear to be something of this kind. Nature is a living and creative energy, which by a sort of instinctive reason works in every individual object towards a specific end" (Butcher

155). The teleological and structural pattern of tragedy seems to have been transferred on to Nature by Butcher. This was a typical nineteenth century view of Aristotelian philosophy.[1] Since the Renaissance, different definitions of Nature have been foisted upon Aristotle's dictum, art imitates Nature. For the purpose of drama, the most disastrous one was that of Realism, which having captured fiction by techniques of portraiture, landscape, and caricature, transferred these on to drama.

Aristotle was clear that the purpose of imitation in drama, was to provide "proper pleasure" by mimetizing *praxis*. ***Mimesis*** of "men in action" was ***mimesis*** of all human life. Through music, the artist mimetizes, "anger and mildness as well as courage, temperance..." (*Politics v. viii.5.134a 18*) and ethical qualities and emotions. Dance, "imitates ethos, pathos and praxis" (*Poetics I:5*). We should be content to note that in drama he applied the general theory of ***mimesis,*** which he thought, was both for the sake of pleasure and knowledge. But even the Aristotelian affirmation of pleasure in art was not sufficient to free art from being constantly compared with its original, the world. This originally Platonic habit, has been strong throughout western criticism which repeatedly gauges art in terms of how truthfully or realistically it represents the world, how much of an understanding of the world can it bring to us, one way or another.

The Concept of Anukaraṇa

The compulsions of the Indian theory of imitation or *anukaraṇa* are different from the Greek ones. The success of *anukaraṇa* is not judged in terms of its ability to represent the world but by its capacity to create a new world. The model is forgotten as soon as the creation is complete. In fact, there has been a long debate in the history of Indian criticism on the possibility of any actual imitation of the original. While refuting Śaṅkuka, Bhaṭṭa Tauta, the guru of Abhinava, seems to have taken great pains to prove that there can be no re-creation of the original historical Rāma or even the character Rāma (as envisaged by the playwright) on the stage. The actor only recreates the dominant emotions (*sthāyī bhāva*) not of the historical Rāma or of the dramatic character, but what he imagines to have been the emotions of Rāma. This argument of Tauta may seem too plain, but it asserts a departure from any attempt at verisimilitude. It theoretically admits no possibility of Realism. Though *nāṭya* has been defined as beneficial in many ways, it was certainly not meant to reveal or hide the world (*loka*).

'*Anukaraṇa*' is only one of the many terms used for imitation, in the *NŚ*. '*Anukaraṇa*', '*bhāvānukīrtana*,' '*lokavṛtt-ānukaraṇa*' '*saptadvīpānukaraṇa*' and '*saṅkīrtana*' are all used synonymously in describing the imitative quality of *nāṭya* by Brahmā *(NŚ*. 1:107- 12). Out of these, *anukaraṇa* and *anukīrtana* are two distinct terms, the rest of the words are made out of prefixing '*loka*', '*saptadvīpa*' etc., to *anukaraṇa.*

Translated literally, '*anukaraṇa*' means an activity (*karaṇa*) which has been in accordance with (*anu*) something else. In this respect, *anukaraṇa* like ***mimesis***, must have an original to be followed and relationship to the original is a point of consideration. The variant terms of *anukaraṇa* used by Brahmā are meant to define this relationship. The *asuras*, after seeing the first ever production of *nāṭya* by Bharata Muni, complained to Brahmā that the production '*Amṛtamanthana*,' retold the story of the defeat of the *asuras* at the hands of *devatās*. They, therefore, wished to destroy this anti-*asura* art. Brahmā tried to placate them by revealing that "Here in (*nāṭya*) there is no characteristic representation (*anubhāvana*) of you two, *asuras* and *devatās*, only; this *nāṭya* is a presentation of the inner feelings and thoughts (*bhāvānukīrtana*) of all the three worlds" (*NŚ 1:107*). Brahmā points out that *nāṭya* only aims at showing the consequences of the good and bad actions. What it shows, can be put as follows:

> Somewhere *dharma*, somewhere play, somewhere money, somewhere war, peace, laughter, sex or slaughter (108). According to their state of mind and taste, the spectators are able to find in *nāṭya*, heroism, learning, excitement, punishment, pleasure

> or sexuality, as *nāṭya* is to be made (*nirmitam*) by the producers keeping in mind the world as their measure (*lokapramāṇa*). The acts (*kṛtya*) of *devatās,* sages, kings, and their families are put to *anukaraṇa* in *nāṭya.* Filled with many emotions and showing many states of being, *nāṭya* has been created by me as *anukaraṇa* of the ways of the world (*lokavṛtta*). The actions of the highest, the mediocre and the lowest people are shown here along with their patience, play and pleasure. *Nāṭya* is a consolation to the sufferers, to the tired and dejected and those hit by calamities. There is no art, craft, branch of knowledge, science, skill, or yoga, in fact no activity which is not to be found in *nāṭya.* Therefore, you *asuras,* should not be angry with the *devatās,* as this *nāṭya* shall always be an *anukaraṇa* of (what goes on in) the seven continents (*saptadvīpānukaraṇa*). (*NŚ 1:112-17*)

It is amply clear that the aim of *anukaraṇa* is human life in all its variety, or "men in action," in the words of Aristotle. Here, besides men, *asuras* and *devatās,* the beings of the upper and the lower worlds are also to be represented. Three dramatic genres, *samavakāra, ḍima* and *īhāmṛga* had purely extra-terrestrial characters. But whatever be the world (*loka*) to be imitated, *nāṭya,* the result of ***mimesis,*** is not seen as falling short of the original. Nor is it supposed to have any Aristotelian aim of improving the original. For *anukaraṇa,* the original three worlds are useful only so far as they are needed to create, *anukṛti* or art, which is not to be judged in terms of the qualities of the original. *Anukṛti,* or art, is a new work, independent and self-sufficient. Although, this is not stated in as many words in the *NŚ* or elsewhere, it is clearly the implication of the fable of *nāṭya*-birth (*nāṭyotpatti*). Bharata Muni says that Brahmā created *nāṭya* out of the four *Vedas.* This 'pleasure-giver' (*krīḍanīyakam*) was also the Fifth Veda. It would not be correct to argue that the Fifth Veda should be thought of as an imitation of four *Vedas.* It cannot be so because it was made from parts of the four. Thus, as knowlege, *nāṭya* is eternal and Brahmā, the creator of the universe has made it so. Art, then, like the Fifth Veda (*nāṭya*) is a recreation. *Anukaraṇa* should be taken as a process of creation or *utpatti*. Just as *nāṭyaveda* was created out of the four *Vedas*, *nāṭya* is created out of the world by *anukaraṇa*. The manual, which shows us the way to do so, is called the *Nāṭyaśāstra*. It is different from *nāṭyaveda* which is everpresent in the practice of drama. In the Indian theory of imitation, then, art is only a manifestation of knowledge, a Veda, expressing itself as a practice (the *prayoga*) along with the rules (*śāstra*) of its creation.

The fable of *nāṭya*-creation also means that the *anukṛti* or art is not to be identified with the real world for good. The *asuras* mistook the actors for themselves and the defeat of *asuras* in the play as their personal defeat. They could not view the play dispassionately and hence became furious. Had they disassociated *nāṭya* from the actual world of personal experience, there would not have been any anger, but pleasure instead. As Brahmā tried to explain to the *asuras*, "whatever are the good and bad results of the activities of yourself and the *devatās*, on seeing them I have made the *nāṭyaveda*" (*NŚ. 1: 106*). Commenting on this verse Abhinava says, "Brahmā meant that there was no burden on the *devatās* or *asuras*" (*NŚ Ab. 1: 106*). In other words, *nāṭya* was not created to put the burden on *devatās* or *asuras* by propagating that the former were good and the latter bad. Instead, even the good acts of *asuras* have been shown as bringing merit. The act of dispassionate viewing has been emphasized as part of *rasa* theory by Abhinava, which I shall take up later, but even for the concept of *anukaraṇa*, the dissociation of the *anukṛti* from *loka*, of art from the object is essential.

Mimesis and *anukaraṇa* while aiming at a representation of the world on stage, do so, through specific media. Let us now take a look at the handling of these media as prescribed in the two theories.

Note

1. A similar view of Nature is attributed to Aristotle by

a contemporary scholar, K.L. Morrison. Aristotle, he says valued most the teleological function of Nature. "Aristotle recognized that 'nature' had many meanings. He narrowed them down to two: (1) the material of which something was composed, and (2) a form into which something grows (as a child grows into the nature of a man)" (Physics 2.1. 193a-b). Aristotle's primary emphasis fell on this second meaning." *Mimetic Action in Greek Thought* (New Jersey: U of Princeton, 1982) 11.

7

Medium of Imitation

IN the Introduction I have argued that the most distinguishing feature of hieropraxic theatre was the unsplintered use of the channels of music, dance and speech. The privileging of the spoken word, which later became a permanent feature of European drama, did not obtain in either Greek or Indian theatre practice. Here, all the channels were equally important and if there was some sort of dominance by one, then it was the visual channel that dominated. In this chapter I shall give a brief account of the various media of imitation that were used in theatre according to the theories of Aristotle and Bharata Muni.

Rhythm, Language, and Harmony

After stating that epic poetry, tragedy, comedy, dithyrambic poetry, flute or lyre playing are all 'modes of mimesis,' Aristotle states that ***mimesis*** in different art forms is achieved differently, and that the object and manner of ***mimesis*** is different in each case (*Poetics I; 2-4*). He states that the three media for all arts are as follows:

> For there are persons who, by conscious act or mere habit, imitate and represent various objects through the medium of colour and form, or again by voice; so in the arts above mentioned, taken as a whole, the imitation is produced by rhythm, language and harmony, either singly or combined. (I:4)

Leaving aside painting and sculpture which use colour and other forms (materials), the arts of performance like music, dance and drạma, use rhythm, language and harmony. Flute and lyre use rhythm and notes only, and dancing uses only rhythm. But for Aristotle, rhythm is not mere beat or a division of time, but movement with regularity, be it the mere movement of the body or that of notes. That is why, dancing, he says "imitates character, emotion and action, by rhythmical movement" (I:5). Poetry or verse whether creative or informative imitates through language alone, but dithyrambic and nomic poetry, tragedy and comedy use all three means. In dithyrambic and nomic poetry all three means are used together, but in tragedy and comedy "now one means is employed, now another" (I:5). What is true of tragedy and comedy can be taken as true of all drama, satyrikon included.

Aristotle's brevity of plan has prevented him from saying anything further about the manner in which rhythm, language and harmony are employed in drama. About the details of language one can gather quite a few things from Aristotle's comments on ***lexis***, categorized as one of the six elements of tragedy. But the nature of harmony or ***melopoiia*** is hardly touched upon by him and so is rhythm never mentioned again in the *Poetics*. No wonder, then, that one has to look elsewhere to gather information about the use of music in Greek theatre. Aristotle perhaps took musical employment in drama for granted and therefore, refrained from stating anything further about it. But the result of what may have been for him a redundancy, was disastrous for the post-Renaissance readers of the *Poetics*. The practical art of theatre-music being extinct, the Europeans reconstructed a picture of Greek drama in which there was hardly any place for rhythm or music. Greek drama was envisaged as a primarily rhetorical affair (an impression reinforced by Roman tragedies) far removed from the balance of channels that hieropraxis depends so much upon. But if Aristotle left out the details of musical application he was at least explicit in stating it as a medium of ***mimesis***. But he not only belittled, but also left out from his description the visual content of Greek performances constitued by the body movements and complex gestures of actors and ***chorutai***. The Greek actor had more than his mask and costume, a repertoire of highly emotive gestures, just as the chorus members performed a variety of dances to create complex visual effect. By restricting the visual to the limited area of stage scenary (***opsis***), Aristotle made posterity forget about the wealth of this visuality. The similarity of dance to sculpture, which Athenacus later observed and recorded, escaped the eye of so keen an examiner as Aristotle.

The Indian Medium of Anukaraṇa

Unlike Aristotle, Bharata Muni nowhere specifically states the constituent elements of *anukaraṇa,* that is, his parallel to the concept of ***mimesis***. But he does say, as we have pointed out earlier, that *nāṭya* as a whole is made up of eleven things: *rasa, bhāva, abhinaya, dharmī, vṛtti, pravṛtti, siddhi, svara, ātodya, gāna,* and *raṅga.* Out of which it is obvious that *abhinaya, svara, ātodya* and *gāna* are the medium that make up the visual and the aural content of drama. We have briefly explained these eleven constituents and from that it can be seen that *ātodya, svara* and *gāna* correspond to rhythm, language and harmony. (*Svara,* in this context, does not mean musical notes or harmony but the *udātta, anudātta* and *svarita* or high, low and circumflex sounds of the vocal chords used in the three registers for producing speech). In fact, *abhinaya* as a concept stands out as something distinct. And an eleboration of this concept is most vital to an understanding of Bharata Muni's idea of *anukaraṇa.*

Abhinaya of Four Kinds

Literally '*abhinaya*' means nothing more than communication. *Abhi* (specially) *naya* (providing) the meaning from the actor to the audience is *abhinaya*. "By which the performance is provided (to the spectators) is called *abhinaya*" ("*Yasmāt prayogaṃ nayati tasmādabhinayaḥ smṛtaḥ NŚ 8:7).* In this comprehensive sense, all media of communication is *abhinaya.*

Rhythm, language and harmony or *ātodya, svara* and *gāna* are *abhinaya,* too, as they are meant to communicate meaning. Why then a separate category for *abhinaya*? The purpose of this classification becomes evident when we look into the four kinds of *abhinayas* postulated by Bharata Muni. They are categorized as *āṅgika,* pertaining to the movement of head, torso and limbs; *vācika,* consisting of speech; *sāttvika,* expressive of deep emotions indicated by subtle facial changes, and *āhārya,* related to the use of costume (*NŚ 8:7-12*). The *vācika abhinaya* is synonymous with the use of *svara,* language as inflected dramatic dialogue (*pāṭhya*) which was not sung most of the time. *Vācika abhinaya* was therefore distinct from *gāna* or song meant for *dhruvā* compostions which were inserted in between dialogues.

In this fourfold division of *abhinaya* or communicative channels, Bharata Muni has laid the base for the complicated work that an actor can do to get across his meaning. This division is not only adequate in describing all that an actor usually does in any tradition, but by creating his division, Bharata Muni has chalked out four distinct channels or languages that acting can use. In the Indian dramatic tradition each of these channels or languages has been provided with an intricate system of signifiers through which the actor seeks to express meaning. His effort is not to use his body or words etc., to project his meaning, but to make his body and words attain the status of the signifiers that are known to contain meaning. It is a presumption in Indian theatre that the body shall not be used naturally but semiotically. Thus drama being *anukaraṇa,* transmutes the worldy or daily actions into its own frame of reference or '*dharmī*'. When this transmutation of things in *nāṭya* is not very far removed from daily life, that status of transformation is called *lokadharmī,* but when the transformation leads to embellishment or intense signfication then the status of dramatic reference is called *nāṭyadharmī*. '*Dharmī*' is the process of semiotization in theatre. It has been enunciated as one of the major elements of *nāṭya*.

Āṅgika Abhinaya

The body *abhinaya* can aim at communicating by concentrating on one of the three ways: by body stances (*śārīraja*), by facial expressions (*mukhaja*) or by movements (*ceṣṭākṛta*) (*NŚ 8:12*). The human figure is divided into 6 major and minor parts. Head, hands, breast, sides, hips, and legs are the major parts and eyes, brows, nose, lips, cheeks, and chin are the minor ones. The *NŚ* then enters into mind-boggling details of the various movements of these parts in an impressive succession of four chapters, (eighth to eleventh) in about 525 verses. Each of these six major body parts, head, hands etc., are then further taken as conglomerates of their smaller parts, for which movements are also prescribed. The head for instance can be moved in 13 different ways. And each of these movement is used for expressing specific emotions or situations. For instance, moving the head up and down rapidly is called '*vidhūta*' and this movement should be employed to express fear, cold, fever or drunkenness. (*NŚ 8:27*)

Head Movements

The head-work, itself, is a conglomerate of 36 eye movements (*dṛṣṭis*), 9 pupil movements (*tārākarma*), 8 ways of looking (*darśana*), 9 lip gestures (*puṭakarma*), 7 brow actions (*bhṛkuṭī*), 6 nostril movements (*nāsākarma*) 6 cheek actions (*gaṇḍaka*), 6 ways of holding the chin (*cibukakarma*), 6 facial expressions (*mukhaja*), and 9 neck actions (*grīvākarma*). The *NŚ* states that all these movemetns are based on the normal behaviour patterns of people ("*svabhāvasiddhamevaitat karma lokakriyāśramam*" *NŚ 8:104*). But a conscious cultivation of these provides the actor with a felicity of expression that he may otherwise lack. Also it is the regional style of acting that gives the actor further distinctiveness which has been defined as '*pravṛtti*' by the *NŚ*.

Hand Postures

As stated in the text itself most movements of the face and its parts are natural and non-artificial. But the hand postures prescribed in the *NŚ* are artificial embellishments of vaguely mimetic signs as arbitrary in make-up as in any other sign language. There are twenty-two ways of holding a single hand and its fingers, beginning with *patākā* pose. There are twenty-two other ways of holding the two hands together beginning with *añjali* pose. A lot has been written with extensive illustrations by scholars and dancers to figure out these poses (*saṃyuta* and *asaṃyuta hastas*). But the usual impression given is that these postures are closed signifiers, that is, they are to be used only for actions as prescribed by the *NŚ*. For instance *patākā* (all fingers and thumb parallel and outstretched) is meant to enact striking, the fall of a sword or a blow, heavy rain, personal pride and many other things. But the truth is that such prescriptions show only some ways of employing *patākahasta*. As the text adds, "the actors should enact tens, hundreds and thousands of things by *patākahasta* of two hands." (*NŚ 8:28*). Adds Abhinava:

> These are not the only subjects for enactment for *patākahasta*, seeing the manner of employement it should be used according to one's imagination. *"Nacaitāvānevāsya viṣaya iti darśayituṃ āha, evamanena prakāreṇa svabuddhayā tāṃ tāmitikartavyatāmutprekṣya prayoktavyaḥ."* (*NŚ Ab. 9:25*).

Besides, the *NŚ* explicitely lays down:

> These two kinds of hand postures, of single and two hands, have been described in brief. But these *abhinayakaras* and others not given here should be employed after knowing their signficance. The learned should themselves contemplate over the shape, movement, signs, and category (of things) and then employ hand postures accordingly. In theatre, no object can be enacted without hand (postures). I have, therefore, described in detail the nature of hand postures as I have seen it before me. Others

> (hand postures) that can be seen in the actions of the people and which are supposed to signify something, should be used appropriately in the flow of *rasa* and *bhāva*. (*NŚ 9:162-65*)

Thus, not only the situations for employment of the codified signs are made unlimited, the repertoire is also open to actor's invention. In addition to these 22 hand-postures, there are 28 *nṛttahastas* or ways of holding the arms with hands while dancing or acting (*NŚ 9:215*). Regarding the use of *nṛttahastas* the text says:

> For making a total dance posture (*karaṇa*) *nṛttahastas* must be used. But where meaning is to be conveyed by *abhinaya, patākā* etc., should be employed. According to the needs of performance the two (*nṛttahastas* and *saṃyuta-asaṃyuta hastas*) are combined and the combination is named after whichever of the two dominates. (*NŚ 9:213*)

Breast, Belly and Leg Movements

In addition to the single (*asaṃyuta*), combined (*saṃyuta*) hands and arm positions (*nṛttahastas*), the total coded wealth of hand-gesticulation is not complete without finger movements (*vartanā*) of four kinds. After hand-work the *NŚ* describes 5 ways of holding the breast. The first position is called '*ābhugna*' in which there is a forward bend, and the shouders are slack. It is used for denoting confusion, melancholia, grief, fear, cold, bending in rain, etc. In the same way there are four others. *Nata*, and four others are ways of holding the sides or curving the torso line (*pārśvakarma*). Then, there are three prescriptions for holding the belly: *kṣāma*, *khalva* and *pūrṇa*. The hip movements are five. The legs are divided into three parts: thighs (*ūru*), shins (*jaṅghā*) and feet (*pada*). For each, thigh, shin and feet, five kinds of positions are prescribed and the dramatic situations for their employment are given.

Leg Postures or Cārī

Just as a great deal of attention has been paid to hand gestures for developing a specified language, similarly, the movements of legs have been codified to suit various gaits, ways of standing, leaps, dances and fighting postures. The hand gestures, have always been used to denote exactly or approximately specific objects in all cultures. It is a natural tendency to supplement the spoken sign with hand sign. The *NŚ* is evidence of a tradition which refined this natural practice to a high degree of proficiency. But the legs unlike the hands cannot speak, they only carry the body. They do, however, indicate by their postures what the body is feeling and doing. *Cārī* is the co-ordinated effort of feet, shins, thighs and pelvis" (*NŚ 10:1*). One leg movement is called *cārī*, two *cārīs* make a *karaṇa*, many *karaṇas* combine to make a *khaṇḍa* and a few of these *khaṇḍas* make a long movement called *maṇḍala*. All leg work is divided into two. When feet are kept close to the ground the *cārīs* are called earthly (*bhaumī*) but when the feet are lifted very high they are called aerial (*ākāśikī*). *Samapada* etc., are 16 earthly *cārīs*. *Simple walk is samapada*. If the forefeet are rubbed into ground the gait is called *sthitāvartā*. *Atikrāntā*, etc., are 16 aerial *cārīs*. "The aerial ones are known as embellished actions and they are employed for enacting archery, throwing the *vajra* and other weapons" (*NŚ 10:46*).

In between movements, the actors have to get into stationary postures (*sthānas*). The *NŚ* has prescribed 6 of them: *vaiṣṇava, samapāda, vaiśākha, maṇḍala, pratyālīḍha* and *ālīḍha*. They are to be used for showing divine and human postures while talking, wooing or throwing a weapon. These postures have been taken as specific prescriptions and are followed in sculpture, icon making and painting. For fighting movements a wide variety of postures called '*nyāya*' are given. All these martial movements, also called *vyāyāma,* are "to be done in proper rhythm" ("*vyāyāmaṃ kārayet samyak layatāla samanvitam/Seauṣṭhave hi prayatnastu kartavyo vyāyamasevibhiḥ*" (*NŚ 10:90*). The aim should be to make it look attractive and decorous.

Gatipracāra or Gait

In describing *āṅgika abhinaya* as medium of *anukaraṇa,* I have so far dealt with details of holding the body and its parts. But this is only an account of the postures as they appear at a given moment. As theatre is not sculpture or painting which capture only a moment, it depicts a continuity of action, a flow of motion containing a series of postures and stances. This motion is called *'gatipracāra.' Gati* is a widely used term in all Indian performing arts; whether it be metre, musical composition, dance or acting. *Gati* is more than motion, beat or rhythm. It can be best translated as the "manner of a walk" or gait. It implies that each moving thing or person has its own characteristic and distinctive manner of locomotion. For instance, an elephant and a horse may be going side by side at the same speed yet each will have its own peculiar manner of moving the body. This peculiar way of movement is called *gati.* Every metre in prosody has its own *gati* even though it may be syllabically equal to many other metres. *Gati* is said to be expressive of feelings or *bhāvas* just as rhythm for the ancient Greeks was expresive of ***ethos,*** " ...for even dancing imitates character, emotion and action by rhythmical movement" *(Poetics I:9).* Bharata Muni's notion of gait is not far from this. The gait of each dramatis persona, is measured by steps prescribed to suit the character. To us moderns the classical actor would seem to be walking in unnatural dance-like steps. The measure and the time for each kind of step is also prescribed *(NŚ 10:9). Tāla* is the unit of space (1 *tāla*=the space between outstretched thumb and middle finger, *NŚ Ab. 10:9*) and *kalā* is the unit of time (1 *kalā*=5 blinks). All divine, royal, as well as high status personae shall make their each step of 4 *tālas* and the time lapse between each step shall be of 4 *kalās.* The middle characters shall use two units and the low characters should use, one. Stately and serious gaits are contrasted with quick and disturbed ones here. But this is only a general injunction. The gait shall vary for each character according to the emotional state and dramatic situation which are enumerated in another two hundred verses. Gaits are also prescribed for depiction of walking in the dark, in rain, in fear and in fun. Also there are ways of walking for merchants, mendicants of different orders, for clowns, old and sick men, those drunk, hurt or stigmatic. Enactment of swimming, climbing trees and buildings, crossing rivers are given. Gaits are prescribed for tribals, birds, man-lion, eunuchs, low women, children and outcastes. These gaits were obviously a matter of codified movements which the knowledgeable audience had no difficulty in deciphering.

In this way we have a comprehensive code of body or *āṅgika abhinaya* which to date is the main part of any traditional actor's training in India. As a medium of mimesis all these gestures and postures of hands, shins and feet, head, neck, breast, belly, sides, pelvis, and thighs are used in various combinations and permutations in both dance and dramatic enactment. As I have suggested earlier, it was dance or *nṛtta* which has been the primordial way of moving the body and which Śiva 'recalled' when he danced, and the *karaṇas* of this dance were passed on to Bharata Muni via Taṇḍu. These 108 *karaṇas* and consequent *aṅgahāras* are made up of nothing but the various hands, head, and leg postures as described in the *aṅgika abhinaya*. To repeat, when these postures are taken as mere movement for attractive presentation ('*śobhājanakam*'), they can be called *nṛtta*, but when they are made to carry dramatic meaning ('*arthabhāvakam*') they are called *āṅgika abhinaya*. This, however, is one kind of *abhinaya*. *Vācika, sāttvika* and *āhārya* are the three others.

Verbal Abhinaya

It is sometimes thought that speech or verbal acting is the prime medium of communication and that the other three *abhinayas* are only subservient to its purpose. "Words are to be rendered carefully as they are said to be the body of *nāṭya*. Body, costume and emotive (*sāttvika*) expressions are meant to render the meaning of words" ("*vāci yatnastu kartavyo nāṭyasyeyaṃ tanuḥ smṛtaḥ/Aṅganepathyasattvāni vākyārthaṃ vyañjayanti hi*" *NŚ 14:2*). But Abhinavagupta cautions us against any simplistic interpretation of this verse which may put the three channels to serve the purpose of one, the verbal. He recalls that in the seventh chapter '*anubhāva*' has been defined "as those postures by which meaning of words, body and emotional expressions are communicated..." (*anubhāvyate anena vāgaṅgasattvakṛto abhinaya iti*"). These three, *vāg*, *aṅga* and *sattva*, are to be taken in succession as being together and yet separate in order of importance; that is, as *vāg*, *aṅga*, *sattva* or *aṅga*, *vāg*, *sattva* or *sattva*, *vāg*, *aṅga* ("*āvṛtyācānvayaḥ vāg ityādiṣvevachedaḥ*" *NŚ* Ab. *14:2*). So if *vāg* is given prominence in a situation, the other channels also express meaning (*"tadyadi vāgbhavati tadetānyarthaṃ vyañjyanti vāksahitāni svārthaṃ vyañjayanti ekatastryātmakataśca vagiti samāsayogenāha" NŚ Ab 14:2*). But they also express their own meaning. Each channel, then, is independent not only in technique but also in purpose, it has its own meaning to convey though a combined effect is what the audience gets to enjoy. The verbal is often given an overriding importance because it capsulates the ***muthos*** or the *itivṛtta* or the story of the play. However, the *NŚ* does not project the author as indispensable though his importance is great if the performance is based on an authored play. We shall consider the details of Bharata Muni's concept of verbal *abhinaya* a little later in relation to Aristotle's ***lexis***.

Sāttvika Abhinaya

There are eight physical transformations such as perspiration, horripilation, etc., which, according to their psychosomatic characteristics, are called *sāttvika bhāvas*. A question is raised in the *NŚ*; how are *sāttvika bhāvas* different from other *bhāvas*, *sthāyī* and *sañcārī*, and why is their enactment given the name *sāttvika abhinaya*? The relevant prose passage in the *NŚ* runs like this:

> Here it is asked—are other *bhāvas* enacted without *sattva* (deep feeling), then why these alone have been called *sāttvika*? The explanation is like this. Here,

> the term *sattva* means that which is born in one's *manas* (consciousness-mind-heart). This *sattva* is said to arise only if the *manas* is concentrated. In high concentration (*samādhi*) the *sattva* comes into being. The effect of *sattva* such as horripilation, tear flow, facial changes and such physical transformations cannot occur without the *manas* causing them. The *sāttvika bhāvas* in theatre are to be enacted as *anukaraṇa* of general behaviour. For example, the states of pleasure and pain are to be made *sāttvika* (that is, to be felt deeply by the actor) so that they appear natural. How can sorrow which causes flow of tears be performed if the actor does not feel any misery and how can happiness be enacted if it is not felt by the actor? Therefore, proper *sattva* is achieved by the actor by becoming miserable or happy, by showing tear-flow or horripilation as needed. Thus, I have defined the *sāttvika bhāvas*. These are *stambha* (stupefaction), *sveda* (perspiration) *romāñca* (horripilation), *svarabheda* (change of voice), *vepathu* (trembling), *vaivarṇya* (change in facial brightness), *aśru* (tears), and *pralaya* (fainting). (*NŚ 7:94*)

Sāttvika abhinaya, as it seems from the passage above, has the touch of a trance. Bharata Muni goes on to enumenrate the emotions which cause these eight psychosomatic changes to appear. For instance, excitement, sorrow, astonishment or bereavement can cause *stambha* or stupefaction.

From this it is clear that *sāttvika bhāvas* are strong psychosomatic states which are generated by other emotions which may be *sthāyī* (dominant) or *sañcārī* (transient). As these deeply felt *sāttvika* states have their somatic or physical manifestations such as trembling, weeping, etc., they are separately categorized as one kind of *abhinaya.* As the manifestations of *sāttvika bhāva* are all entirely universal, they cannot be, or rather need not be made into signs or codes with posited meaning, the way hand gestures (*saṃyuta* and *asaṃyuta hastas*) have been used to denote specific objects. The *sāttvika* gesture directly indicates a strong emotional state without revealing the reason for the occurrence of the state. Tears indicate sorrow but not how it came to be whereas sorrowful words may also contain the reason of grief (*"avyaktarūpaṃ sattvaṃ hi vijñyeyaṃ bhāvasaṃśrayam" NŚ 22:3*). About the importance of *sāttvika abhinaya* the *NŚ* says, "It is to be done with meticulous application as *naṭya* is most dependent upon *sāttvika abhinaya*. When there is ample use of the *sāttvika*, acting is called excellent (*jyeṣṭha*), when its use is moderate, acting is considered mediocre, but when there is none, acting is called poor" (*NŚ 22:1-3*). *Sāttvika abhinaya*, then, makes drama a deep experience in emotional comunication. It is also the most subtle and effective of the four kinds of *abhinayas*. It conveys directly and unambiguously the emotions which *āṅgika* (physical) and *vācika* (verbal) can merely suggest or imply. Besides, other *abhinayas* can be done as mechanical exercises without actually feeling any emotion. But the *sāttvika* can only be done by involving both the heart and the head. In fact, "....acting is called praiseworthy only when *sāttvika* is combined with *āṅgika* or *vācika*, or both, and is made to dominate the combination..." (*NŚ Ab. 23:3*)

In a way, *sāttvika abhinaya* is practised upto a degree in all acting, whether European or Asian. However, as a concept *sāttvika abhinaya* has been formulated and put to use with special emphasis only in the Indian tradition. As a matter of cultural behaviour uninhibited expression of emotions has always been appreciated by the Indian audience. Dwelling upon a mood or an emotional state, exploring its pervasiveness, all the while maintaining its intensity and depth, is the standard practice in Indian poetry, music, as well as dance. Such a preoccupation with emotions may seem repetitive and cloying to an untrained audience, particularly of the West, but this was not the case with ancient Greeks who were fond of strong emotional experiences in their drama as W.B. Stanford has shown in *Greek Tragedy and the Emotions*. Plato in his *Republic* gives evidence of the "utterly alarmingly" emotional power of tragedy:

> ... even the best of us, when we listen to a passage from Homer or from a tragedy in which a grieving hero represented as dragging out his sorrows in a long speech and people sing and beat their breasts—then, as you know, we delight in surrendering ourselves..." (qtd. by Stanford 3)

For all those who are free from the cult of the stiff upper lip, the hieropraxic experience can readily be understood as a justified indulgence in emotional letting out. I shall compare Greek tragic emotions to the Indian categorization of *bhāvas,* in a later chapter. Here, in the context of *sāttvika bhāvas,* it is relevant to note that in his *Nicomachean Ethics* (*1128b, 10ff*), Aristotle observes that emotions are accompanied by somatic symptoms; shame by blushing, terror by blanching or paling of complexion. The parallel with *sāttvika abhinaya* is obvious. In addition to this, one should not overlook another parallel. ***Ekplexis*** (stupefaction) is enacted quite often in tragedies, particularly at ***anagnorisis*** just like *stambha* or *pralaya* is portrayed as *mūrcchā* (fainting) in the Indian plays. The working up of emotions to a high pitch was perhaps common in Greek and Indian cultural situations, if literature is any evidence. Sappho's "Ode to Anactoria," describes an acute state of erotic fever in a woman:

> As she gazes on her beloved, her voice fails, her tongue grows rigid, a fiery sensation runs under her flesh, her eyes grow blind, her ears hum, sweat flows freely over her, her whole body trembles, she is paler than withered grass (or greener than fresh grass), and she seems almost to be dead... (qtd. by Stanford 37)

The ten stages of fever caused by *kāma* (erotic desire) are described not very differently in the *NŚ* (*22:170*).

Āhārya Abhinaya

Preparations made in the green room are called *āhārya* (*āhāryābhinayo nāma jñeyo nepathyajo vidhiḥ, NŚ 21:3*) i.e., the actor's costume and the stage props. Though *āhārya* is the last category of *abhinaya* to be dealt with in the *śāstras* on theatre it is certainly not the least in importance. "The whole performance is located in *āhārya abhinaya*" (*NŚ 21:1*). Adds Abhinavagupta:

> *Āhārya* is the wall on which the painting of all kinds of action is drawn upon. Even if all other channels of *abhinaya* cease to be, by its particular adornment, *āhārya* should be able to express its own of meaning. Some people denigrate *āhārya* by saying that there is continuous change (variety) in other *abhinayas* but *āhārya* for an actor does not change in the same manner. Nonetheless, the value of *āhārya* should be acknowledged. Even though emotional states and actions vary, it is *āhārya* that keeps them all together in a unified string of experience and is thus instrumental in the realization of *rasa*. (*NŚ Ab. 21:1*)

These observations of Ācārya Abhinavagupta on the significance of costume indicate that in ancient theatre, costume/dress was used as a sign for defining dramatis persona ('*avasthāḥ prakṛtayaḥ pūrvaṃ nepathyasādhitāḥ*" *NŚ 21:2*). In this drama, characterization did not aim at a delineation of individual particularities nor at the portrayal of an individual's psychological world. Instead, it tried to capture the plight of a rather representative individual going through crucial situations of life. The rank, status, and age of a character were prominently indicated to avoid any ambiguity and to mark these, some standard costumes were chosen as accepted signifiers. It should also be remembered that in ancient societies many kinds of clothing, head gears, hair styles or marks were reserved for particular castes, ranks, ethnic groups and regionalities. Drama had ready material to make them into theatre-signs to suit its own purpose. They could then be made to reflect the essential meaning of a persona and its ethos. The same aim was fulfilled by the use of mask in Greek theatre. The codified costume and the mask both eliminated the personality of the actor—something upon which Naturalism, particularly of the Stanislavskian kind, depends most. They instead established the personality of the mask (***prosoopon,*** which in Greek means face, mien, look, appearance and what in Indian terms may be called the *sthāyī bhāva* of the actor wearing it). The actor is supposed to enliven the personality of the mask or *āhārya* to express the meaning, emotion or *bhāva* that the mask/*āhārya* signifies or to express what Abhinava called *āhārya's* "own peculiarity." He should become subservient to mask/*āhārya* or rather be possessed by it. The persona is supposed to exist by itself as the actor does not create it. He only brings it to life on stage. The persona 'descends' on the stage as is indicated by the term *'raṅgāvataraṇa'* which indicates the 'descent' of the persona and not the actor. The force and the icon of the persona, whether human or divine pre-exists, the actor is only a medium for its manifestation. He sets aside his own personality. As is made clear by Bharata Muni, "*Ākṛti* (shape or form) should be made of *prakṛti* which is to be taken up (by the actor) just as a being leaves his own nature and takes up the nature (*prakṛti*) of another body (on rebirth). The man (actor) covered up by the dress and complexion of the new body takes up a new nature" (*NŚ 21: 89-90*).[1] The simile of rebirth makes it quite clear that when the actor takes up a role he or she has to die as a person and live the role as a different being. This is antithetical to the practice of great cine-stars who interpret every role through their own personality giving it their own characteristic flavour.[2] Ancient drama was above this confusion created by Realism. The person and the *āhārya*, the actor and the ***prosoopon***, have always been distinguished even by the common Indian theatre-goer. Even today the actors of ritual dramas like *Rāmāyaṇa* etc., are worshipped as Rāma, Sītā etc., but only when they are dressed up as "*svarūpas.*" The people are clear in their minds that they are praying to the *svraūpas* and are not adoring the actors. Such a belief in the persona as an entity can be entertained by polytheists only and not by monotheists (Napier 25-27). From the Christian view-point there is only one Force or Spirit, that is God with which man is allowed to communicate. Fusion or union of man (even as actor) with another force is unthinkable, it is taboo even with God. To give up one's own personality and become another or to surrender to a different persona is diabolical. As early Christian fathers expounded, "a man cannot be a Christian and remain an actor, because he is serving pagan gods, and the audience are his abettors" (Garton 37). The decline of classical mask in Europe was a result of this bias. According to Napier:

> From medieval times onwards, the prevalent interpretation of the mask focuses on its role as an evil disguise. Such an association is perhaps nowhere more obvious than in its connection with the word larva, a word meaning, according to Skeat (1879-82, 1974, 330), 'a ghost, a spectre, or mask; the insect's first stage being the mask (disguise) of its last one... (11)

Āhārya, then, from the Christian dogmatic view-point is an evil disguise, a devilry that would condemn the actor's soul to hell and to save which he must stay naturally himself. At the most, he may enlarge himself to absorb the persona in him but he should never become the persona. The costume should also be personalised to suit the actor. As a result, because of the projection of his particular personality, the actor's representation cannot become a conventionally accepted sign. The Christian attitude, then, is the reverse of the Indian or Greek one. It was one of the factors responsible for the reduction and devaluation of the visually symbolic in European theatre.

Kinds of Āhārya

Āhārya is said to be of four kinds by Bharata Muni. *Pusta* (stage props), *alaṅkāra* (ornaments of flowers and metals), *aṅgaracanā* (costume), and *sajīva* (moving objects). The Indian classical stage was not entirely bare or propertyless. Decorative models of mountains, chariots, air-vehicles, elephants, etc. were made out of cloth, skin, leaves or bamboo (this mixture was called *sandhim*), or out of woven threads (*vyājim*), or out of wax and straw (*veṣṭim*) (*NŚ 21:6-9*). There was no attempt to make these models look realistic in any way, on the contrary they were meant to be ornamental. Similarly, there were prescribed sizes for all weapons for stage use, as also for the *jarjara* pole, which was also part of *pusta āhārya*. The second major category of *āhārya* is ornamentation, *alaṅkāra*. It seems that unadorned bodies were unimaginable on this stage. Even ascetics had to be adorned with flowers and fancy garlands. Women of all ranks were well-laden with jewellery and ornaments, the designs of which differed according to status and region. The royal and the rich of both sexes would wear ample garlands and ornaments which need not have been of actual gold but light imitative material (*NŚ 21:44*). The *NŚ* list of ornaments to be born by human, celestial, *gandharva* or *rākṣasa* women is quite staggering. A salient feature of *aṅgaracanā* was the painting of faces in prescribed colours (*varṇaka* or *vartana*) (*NŚ 21:89*). Gods, *yakṣas, apsaras*, sun and such characters were to be painted fair (*gaura*); fire, etc., in red; *Nārāyaṇa*, serpents, *rākṣasas* and hill folks were given dark faces; kings were to be given fair, rosy or even dark facial complexions; northerners were shown as fair; ascetics, the mean and the diseased were made dark and so were the people of *kirāta, barbara, draviḍa, āndhra* tribes. *Śakas, Yavanas* (Greeks), *Pahlavas* were made fair. Brahmins and *kṣatriyas* were given fair faces, the *vaiśyas* and *śūdras* were made dark as a general rule. But considering the total data given and the concept of '*lokānukṛti*', it seems that complexions were chosen more according to regions of India and less along caste lines. All costume was of three types: simple (*śuddha*), ornamental (*citra*) and plebian (*malina*).

All moving things on the stage were called *sajīva*. They were 'four-legged' (animals), 'two-legged' (men, women and birds) and 'unlegged' (serpents). It is my guess that this sort of classification by legs was done keeping in mind the application of gait (*gatipracāra*).

The Unification of Four Abhinayas or Samānīkaraṇa

After dealing with the four kinds of *abhinayas—sāttvika* in chapter 7, *āṅgika* in 8-12, *vācika* in 14-17 and *āhārya* in 21,

Bharata Muni gives an account of the situations and characterizations where the four *abhinayas* are applied in unification. It is, of course, an unstated presumption that all these four channels of *abhinaya* are mixed in drama, all the same, classifications are necessary to facilitate a descriptive analysis of each *abhinaya*. This mixing is called *sāmānya abhinaya* which in net result is neither dance, nor poetry, nor song but dramatic acting. "*Abhinaya* made out of words, body movements and *sāttvika* feelings is called *sāmānya*" ("*sāmānyābhinayo nāma jñeyo vāgaṅgasattvajaḥ NŚ 21:1*). Here a question may arise. Why is *āhārya* not spelt out as the fourth constituent of *abhinaya* in this definition of *sāmānya abhinaya*? To this Abhinavagupta says:

> *Āhārya* is of lesser magnitude (in terms of effort) as compared with other *abhinayas*. As its existence is obvious, it is not pointed out here. *Āṅgika* and *vācika* are actions, which *āhārya* is not. It is natural in theatre that one *abhinaya* is done after another and, therefore, *sāmānya abhinaya* which seeks to unify them all, is achieved by great effort only. In that (*sāmānya*), *āhārya* is included as it comes into existence without any special effort. (*NŚ Ab. 22:1*)[3]

Abhinava rejects the view of some commentators that *āhārya* is not to be included in the process of *samānīkaraṇa* or unification, as it denotes no feeling and that it is not live but inert. Some critics in Abhinava's time, also questioned the validity of the relationship between certain feelings and colours or costumes. They argued that this relationship is not causal but conventional. For example, the erotic mood is denoted by splendid white is only a convention, they said. Erotic feeling, they said, is a personal affair; an individual may not be erotically aroused by white. Therefore, *āhārya* cannot be definitely related to emotions. Against such a view Abhinava asserts that such arguments contradict the principles of aesthetics as stated by Bharat Muni. In his system the sign function of *āhārya* is upheld as valid and effective, says Abhinavagupta, and therefore, its inclusion in the unification of *abhinayas (samānīkaraṇa)* is acceptable. (Abhinava, it seems, takes it for granted that all signs are conventional and not causal and he believes that such was also the position of Bharata Muni.) "*Sāmānya* means, brought together, that is, where each major and minor part of action is so combined that the result is a unified whole like the image of an *alātacakra*" ("*sāmānyasya sāmānīkṛtasakalāṅgopāṅgakarmaṇā sato abhinayanaṃ yena alātacakrapratimatā prayogasya jāyate*" *NŚ Ab. 22:1*). If a firebrand (*alāta*) is rotated, an illusionary circle is created. In reality, there is no circle, but it appears to exist by the skill of rotation. Similarly, the four *abhinayas* are all distinct and separate acts but by the skill of mixing they appear as one in a dramatic performance. This was Abhinava's simile, which Bharata Muni has himself used in a later chapter. "Thus *gāna*, instrument playing, and drama consisting of various constituents (*abhinayas*), are to be performed (to appear as a unity) like a fire-circle by the producers of theatre." ("*Evaṃ gānaṃ ca vādyaṃ ca nāṭyaṃ ca vividhāśrayam/ alātacakrapratimaṃ kartavyaṃ nāṭyayoktṛbhiḥ*" *NŚ 28:7*).[4] Abhinava uses yet another example to illustrate the unification of *abhinayas*. "Just as the perfumer brings various constituent materials from the house of a herb-gatherer (*kirāṭa*) and then mixes them, some first, some later, in the same manner the *abhinayas* are dealt with in this chapter" (*NŚ Ab. 22:1*).

Thus, I have attempted to show that there has been a clear understanding of the multiplicity of the media of ***mimesis*** or *anukaraṇa* in the minds of both Aristotle and Bharata Muni. The nature, purpose and application of each medium is well worked out by them. As a matter of principle both the theorists uphold that performance is a unification of all channels and that there is a system of unification to achieve the desired effects. Aristotle, owing to the compact nature of his work has been brief but Bharata Muni is amplificatory.

Notes

1. *Ākṛtistasya kartavyā yasya prakṛtirāsthitā/ Yathā jantuḥ svabhāvaṃ svaṃ parityajya anya daihikam// Tatsvabhāvaṃ hi bhajaṭe dehāntaramupāśritaḥ/ Veṣeṇa varṇakaiścaivācchāditaḥ puruṣastathā// Parabhāvaṃ prakurute yasya veṣaṃ samāśritaḥ. (NŚ 21:89-91).*

2. "The movie star wears a different story and costume in each film. But he is groomed for one limited set of traits and these vivify all his roles. The cynical easy violence of Bogart, the austere integrity of Cooper, the slurred, rough goodness of Wayne; the virgin who will fuck of Doris Day; the slut who is good of Marilyn Monroe..." Richard Schechner, *Essays on Performance Theory 1970-76* (New York: Drama Book Specialists, 1977) 29.
3. *"Āhāryo hi yadyapi abhinaya antarebhyo nyūnastathāpi tasya siddhasvarūpatvānnātropādānam. Āṅgikādikriyāṇāṃ hi purvā-parībhūtarūpatayā sambhāvanīyaviśeṣabhāvanādekīkārātmā sāmānyābhinayo yatnasampādya eva. Āhāryasya tu tanmadhye sthiratvena avasthānāt ayatnasiddha eva asau. Ata eva āhārye api bhaviṣyati sāmānya abhinayacintā. Na tu sarvathā eva asya tatra tyāgaḥ" NŚ Ab. 22:1).*
4. In spite of the '*alātacakra*' simile, the misunderstanding persists that in classical theatre the written text was of primary importance. As Sisir K. Das puts it, "The popular theatre is often described as a 'total theatre' where music and dance and costumes and words are woven together to present one whole. The primary importance in a Sanskrit drama is given to a written text which is presented through *abhinaya* (acting) without resorting to dance and music as devices of narration or presentation. Some scholars, however, think that the popular theatre evolved out of classical tradition." "Medieval Indian Theatre: A Study in Terminology." *Journal of Comparative Literature* 24 (1986) 94-123.

8

A Comparison of Greek and Indian Theatrical Space

WE may now consider the nature of performance spaces used by the sacred drama of ancient Greece and India. The manner in which the performance area is divided and made available to the spectators clearly reflects the kinds of theatrical devices and communication channels that a given performance tradition has made use of. As argued earlier, both the traditions under our present purview are hieropraxic, but still there are some major differences in their ways of using theatrical media and hence in the method of using performance spaces.

It may also be stated at the very start of our exposition, that an analysis of performance space is not part of any ancient dramatic theory. The *Poetics* has hardly anything to say about the nature of a ***theatron***, and the *Nāṭyaśāstra*, even though it provides details of its measurement, does not reveal anything which might indicate any thinking on the manipulation of space to create variations in the performance environment. In fact, for the ancients, the subject of performance conditions was not a matter of selecting from variables. For them, there was only one system which each culture took for granted. It is now for us to analyse performance space as a varying structure that can be adapted to the needs of the performing techniques as we may wish to employ them. For that a study of the traditionally and historically available variables is required and a comparison between the Greek and Indian spaces can be fruitful for this purpose.

Here, I shall not repeat the task of describing the dimensions and other physical properties of the Greek and Indian theatre houses, as the subject has been extensively dealt with by many scholars. I shall here limit myself to a discussion of only those features of performance area and its distribution which influence the performance text, that is acting, costume, music, speech and so on.

Hieropraxic Division of Space

Use of space in modern theatre can hardly give us any idea about the hieropraxic management of space, where it is divided into areas which are reserved for predominantly three representational categories; speech activity, dance motions and musical expression. One activity-area does not exclude other activities entirely, but it certainly allows one kind of activity to dominate. For example, in Greek theatre the orchestra is the area where dance predominates, though actors also keep coming in and out of it. Division of space into melopoic, rhetorical and orchestral reflects the equal importance of the channels of music, speech and dance in the total performance script. Moreover, hieropraxic theatre permits a flexibility, in changing the same area from one supposed location to another by mere verbal or gestural indication without changes in cumbersome realistic stage props. This denotational variability of space is possible only if the performance space is not treated as if it existed within a single three-dimensional perspective frame. Any pre-realistic theatre, like the pre-Renaissance painting, must reject the distribution of the acting area as located within the perspective of a single hypothetical viewer. On the contrary, in hieropraxic theatre space, there is the existence of not one, but many frames of view. The technique is similar to that of the cave frescos of Ajanta in Western India or the medieval miniature paintings of Mughal and Rajasthan style, where the stature of a given figure is determined by the importance of its role and not by naturalistic proportions, and where other figures not so significant get greatly diminished. The action on hieropraxic stage is constantly reordering space by shifting the focal point or the centre to any corner of the space as needed. What is more, this is done not only through the channel of speech, but of dance or music as well.

The Greek Performance Space

The demarcation of performance space in Greek theatre was primarily to suit the large gatherings of city festivals. The sheer size of theatre was so great that but for the archaeological sites at various places, nobody would have readily believed Plato's testimony that eighteen thousand people gathered in one ***theatron.*** Not only the size but the design also tells the story of the assimilation of earlier rituals of Dionysian worship into the dramatic forms of tragedy, comedy and satyrikon. The closeness of the theatre in Athens to the age-old temple of Dionysus only serves to reinforce the belief that ur-tragedies were played either within the precincts of the temple or at a spot where the annual procession of the god's ***eidolon*** terminated. The evidence that plays were performed in the ***agora*** before a permanent ***theatron*** was built, does not necessarily mean that there was no link between tragedy and the Dionysian ***eidolon.*** The god, who in classical and later Hellenistic period stood in the orchestra of the ***theatron,*** could as well have been taken to the ***agora***. In any case, the celebrations of Dionysus Eleuthereus consisted of a procession (***pompe***) which went around in many parts of the city before it reached the main temple of Dionysus. (Pickard-Cambridge, *Dramatic Festivals of Athens* 61). As one activity of this ***pompe***, the ***eidolon*** could have been carried to any part of the city where the temporary theatre may have existed before the building of the permanent one. But even if no ***eidolon*** was carried in very early times, all the same the ***pompe*** had to be accommodated into the ***theatron,*** and therefore what needs to be noted most of all, is the suitability of the design of the open ***theatron*** which lent itself to be used by the festival celebrants with utmost ease. As we have pointed out earlier, dramatic activity here was just one ritual in the whole festival and that the theatre space was arranged in such a way that it absorbed the whole procession at the required hour.

In Greek theatre, the orchestral space was the focal point of attention. It should not, however, be supposed that mere circularity of design was instrumental in making it so. It was above of all, the Greek fascination with dance and a belief in its effectiveness as a dramatic channel, that attracted the attention of the audience. It is true that the majority of the surviving ***theatrons*** are horseshoe shaped in which the audience formed a nearly complete circle around the orchestra, leaving out a small space for ***skene***. However, the seating arrangement need not have been circular throughout the fifth century B.C. and earlier. The orchestra at ***agora***, where on the testimony of Photius, "***Dianusiakoi Agones***" could be performed (Pickard-Cambridge, *Theatre of Dionysus* 13), was, perhaps, not well-defined in shape. May be, during this period, the scaffolding for the seats (***ikria***?) was erected on one side of the orchestra only. This speculation is supported by the evidence of the seating arrangement found in some of the archaic ***theatron***-sites such as at Argos. Here, the original seating plan shows that the seating lines were not circular but were laid in parallel straight lines on a hill slope. At the bottom of the slope, an orchestra was carved out which later Roman remodelling made circular (Izehnour 11). Thus, perhaps, not till the time of Sophocles did the classical ***theatron*** acquire its well-known circularity.

But whether this circularity existed right from the beginning or developed later, it is the reservation of orchestra for dance and music that bestows upon it a special significance. The ***paradoi*** on two sides of the orchestra were added for the same purpose. These were spaces for specific usage, i.e., the formal entry of the chorus, an affair to be executed with great finesse and dramatic appropriateness, but nonetheless to be presented as a dance movement. Furthermore, the orchestra was not only a dance area but also a musical area as the dancers were the singers, too.

The provision for non-acting singers and players in Greek theatre was nill and the number of the musicians was small. It was mostly a single ***aulos*** player who did the job. His flute was efficient in producing a very loud, low pitched, penetrating sound that easily filled the whole ***theatron.*** He may have stood at the ritual altar of Dionysus, made in the very centre of the orchestra but distinct from the altar, "at which suppliants in various plays made their entreaties" (Pickard-Cambridge, *Theatre of Dionysus* 131). The peculiar manner of this choric employment of music, kept the Greek theatre productions bound to the framework of group action till the time of Euripides. The dialogues, whether spoken or sung by the actors, were interwoven into the scheme of choral singing which always brought back the attention of the spectators to the orchestra. In this respect, early Greek theatre has a unique place in the whole history of performing arts. Through group action of music and dance, the chorus reinforced the magnitude of the tragic themes by providing an emotive profundity to the spectacle. Even though the number of choral members was not large, usually twelve, some scholarly speculation claiming it to be fifty, the large space that they occupied, gave them a semiotic significance that no theatre has perfected ever since.

At this point it may be worthwhile to note that the ratio between the spoken and the sung parts of the text of the Greek plays, was the same as the ratio between the speech space and the orchestral space in theatre. The spoken passages of early tragedy and comedy in iambic trimeters, were only a small quantum of the total aural content of the play (the rest of the play in verse, was either chanted or sung, as ***parakataloge*** or ***strophe***.[1] Similarly, the early ***skene-logeion*** area was only a small fraction of the total performance area (the rest of it being the orchestra). It may be pointed out, however, that this rhetorical and orchestral division was not absolute, as part of the orchestra was often used for speech making. This happened when a character holding an intimate dialogue with the chorus moved into their midst for this purpose. For example, in the opening scene of *Agamemnon*, Clytemnestra might have stayed a long time close to the chorus of the twelve elders of Argos. This would have been easy for the actor of the early classical period when there was no raised ***logeion*** as speculated by Pickard-Cambridge in his *Theatre of Dionysus*.

Similarly, the Electra of Sophocles would have been able to converse with the chorus of Mycenean women by walking straight into the orchestra. She could have carried on the dialogue while the women danced around her. Her walk over to the chorus area would have seemed natural as the scene showed a courtyard located in the front of a royal palace. However, by the time of Euripides' play on the same story, the ***theatron*** had changed. The ***skene*** was by now more elaborate and the distance between the middle of the ***skene*** and the orchestra was much greater. Although the scene is set again in an open area, a cottage-front instead of the palace-front, Electra would now be required to travel a greater distance to intermix with the chorus. The new ***skene*** was big and extended even if there was no raised ***logeion*** till this stage of development in Greek theatre. Besides, there were other changes that made the intermingling of the actor and the chorus difficult. The speeches of the main characters had become more elaborate and the choral ode had started shrinking. In later drama, the gap between the dialogue and the choral song became very great with the near extinction of choral passages. The division of performance space into rhetorical, melopoic and orchestral, now became redunant. The evolution of a raised ***logeion***, the ***paraskenia*** and the elaborate double storied ***skenion*** was suited to provide an enlargement of the speech dominated area as required by the new scripts. The older orchestral area now seemed superfluous as the choral odes were no longer part of dramatic action.

The Effect of the Mask on Theatron Size

Besides the rhetorical-melopoic-orchestral space division which required the performance area to be big enough to accommodate group dancing, another factor which favoured the hugeness of Greek theatres was the use of masks by all actors. The chorus, it is believed, was not always masked. Perhaps, sometimes as in *Birds*, it was desirable for it to be so, but more often, as in the tragedies, there was no such need or convention. The main actors, however, were always masked. It is to be expected that an actor in mask, and that too in broad daylight, would need a greater distance between himself and the spectators to achieve proper histrionic effect. At very close quarters, the mask may not come alive. This, of course, is not universally true. In Noh, and many other African and Asian theatres, the actor-audience distance is relatively small and sometimes plays are done in daylight. Even then the mask is used with great success. The Greek masks, however, were made differently. They depended upon broad exaggerated features to convey an impression of things larger than life and, therefore, needed to be distanced from the audience. An idea of these masks can be obtained from the scenes in Greek and Roman bas-reliefs, but more precisely from the excavations at Lipari by the archaeologist Luigi Bernabo Brea done in the sixties and the seventies.[2] These excavations which provided the scholars of theatre history with terracota models of about twenty-two masks of Menander's comic characters, give us the best possible idea of a Greek mask. Although these masks belong to a late period, there is no reason to believe that they had not evolved from the masks of classical comedy. It is safe to presume that they were more or less like the earlier masks. From them we gather that a Greek mask covered the whole face and was, in fact, larger than a normal face. It was obviously meant to be appreciated at a distance and it helped to maintain the largeness of the ***theatron.***

The absence of mask from mainstream theatre was a cardinal reason for keeping the auditorium size comparatively small in India. The *NŚ* seems to have no word for mask (*'pratiśirṣa'* could have been a mask, but more likely it was a headgear). The *NŚ* has not even mentioned it as a dramatic device. In the wider performance tradition the mask is frequently used in many dance costumes, such as Purlia Chau, etc. but in the classical mainstream theatre it never seems to have had a significant place.[3] At a very early stage in theatrical development in India, the art of *sāttvika abhinaya* came to be developed highly. As *sāttvika abhinaya* depends upon a minute manipulation of the facial gestures and movements of eyes, eye-brows, lips and nostrils, it requires close watching. Hence, arose the need for smaller theatre houses in India. But all Indian theatre-houses were not small and the larger ones made for festivals must have been as large as the Greek theatres.

The Indian Performance Space

Regarding the data on ancient Indian performance space, it must be said that there is very little archaeological or literary evidence other than what is found in the text of the *NŚ* itself. The situation here is the opposite of the one on the Greek side, where many ruins, even though of shapes reworked and modified by Romans, have survived to help us make credible guesses about the nature of ***theatrons*** in which early Greek drama was played. On the Indian side, we have a detailed account in the text of the *NŚ* but not a single surviving ruin. And here none could have survived, as the theatre-house as described in the *NŚ* was made of wood and was supposed to be a temporary building. The ethos of the performance-culture of the time required that a fresh building be constructed for every performance cycle and then be abandoned. This tendency must have been very strong as no permanent stone structure was ever attempted till very later ages. As shown earlier, the making and consecration of the Indian *nāṭyaveśma*, had a ritual and festive function, which could not have been abandoned for the sake of taking advantages of a stone building. When the major performance tradition delcined, this theatre-house sunk into oblivion. Only a description has survived. By the time of Abhinavagupta (eleventh century A.D.) it had become a thing of the past. By then, many controversies arose among various commentators of the *NŚ* over the exact nature of almost every part of the theatre building. This is evident from the text of the *Abhinavabhāratī* itself. As my primary purpose in this chapter is to analyse the performance space used by the various channels of theatrical communication, I shall not go into the details of the controversies about sizes and parts of the ancient Indian theatre-houses.

The *NŚ* describes three kinds of theatre-houses; rectangular, square and triangular. Three general sizes are prescribed; the largest of 108 'hands,' the medium of 64, and the small of 32 (*NŚ 2:8-14*). A 'hand' is taken as equivalent to one and a half feet by most scholars, but the traditional temple-architects, the Sompuras of Gujarat, take it as two feet. All the shapes could be of large, medium or small size, but generally, says the text, the small is triangular, the medium is square and the large is rectangular. The *NŚ* further suggests that the large theatre is meant for the gods, the medium one for kings and the small one for others. Abhinava interprets it thus: "for gods means where gods (*deva-asura*) are the chief characters as in the genre called *ḍima*, which is played in *ārabhaṭī* (action oriented) mode with plenty of drumming and running around in lengthy (dance) cycles which are impossible to play on a small stage" (*NŚ Ab. 2:11*). He goes on to add that the medium size square auditorium is meant for kings, that is to say, kings as characters in the *nāṭaka* genre; the small triangular stage is suited for *bhāṇa* like genres which have single actors or for *prahasanas* which contain a small cast of low characters. Abhinava's suggestions seem very practical from the point of theatrical production, but whether it was actually the practice in ancient times is anybody's guess.[4]

In all the three kinds of theatre-houses, the division of total space of the building was made into three parts as follows: the dressing room (*nepathya*), the stage (*raṅgaśīrṣa* plus *raṅgapīṭha*), and the auditorium (see fig. A in end notes. Thus, the seating arrangement was not very different from the one found in later European and contemporary theatres. The *NŚ* also recommends that seating be raised in the manner of a stair-case. This increases the similarity of its auditorium with modern ones. In other words, here there is no circular seating, reminiscent of the primitive theatres or the Greek ***theatrons***. However, it seems to me, that there is a possibility of the Indian audience of *NŚ* times might have seated themselves on the three sides of the stage. This could have been done by using the so called *mattavāraṇī* for seating certain select spectators. The part of stage named *mattavāraṇī* (*NŚ 2:63-67*), has been a source of divergence of opinion among scholars for more than a thousand years. Most modern Indian scholars have tried to interpret the *mattavāraṇī* in such a manner that it keeps up the resemblance of the ancient theatre with the European procenium stage.[5] But the interpretation given very confidently by Abhinavagupta, based on traditional teaching, if not direct observation, suggests that the *mattavāraṇī* was a peculiar space that does not fit into any known pattern of stage design (see Fig. B in end notes). For Abhinava, the *mattavāraṇī* was a space, or rather set of spaces, which were located on both sides of the front stage (*raṅgapīṭha*). They stood in addition to the rectangular stage area, and they (that is the two *mattavāraṇīs)* extended beyond the side walls of the auditorium. According to some specialists of his time, remarks Abhinava, the *mattavāraṇī* was an eight 'hand' square, but others interpreted it to be as deep as the stage itself, thus making it into a rectangle of 8 x 16 'hands'. Some commentators held that the *mattavāraṇīs* were a 'hand' and a half higher than the stage, *(raṅgapīṭha)* but Abhinava suggests that their floor was of the same height as the stage, which itself was a 'hand' and a half high. As the *NŚ* text explicitly says that the *mattavāraṇī* was adorned with four pillars, it is commonly accepted that these pillars were to support some sort of a ceiling or a canopy over the *mattavāraṇī* area. Thus, for Abhinava, the *mattavāraṇīs* are two side spaces augmenting the stage, decorated with pillars and ceilings, modifying the total shape of the auditorium. (One is tempted to think of them as resembling the ***paraskenia*** of the Greek stage). However, Abhinava, like Bharata Muni nowhere mentions the use these *mattavāraṇīs* were put to. Were they performance space? The *NŚ* chapter on the division of acting space (*kakṣyā vidhāna*) while laying down which part of the stage is to be used for what purpose, makes no mention of the *mattavāraṇīs* as acting area. Nor it is suggested anywhere in the *NŚ* that the musicians sat in them. The place for the muscians was at the rear of the backstage. I am, therefore tempted to believe that the *mattavāraṇīs* could have been used as seating space for exclusive members of the audience, for couples of the royal household, or for the sponsor's family. '*Vāraṇa*' or '*mattavāraṇa*' in the architectural texts seems to denote a structure, embellished or otherwise, used for the purpose of sitting at leisure.[6] Thus, perhaps, the most leisurely class was seated in the *mattavāraṇa* of the classical Indian stage. In that case, the acting area was encircled by the audience from three sides. And if the *mattavāraṇīs* are accepted to be as full deep as the stage itself, then the bulk of the audience would not have been on one side of the stage. In other words, such a use of the *mattavāraṇīs* renders the Indian theatre seating arrangement similar to that of the Greek theatres, in the sense that it makes the audience fully surround the performance space. However, this must remain a mere speculation, until some further evidence on the *mattavāraṇīs* permanently deciphers them for us. I shall now analyse the way in which the division of theatrical space into musical, orchestral (that is of dance), and rhetorical areas took place on the Indian *raṅga.*

Space for Musical Activity

The Indian stage had an area unambiguosly marked area for the seating an ensemble of musicians called *kutapa.* "That which sustains the words and that which enlivens or brightens the stage is called *kutapa*" ('*kutaṃ śabdaṃ pāti, kuṃ ca raṅgaṃ tapati ujjvalayati....*' *NŚ Ab. 28:2*). Here, the function of the ensemble, or musicians, as the promoters of the spoken words in drama and as the embellishers of the visual content, is clearly spelt out. This ensemble consisted of some seven to ten persons. They sat on the centre back-stage by the rearmost wall which divided the stage from the *nepathya* (actors' dressing room). Two doors, one to the right and the other to the left were made in this wall, for entry (and exit) from the *nepathya*. There were no side entrances. With doors on both their hands, the *kutapa* sat on the floor of the stage (*raṅgaśīrṣa*) in the large rectangular theatre. In the square, medium-size theatre they were provided a small dais. The dimensions of the dais (*vedikā*) are not specified. The *vedikā* did not exist in the rectangular theatre, perhaps because the *raṇgaśīrṣa*, or the rear stage in the rectangular theatre, was a little higher than the front stage (*raṇgapīṭha*). There was never any change in the positioning of the *kutapa* in any theatre, rectangular, square or triangular (*NŚ 34:215*).[7] In a dramatic performance the very first action sequence was the entry (*pratyāhāra*), the taking of seats (*avatāraṇā*), singing (*ārambha*), and the tuning of instruments (*āśrāvaṇā*) by the *kutapa* musicians. They would now be there on the stage till the end. Thus, the musical space became the most central thing in a spectator's vision. He experienced the sustenance that music provided to the total performance. Even for our hypothetical spectators in the *mattavāraṇī*, the *kutapa* had its centrality in the scheme of the theatre-layout. This position of the *kutapa* is quite similar to the centrality of the ***aulos*** player on the Greek orchestral floor, who stood at the central ritual alter to guide the choric dance around it. However, it must not be forgotten that the ***aulos*** player would have been moving around as well, whereas the Indian *kutapa* musicians were stationary. Their position was such, that all action took place in front of them, often covering them from view. They were, of course, not meant to be watched nor were they considered as disturbance or illusion breakers of the world of drama. It may well be added that their presence served the very desirable purpose of affirming the fact that drama was only a make-believe (a play-thing or *krīḍanīyakam)* but nevertheless a true emotional reality.

Dance Space

The stage area in front of the musicians was the acting as well as the dancing space. Whereas, in Greek theatre, there was no exclusive melopoic space, as the chorus danced and sang at the same time, on the Indian stage there was no exlcusive dancing space. Here, the actor/actress was the dancer, too. As the need arose, he or she would mix dance with role-playing. A small amount of singing was done by the actor as a few lines were sung. But mostly the singing was done by the *kutapa*, The musical space overlapped with the acting area, but the dance space was always the same as acting space. All the ritualistic dancing in *pūrvaraṅga* was done on the acting area to consecrate the stage. Here they also performed dancing which was often a part of some feminine roles, such as of Mālavikā or Ratnāvalī. The masculine war-drill dances were also done on the main acting area.

Division of Acting Area, or Kakṣyā Vibhāga

The *NŚ* has used a particular term for acting that also indicates a dramatic location. It defines a supposed location as '*kakṣā* and the acting done in the area as '*kakṣyā*.' On a bare stage a location can be indicated only by gestures and words. Once a spot is marked out on the stage, it has to be defined in relation to other spots. For dividing acting area, the *NŚ* first marks out the *kutapa* area (melopoic space, as I have called it). "The space between the two doors of the *nepathyagṛha* (green-room) is the area (at rear stage) where the instrument players are to be seated..." (*NŚ 13:2*). In the remaining space, the "division of *kakṣyā* is to be made by going round the *raṅgapīṭha*. Other *kakṣyās* may be specified by moving around on the *raṅga* (in special ways)" (*NŚ 13:3*). Here, two things may be noted. First, that all acting is performed on the *raṅgapīṭha*. Only a little part of the *raṇgasīrṣa*, that is rear stage, was left unused by the *kutapa* and no acting was prescribed in the *mattavāraṇī* area. In the context of acting space the *mattavāraṇī* is not mentioned at all by the *NŚ*. This only indicates that it was not a performance space of any kind, and therefore, all speculations by scholars who have imagined it to be a place for resting, or for withdrawal of players, or a sitting space for members of the *kutapa*, deserve to be rejected outright. Secondly, the *NŚ* verses imply that the manner of an actor's gait, the way he goes round the stage (*parikramā*), and the door he uses for entry, are enough to indicate the *kakṣyā* established on stage. Whereas on the Greek stage, particularly for tragedy, we are usually required to imagine a few locations such as a palace courtyard, a temple front, a sacred grove, or a graveyard, the places shown on the Indian stage were limitless. We are required to imagine gardens, rivers, *aśramas*, sea, land, outer space, lands beyond India (*Ilāvarṣa, Harivarṣa*, etc.), mountains, the upper and the nether worlds, houses, forests, and almost anything movable or unmovable found in the three worlds ("*trailokyaṃ sacarācaram*").

To whichever place a conversation or an action leads the actors, that spot is indicated by a *kakṣyā*. A *kakṣyā* or a spot is imagined to have an outer, an inner and an innermost region. Those who have entered a *kakṣyā* first, make the region of their locus as the innermost and those who enter (on to the stage) later are to be imagined as located outside a *kakṣyā*. Before entering the innermost region of a *kakṣyā*, a newcomer should turn his face to the right and announce his name and parentage. (*NŚ 13:7-10*)

There were certain conventions to be followed to help the spectators understand the imaginary marking of spots and regions. Some were very simple, such as a person leaving should use the same door which he had used for entering from 'outside' (*NŚ 13:13*), while others consisted of specified gestures which were supposed to indicate climbing, driving, flying, swimming, etc. (*NŚ 12:88, 89, 102, etc.*). Certain specific leg movements (*cārī*) were also employed to make up the gaits that were supposed to depict the actions of flying etc. The chapters ten, eleven and twelve give a detailed account of the movements that provided an actor with a wealth of gaits which are mimetic of almost any human or animal movement and which also spell out both the nature of a character and of the ground or the air or the water where the action is supposed to be taking place. For instance, by such coded gestures, gods could be represented as wandering or appearing in any kind of terrain (*NŚ 13:22*). These *cārīs* also freed the Indian producer from the need of employing theatrical devices such as the Greek ***mechane*** to show flying gods. Apart from these body movements, certain ways of encircling the stage were meant to denote characters. Western people and southerners were supposed to encircle the *raṅga* in the clockwise direction; those from the middle country (*pāñcālas*) and from the east (*ūḍhramāgadhas*) were supposed to move in the opposite manner.

Open Theatres

Given the wide variety of dramatic practices in ancient India and the diversity of occasions on which they were held, it is impossible that a provision would not have been made for holding performances in the open. Perhaps, open air productions were held more often than the housed ones. Some of the action-oriented genres such as *ḍima, samavakāra* and *vīthī,* besides being held in the large theatres, would have been very naturally held in the open. The *NŚ* lays down quite clearly:

> In an open performance, not done in a theatre, the *raṅga* may be made to face the wrong direction (that is, other than the east) under the orders of the patron. With the musicians (*kutapa*) at their back, the direction faced by the players is called the 'east' by theatricians. After fixing the direction and the dimensions of *raṅga* it may be said that such a *raṅga* can have upto six doors and to suit the conditions of *nāṭya* these can face the east or the west. When the stage has not been set in accordance with the prescribed measure and direction, then by seeing the doors and the position of the *kutapa,* one should mentally fix the east. (*NŚ 13:65-67*)[8]

Thus, all other features of the stage can be altered, dispensed with or varied, but the *kutapa*-door pattern is the invariable around which the remaining structure of the *raṅga* is laid out.

Let me summarize our comparison of the Greek and the Indian performance space. In both cases, space is divided into areas which are meant predominantly, if not exclusively, for musical, dance, or speech purposes. But the distribution is in different shapes. The musical space is identical with the dance space in Greek theatre, and is placed at the end of the performance area and is closest to the spectators. In the Indian case, it is unmixed and is placed furthest away from the spectators. The ***skene*** and the *nepathya* have identical locations in both cases. But it is the location of the musical space, whether as orchestra or as *kutapa,* which is of cardinal significance. It shapes the usage of the remaining performance area. This importance only reflects the signi- ficance of the music-dance channels in the totality of a sacred drama performance script.

Figures

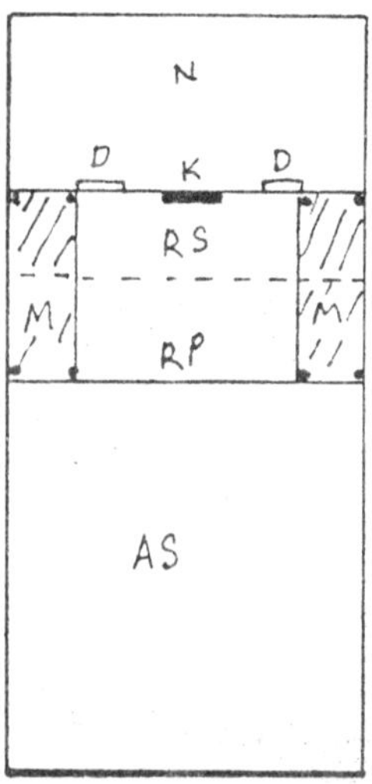

A

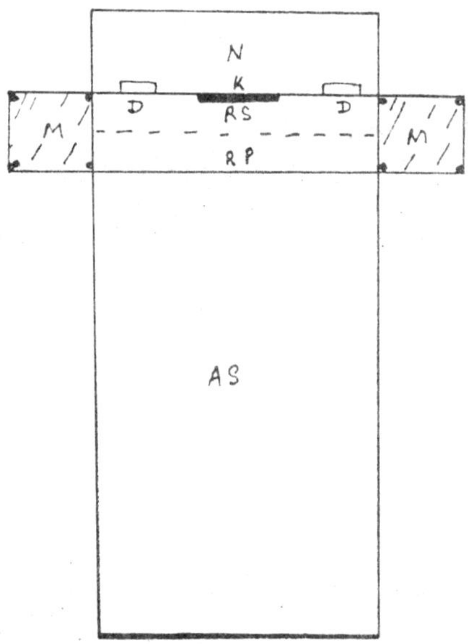

B

N *Nepathya* (Green Room)
RS *Raṅgaśīrṣa*
RP *Raṅgapīṭha*
M *Mattavāraṇī*

K *Kutapa*
D Doors
AS Audience Space

Notes

1. "The only parts of tragedy or comedy that were spoken are the passages in iambic trimetres, the metre of dialogue verse, which it used to be natural to translate into English blank verse, and for which in modern English verse there is no obvious equivalent." Leo Aylen, *The Greek Theatre* (London: Fourleigh Dickenson UP, 1985) 104.
2. Mario Prosperi, "The Masks of Lipari," *The Drama Review 26.4* (Winter 1982 T96): 25-36.
3. Whereas the regional languages have names for the masks that players use, the *NŚ* has offered no name. It is no wonder that David A. Napier in his book on masks has used the term '*kīrtimukha*' as Sanskrit for mask. He has not given the reference of any dramatic or literary text from where it might have been taken. The elephant's head placed on Gaṇeśa's shoulders after Śiva severed his original head, has been called '*kīrtimukha*' by Napier, but neither in any Sanskrit lexicon nor in any work of dramaturgy do we find this term, or any other term, for mask. The *NŚ* has used "*pratiśīrṣa*" for head gears of all kinds. David A. Napier, *Masks, Transformation and Paradox* (Los Angeles: U of Cal. P, 1986) 2-3.
4. It cannot be presumed that all Indian theatre-houses were smaller than the Greek ***theatrons.*** The diameter of the Lycurgean orchestra was 66 ft. The ***paraskenia*** and the ***logeion*** should be approximately 70 ft. And the distance between the ***logeion*** and the last row of audience was about 120 ft. The *NŚ* theatre of medium size (36 hands) was 72 ft. (or at least 54 ft if it is presumed that 1 hand = 1.5 ft.). Thus, the stage here, was as broad as the Greek one. The length of the auditorium, however was not much. It was only 48ft. (24 'hands'). But, if it is believed that the 108 hands rectangular theatre actually existed, then, its stage was 64 hands wide (i.e 108 or 96 ft.). There is every likelihood that these so-called large theatre-houses

(*jyeṣṭha vikṛṣṭa maṇḍapa*) were really huge. How else would they have accommodated the festive crowds that came from distant regions on great occasions? The idea that ancient theatre was a harem affair, accommodated somewhere in the courtyard of the royal palace, is a figment of the imagination of early Orientalists. It should be remembered that the ideal size of the play-house that Bharata Muni has in mind is (64x32 hands) (*NŚ 2:17*).

5. To achieve this end they (M.M. Ghosh, D.R. Mankad and later G. Panchal and G.K. Bhatt) and many others scholars have imagined the *mattavāraṇīs* to have existed on the right and left extremities of the stage itself. Now, the *NŚ* says, "The *mattavāraṇī* should have four pillars, be of the same *pramāṇa* (measure in depth or width or both?) as the *raṅga*. It should be raised by one and a half hand" (*2:64*). If it is postulated that the *mattavāraṇīs* existed on stage area, and were two in number then the eight pillars of the *mattavāraṇīs* would have also stood on the stage. Four of these, may have been placed by the side walls, but four of them would have occupied the stage. Most modern scholars are willing to accept this obstruction, while Abhinava's interpretation seems preposterous to them as it is so far removed from their 'normal' idea of the stage (the European model being the 'normal' for them). D. Subba Rao goes to the extend of ridiculing Abhinava, modifying his name to 'Anubhavalupta' (experience-less) and proposing that the *mattavāraṇī* was nothing more than a sculptural relief, a row of elephants tied to four pillars, made on the front elevation of the stage. For him, a totally European proscenium like stage with elephant pictures was Bharata Muni's theatre (*NŚ* ed. by R. Kavi. Baroda: Oriental Institute, 1956, Appendix VI 441- 45). Some modern pundits have suggested that the *mattavāraṇī* was a barricade erected between the stage and the spectators. It was supposed to obstruct (*vāraṇa*) the

unruly (*matta*) watchers from climbing the stage.

6. *Mānasāra,* the famous manual of architecture, gives eight words which are synonyms for '*mattavāraṇa.*' They all suggest that the structure meant by them was some sort of an area with a canopy, projection or ceiling. "*kapotaṃ prastaraṃ caiva mañcaṃ pracchādanaṃ tathā/ gopānaṃ ca vitānaṃ ca valabhī mattavāraṇaṃ/vidhānaṃ ca lupaṃ caivamete paryāyavācakāḥ*" *Mānasāra* (*16:9-10*) qtd. in the *NŚ* Ch. I and II, ed. with commentary by Satyaprakash Sharma (Varanasi: Chaukhamba Surbharati Prakashan, 1978) 87.

7. The *kutapa* should be seated in between the two doors of the earlier described *nepathya.* There, the *muraja* player is made to sit facing the *raṅga* (east); the *paṇava* player and the *dardara* player are seated to his left. This is the seating for drum players in the *kutapa.* The singer shall face the north and on his left side shall sit the *vīṇā* player. On the right of the *vīṇā* player should be the seat of the flute player. The lady singer is to face the male singer." ("*tatra pūrvoktayornepathyagṛhadvārayormadhye kutapavinyāsaḥ kāryaḥ. Tatra raṅgābhimukho maurajikastasya pāṇavikadardarikau vāmataḥ. Eṣa prathamamavanaddhakena tasya tataḥ kutapavinyāsa uktaḥ. Tatrottarābhimukho gāyakaḥ. Gāyakasya tu vāmapārśve vaiṇikaḥ. Vaiṇikasya dakṣiṇena vaṃśav-ādakau. Gāturabhimukhaṃ gāyikā. Iti kutapavinyāsaḥ.*" (*NŚ Ab. 34:215*).

8. "*Atha bāhyaprayogeṣu prekṣāgṛhavivarjite/ vidkikṣvapi bhavedraṅgaḥ kadācidbharturājñayā// Pṛṣṭhe kṛtvā kutapaṃ nātye yuktā yato mukhaṃ bharatāḥ / sā pūrvā mantavyā prayogakāle tu nāṭyajñaiḥ// Dvārāṇi ṣaṭ caiva bhavanti cāsya raṅgasya digvibhāṇḍaviniścitāni/ nāṭyaprayogeṇa khalu praveśe prācyaṃ pratīcyāṃ ca diśi praveśaḥ // Vidhānamutkramya yathātra raṅge vinā pramāṇadvidiśaḥ prayoge/ dvāraṃ tu yasmāt samṛdaṅgabhāṇḍaṃ prācīṃ diśāṃ tāṃ manasādhyavasyet.*" (*NŚ 13:65-68*)

9

The Visual Content

IN the chapter 'Medium of Imitation,' we noticed that the visual element was a major constituent of the medium of ***mimesis*** as postulated by both Aristotle and Bharata Muni. Here, I propose to deal with the actual appearance of the visual element in the two theatres. Aristotle has precious little to say by way of description of dance, gesture or spectacle in his *Poetics*. There is no choice, then, but to turn to other sources. Bharata Muni on the contrary has said so much on the subject that we can deal with it only selectively. Sources other than his, but of the same era, are not available.

The visual in theatre can be divided into gestures and movements of the actor, costume, mask, stage scenery and theatre lay-out (performance area versus spectator seating). The last I have already dealt with. Mask, props and costume, I shall not touch upon for fear of expansion. The theory behind their usage has been touched upon. Attention is given here mainly to the actor's body work as it was used in the ancient theatres in a manner which was entirely in contrast to the later European Realism.

Greek Gesture and Dance

Let me begin by recapitulating a Greek performance. All plays began with a prologue, spoken by a single actor or at times by two. The chorus then entered, often from the right side (spectator's view) singing and dancing. The tragic chorus consisted of five files (***xuga***) and three ranks (***stoikhoi***) and the comic of six files and four ranks. Sometimes, this entry, called ***parodos,*** may have been in a single file (Pickard-Cambridge, *Dramatic Festivals of Athens, 239-40*). As in all choric arts the ***aulos*** player came in with the chorus. Positioned in the orchestra, the chorus danced till the ***parodos*** was over. Their leader, ***koruphaios***, was number three in the first file which also was the closest to the stage area. Then followed a dramatic episode or an act in which the actors spoke or sang to each other and the chorus also reacted mostly in song. At the end of the episode the actors withdrew and the chorus sang a choral ode, a system consisting of strophe, antistrophe and epode. This unique feature of Greek drama was pure song, dance and mime, with the flute player also playing and dancing. The chorus presented a dramatic response, in continuation of the dramatic action, to the episode, making it an expression of hope, sorrow, despair or happiness through song and dance. The actors, then, entered again and the same cycle was repeated. On the termination of the final episode came the ***exodos***, consisting of an ode system, some dialogue and a brief song. The chorus then went out in the same formation of files and ranks.

Thus we find that acting was sharply divided between the actors and the chorus. Whereas the actor or actors would speak, recite or sing, the chorus with some exceptions, only sang. As is commonly accepted now, their song was always accompanied by dance. It is difficult to say what kind of relationship may have existed between the gestural code used by the actors and the one used by the chorus. We know that the use of gestures for orators was prescribed by the Greek rhetoricians for arousing emotions and effective communications. Quintilian has given an account of how the head, face, arms, body and feet can be made to express joy, sorrow, humility, abhorrence, wonder and many other emotions. But the orator, he suggests, should not use mimetic gestures and be as unlike a dancer as possible. He adds that an actor should not even attempt to imitate the voice of the character (Stanford 85). From this one can only guess that gestures of the actors were non-orchestric and rather oratorial. But of this there can be no surety as Quintilian wrote nearly four hundred years after the waning of classical drama (circa A.D. 35).

Whatever the nature of gestures, it is believed that the acting in classical period was not statuesque. Even in tragedy the high seriousness did not compel actors to eliminate the variety of gait and continuity of gestures. The flow of movement was often rapid and violent (Pickard-Cambridge, *Dramatic Festivals* of *Athens 171*). If acting was benumbed, the dramatist Myniskos could not have ridiculed his rival Kallipedes by nick-naming him 'monkey' (Pickard-Cambridge, *Dramatic Festivals of Athens 174*). One can infer that gestures of many kinds must have been employed as revealed by a close reading of some plays. From *Libation Bearers* (lines 24-31), *Suppliant Women* (lines 110-11), *Electra* (lines 146-50) actions like veiling the head, beating the hand and the body vigorously, tearing and hair pulling, gnawing the face with finger-nails and tearing garments can be inferred easily. Supplicants would frequently postrate themselves to touch the protector's knees and extreme appeals of pity by women would be accompanied by the gesture of baring their breasts, as was done by Clytemnestra in *Libation Bearers* (lines 896-98) and by Electra in *Electra* (line 1207), and by Polyxena in *Hecuba* (line 560). Embracing, caressing, hand-clapping and even kissing, in spite of a mask, are described in *Alcestis* (line 402); *Trojan Women* (line 763); *Phonecian Women* (line 1671) and *Heracles* (line 186).

Orchestral Activity

The gesture and movement of the dramatic chorus was a very different story. All of it was situated within the framework of dance which was the major constituent of visual element in Greek drama. As I have pointed out earlier, while discussing the division of performance space into verbal, musical and orchestral, the last division takes up the largest area to privilege the position of dance in the performance script. Dance was in fact an ever present reality in this theatre as the chorus all the time performed in some unobtrusive way. Even when the actors rendered their lines, except in ***stasimon,*** it did not stand still. Dance, then, was synonymous with ***opsis*** and its employment in theatre was reflective of its pervasive presence in Greek life.

While trying to visualize the exact appearance of choric gestures and movements we are again faced with scantiness of evidence. The names of a very large number of dance from the Cretan ***curetes*** to the Greco-Roman ***pantomimi*** are known. But the available fragmentary descriptions of these dances, even when put together with the evidence of vase paintings, are not sufficient to give their exact appearance. An authority on the subject like Lilian B. Lawler is forced to admit:

> As we have seen, a great deal of information has come down to us on the dance of Greek tragedy. However, the exact appearance of those dances eludes us. No director of a Greek tragedy can claim to set forth an 'authentic' reproduction of the ancient dances (85).

However, in an attempt to vaguely visualize what the dance movements may have looked like we can draw upon the following sources of information. First, upon brief descriptions of various dances that were performed on ritual, festive and sportive occasions; upon dances included in art forms like dithyramb and tragedy, nomoi, paean; and upon entertainment dances like ***huporkhema*** and ***pantomimi*** performed by professionals. Secondly, there is a rudimentary dance theory found in the writings of some late authors like Athenaeus, Lucian, Pollux, Quintilian and Plutarch. They all indicate that a definite choreology for the purpose of teaching and practising dance existed in Greece. Perhaps it was not considered a subject serious enough to deserve the attention of philosophers, but Sophocles is said to have written a book on it which is now lost (Lawler 82). In Greece, as in all cultures, dances of the people may have been transmitted informally. Dances of shrines and mysteries may have been taught in ***thiasoi*** but in the theatrical tradition a choreology must have been essential to sophisticate and assimilate the popular dances into theatric dance forms. For this reason, a book from Sophocles on the subject is no impossibility, others may have written too.

Greek Choreology

Greek dancing was part of the unified art of ***mousike*** which included singing and instrument playing. There also existed a general acceptance that dance was not mere exuberance of body but that its motions were meant to convey a specific meaning. As Pickard-Cambridge points out, "the Greek regarded all dancing as mimetic or 'expressive,' especially in its employment of rhythmical gestures and motions" (*Dramatic Festivals of Athens 247*). The gestures and postures of dance had come to acquire a fair degree of semiotic significance or else they could not have been used as transferable signs from dance to military drill to scuplture and vice-versa. Athenaeus, says Pickard-Cambridge, "compares choral dancing with military drill...and speaks of connections between dancing (in the wide sense including gestures) and the work of ancient sculptors" (247). The gestures, having their own significance were according to Pollux, "intimately associated with the words from moment to moment especially in ***huporkhematikon genos*** as if words and parts of body were connected by strings which the former pulled" (249). The unification between dance movements, both of gestures and posture, and the words, spoken or sung, was a common practice in some mimetic arts. While defining the media of mimesis, Aristotle stated that in drama language, rhythm and harmony were all used together. In dance, ***kineseis*** (movement) was divided into three by Plutarch: ***phoroi*** (motions), ***schemata*** (postures), and ***deixeis*** (indications). Lawler thinks that while talking about this three-fold division Plutarch is "confused and illogical" (25), though she concedes that he may have been using earlier works now lost. But it seems to me that there is no reason to doubt the validity of this basic division nor is it so incomprehensible, particularly if we keep in mind the parallel Indian system. (Lawler knew of Indian *nṛtta hastas* and therefore became a strong advocate of Greek ***cheironomia***. Indian *karaṇas* etc., were not known to the West by Lawler's time.) Let us consider them one by one. ***Schemata*** is an "attitude in which each motion terminated, suggesting it might be Apollo, Pan or a Bacchant" (Pickard-Cambridge 249). To the Greek audience, deciphering the sign system would have been no problem. It was like the *sthānakas* or *piṇḍībandhas* of Indian dance that denoted the various deities, as described earlier. Some of the names for ***schemata*** are : "'little basket,' 'snub-hand,' 'hand flat down,' 'seizing a club,' 'the split,' 'tongs,' 'go past the four,' 'sword thrust,' 'own,' 'bunch of grapes,' (Lawler 25). To Lawler these do not suggest definite postures or 'poses in which movement ends.' It seems, Lawler, presumes that a ***schema*** was a static thing used in isolation only. Whereas names mentioned suggest that a ***schema*** was an attitude which was employed in combination with other ***schemata*** and a whole sequence was expressive of a character or a deity or of an action. A single ***schema*** was perhaps something corresponding to a '*karaṇa*,' i.e., a single definite posture, but that a sequence of many a ***schema*** was called ***schemata***. About ***phoroi***, examining it etymologically, Lawler suggests that it comes from the verb '***phero***' which meant to carry. She adds:

> Greeks writers speak of the ***phora*** of heavenly bodies through the sky, of the wind, of a missile thrown at mark, of the waves of the sea. In dance ***phora*** would seem to imply 'carriage.' It may be applied to the feet of the dancer, to his hands, or to his whole body. In general it would seem to denote the way in which the dancer carries himself, moves from place to place—a combination, in fact, of our words 'step' and 'movement.' It would include such movements as walking, running, leaping, twisting or bending the body limping, skipping, hopping stomping. (26)

One can hardly refrain from observing that ***phora*** is an exact equivalent of Sanskrit '*gati*' and the Indian concept of '*gatipracāra*' on stage would be the same as ***phora***.

However, another critic Leo Aylen has interpreted the many ***phoroi*** differently. To him they stand for mime and "clearly involved a conventional dance language such as we find in Indian dancing" (118). The third category, ***deixeis*** is mostly taken to mean pointing at things. But Lawler suggests that coming from the very '***deiknumi***' it means, to show, display or portray in dance, "of flame, of flowers." Obviously, gesture or ***cheironomia*** would play a part in such portrayal (26-27). ***Deixeis,*** then, would mean a particular application of ***phoroi, schemata*** and ***cheironomia.***

Of all the terms of Greek choreology, ***cheironomia*** is the least disputed. It was a system of manual gestures with known signification totally parallel to the Indian system of *saṃyuta* and *asaṃyuta hastas.* No name of any particular ***cheironomic*** gesture has survived as have the names of ***schemata,*** but its employment from the very early times in Homeric ***huporkhema*** to the late Roman ***pantomimi*** is widely recorded. Like the *nṛtta hastas,* ***cheironomia*** lends a sense of certainty to the meaning sought to be conveyed by postures and movements of the other parts of the body. And therefore, it was said that the Muse Polyhymnia "expresses all things with her hand and speaks with gestures" (pseudo Ausonius qtd. by Lawler 12). Classical authors mention that the effect of ***cheironomia,*** even upon foreigners, was powerful and convincing.

Greek Dance Genres

Schemata, phoroi, deixeis and ***cheironomia*** provided only a choreology for instruction and analysis. For actual creation of the dances employed in theatre, it would have been necessary to base the choreography upon those dance forms which were widely popular in Greek life. We do know that the dance used in tragedy was called ***emmelia*** and that in comedy was called ***kordax,*** but just one dance in a whole play would not have been sufficient to provide all the choreographic variety of choric action. It is, therefore, not unfair to conclude that in order to portray various situations in drama, dances associated with those situations in Greek life would have come handy. For instance, employment of the sacred dances in the religious context and of ***paeon*** or ***purrixe*** in the martial context would have been very effective. Dance gestures could have also helped to indicate regions and races. Dance genres prevalent in Greece had been absorbed from sources as far and wide such as Egypt, Phrygia, Thrace, Asia and in a major way from Cretan and Mycenean cultures. "Even in classical times the inhabitants of Crete boasted that much of Greek religion (which would, of course, include the Greek dance) was of Cretan origin" (Lawler 39). Cretan dances performed before the goddess, called Rhea by the Greeks, in caves, groves and sanctuaries were ancestors of many a later Greek orgiastic dance. The dance called ***curetes*** was noisy and leapy, and depicted slashing by weapons. It could have been used for violent dance in the theatre. Other dances like ***orsites, epikredios, telesias*** led to the later ***purrixe*** and remnants of which could have been used for theatric marches of the chorus. Cretan ***kernophoron orchema*** was the basis for many Greek first-fruit dances which theatre must have surely drawn upon. Among the dances of Mycenaean origin, the best known was ***geranos***. Pollux has described it as labyrinthine movement in ***anamix*** (men mixed with women) style for meandering around a horned alter. It is said that Theseus first performed it at Delos after killing the Cretan Minotaur. ***Geranos*** could have been employed in theatre to suit the mood of solemn but reconciliatory celebration at the end of *Orestia*.

In the dramatic episodes related to mysteries and secret cults, the chorus perhaps drew upon the choreography of the Thesmophoric dances of Demeter. May be, Aristophanes did, in some way (hopefully not in parody) use, the Eleusian nocturnals in his play. All that is known about the nocturnals is that torches were used by the dancers. Most of these cult dances were ecstatic, clamorous and frenzied and were held in secret by the ***thiasoi***. Some dances were open to everybody like the Corybantes performing before Cybele which were also supposed to cure the mentally ill. Among the sexually sensational dances were the ones held at the temple of

Artemis where girls and young women performed in a single ***chiton***. Religious dances often required snake handling (perhaps at times of dough) as in ***oreibasia*** or at Apollo's Delphic shrine where his victory over Python was orchestrally enacted. Theatre must have used such ***agalmata*** (sacred emblems like snakes, etc.) and the conventional costume to help the audience identify these dances. For example, fawn skin, fox pelts and panther skins were used by Dionysian dancers, particularly by the feminine ***bassari***.

Of the non-cult kind, though not exactly secular (for no such thing could have existed then), were the dances performed at public occasions. Nomic songs, poetic accounts of heroic and divine adventures sung by a singer or by a chorus with flute and lyre accompaniment, ***paeans,*** supplications for battle victory and for warding-off pestilence or calamity, were amongst the many kinds of public performances and prayers which included dance. ***Huporkhema*** was a well-known dance form in vogue as early as Homeric times in which song, dance, instrument and pantomime were used in combination. It was often held in the honour of Zeus. Of the war dances and exercises, the ***purrixe*** was most famous. In Sparta, the performances of ***purrixe*** were rough but in Athens they were soft and graceful.

Of all the dance forms that provided entertainment ***pantomimi*** was perhaps the most intriguing. Though its hey-dey came after the decline of theatre, its history as a mimicry based dance goes back to prehistoric times. It is said to have been invented in 22 BC by Pylades of Cilicia and Bathyllus of Alexandria. Later on it became a rage with the Roman rulers. It was a highly coventionalized performance where the single dancer called ***pantomimus*** portrayed a story from myth or legend by playing all the roles. The episodes of the story were separated by musical interludes. The dancer/actor wore a closed mouth mask, as he remained mute throughout. He dressed in sumptuous costumes of Eastern silks. In the musical accompaniment, there was a change from the earlier simplicity of a single flute or lyre in favour of an ensemble of tympana, castanets, pipes, cymbals and other loud percussion instruments. An off-stage chorus of singers performed before and in between the dance episodes rendered by the ***pantomimus.*** The show began with a herald announcing the story content to be enacted. For every episode the actor changed his costume and mask. He had about five scenes to go through. As an acting technique ***cheironomia*** was used extensively. It was so effective that a dancer when challenged by Cynic Demetrius performed only by ***cheironomia.*** He kept aside the instruments and chorus, and told the whole story so well "that the amazed and convinced Demetrius called out, "Man, ***pantomimus***, I hear what you are doing. Not only do I see you, but you seem to me to be speaking with your very hands" (Lawler 141). As one can easily discern, ***pantomimi*** contained elements which seem to have Indian parallels. The herald is like the *sūtradhāra*, the instrument ensemble like the *kutapa,* the major dependence on ***cheironomia*** is like the Indian use of *nṛttahastas* and the one actor mime is like the *bhāṇa*. It is not impossible that ***pantomimus*** may have developed from the earlier ***huporkhemic*** tradition under an Indian impact. Its inventors, who were freed men, could have travelled outside Greece and absorbed Asian techniques. I have mentioned ***pantomimus*** in this detail only to show that it catered amply to a need which theatre had been fulfilling earlier, the need to see a unified expression of song and gesture.

Theatrical Dances

The dramatic genres themselves are said to have developed from dance genres like dithyramb, phallika or ***komos***, all of which were associated with the worship of Dionysus. The dances of this cult must have contributed to the choreography of dramatic chorus in a major way. These dances were the oldest dance genres, preserved through the worship of Dionysus. The Dionysus cult was thought to have been brought from Thrace and Phyrigia as a reintroduction from these places into the mainland, being originally of Mycenaean and Minoan descent. The exact procedures of this worship were a secret, but it is known that in the Dionysian dances called ***oreibasia, thyrsi*** (torches) were taken into woods where screaming women (***maenadas*** or ***bachantes***) were 'entered into by the god' (***enthousiasmos***). In the resultant frenzy, they raged about in the woods tearing apart small animals. The impressionable among watchers were sucked into this hysteria in huge numbers. Such rites were opposed in vain by some kings but were eventually accepted in revered fear (as depicted in *Bacchai*). By classical times they had toned down to become formal ceremonies performed at shrines and feasts. Similar to ***oreibasis*** was the dance of dithyramb called ***turbasia,*** the word meaning to revel in frenzy (***turbe***). But its madness was induced by wine not visitation. The introduction of the actor, or rather the conversion of the ***exarchon*** of the dithyrambic chorus, is said to have resulted in the development of tragedy. But how much of ***turbasia*** was retained by the tragic chorus and in what way, is only a guess. Perhaps it was employed to show violent movements.

It is commonly accepted that the noble and dignified ***emmelia*** was the dance of tragedy. But it is not clear whether all the dancing in a tragic play was called ***emmelia*** or the movements of the chorus in tetragonal formation at the time of marching in and out of orchestra alone were called so. The definition of Suidas includes, "dancing with song and dancing in accompaniment to spoken words, i.e., gestures..." (Lawler 83). This is not sufficient to specify the nature of ***emmelia.*** Moreover, whether ***emmelia*** was a separate dance form or a tragic dance, theatrical productions were required to draw upon many other dances besides ***emmelia***. In Euripides' *Suppliants* (71-78) chorus members urge each other to stage that particular dance which alone pleases Hades. Sophocles himself is known to have done the ball dance in his *Nausicaa.* In Euripides's *Hercules Eurenes* (*785-89*), the participants are asked to dance the joyous ***killinikos,*** as a mark of victory. Leo Aylen cities the ancient evidence on the dance variety in drama thus:

> Pollux gives the following tragic dances: hand upturned; basket; hand downturned; receiving the wood...double; pincers; somersault; passing four; Athenaeus' list includes a dance that involves kicking

> the buttocks with one heel after another; two kinds of owl dance, which is interpreted as stooping and gazing movement with one shading the brow, a dance mentioned in Aeschylus' *Envoys;* pounding the mortar; pouring out barley; cancelling debts, whatever movement that implied; spinning top; a dance involving some kind of movement with the elbow; he also mentions Pollux' hand upturned and down turned, the basket, baton passing, and pincers, and goes into some detail with the ***kallabides.*** (117)

The dances of comedy had many things to portray, not just a variety of humans but also strange beings, animals, clouds, and birds. The popular animal dances and mask dances would have been drawn upon by the comic poet to make up his chorus. The proverbial dance of comedy, the ***kordax*** would have hardly sufficed. ***Kordax*** was lewd, sexually blatant and vigorous. Much emphasis, all sources say, was on a lascivious rotation of belly and buttocks to create an image of lowliness suitable to comedy. In the satyr plays a similar dance called ***skinnis*** was performed by the fat and ugly ***sileni*** who were given a horse's ears, tail and hooves, and a ***phallos***, costume of goat skin looking very much like the satyrs of Dionysus. But as the satyr plays were short and limited in scope, perhpas other dances were not needed in them. In any case, it is difficult to say much about this genre as only a single satyr play has survived.

Unification of Dance with Words

I have stressed that a primary feature of hieropraxis or sacred drama was the unity of the visual and aural channels. As Aylen puts it:

> The choruses of fifth century drama include some very great lyric poems. But when they performed, they were received as Gesamtkunstwerk–song, dance, groupings, colour and spectacle together ... It is this unity that we must never forget. To understand and recreate this, it is with the unity, of word and dance

that we must start. (Aylen 115)

Not only was all dance meant to mimetically express the meaning of the verse, its rhythm was also required to match the metre of the verse. Taking a cue from T.B.L. Webster, Aylen contends that particular dance movements were connected to particular metres used in the choral lyrics. "Not only do all Greek lyrics contain a built-in-rhythm score; they also contain choreographic instructions in the metres they use" (Aylen 118). He postulates that dochmian metre was employed in tragic lyrics to suit violent movement of the chorus. Similarly, Aylen thinks that the cretic metre could have been useful to the kicking in ***skinnis*** and the slow ionic metres would have matched well with sinuous motions of the back bends of the ***maenads***. Dactyls would have helped stately movements (119).

Even though it is not stated anywhere, it is not wrong to presume that the Greek concept of rhythm was comprehensive enough to cover in its ambit both, the metre of prosody and the steps of dance. The Indian system worked along the same lines as we shall see later. Aylen is right in presuming that "unless music and dance worked with the metre all the time, then the point of metre would be lost. And if the point of the metre is lost in performance, then there is no need to torture oneself composing in that metre..." (120-21).

After observing that in the system of choral odes, the strophe was rhythmically (in metrical terms) identical to antistrophe, Aylen suggests that "both music and dance in antistrophe were an exact repetition of the music and dance in the strophe" (120). He has made such a postulation placing full faith in the observation of Triclinius, who, though he lived long after the heyday of chorus dancing in theatre, had recorded that in the strophe the chorus moved to the right and in the antistrophe to the left and in the epode it stood still. Analysing the meaning of strophe and antistrophe in many systems from diverse plays, Aylen suggests that a choreography arranged to suit the meaning of a strophe could be repeated as such in the antistrophe. The action depicted in the antistrophe was such that the same choreographic activity of the strophe would match the meaning of the antistrophe also. Though Aylen's argument seems commendable, it is not necessary that the repetition of metric rhythm should compel a repetition in ***phoroi*** and ***schemata*** as well in the antistrophe. May be the repetition was limited to the beat of dance, that is motion of rhythm in dance were repeated to suit the repetition of metre, but the gestural choreography could have been easily different. Besides, too much credibility is being accorded to Triclinius whose observation is not confirmed by any other source.

Visual Content in Indian Drama

The Indian performance began with an attractive preamble of song and dance (*gītādiprakriyā*) called *pūrvaraṅga.* It was meant to make the spectators forget their world of stress and care; in the words of Abhinava, "to untie the knots of grief, anger and loss in their hearts." The total run of a *pūrvaraṅga* was done in a succession of 19 steps. The first nine steps were performed while the curtain (*yavanikā*) was held somewhere midstage. The action of 9 steps was not visible to the audience, but presuming that the *yavanikā* was made of transparent material, then they half saw it. In the first step called *pratyāhāra,* the instrument players *(kutapa* members) entered from the doors of the *nepathyagṛha* and took their seats at the prescribed place, i.e., centre-back-stage by the wall. The second step was the entry of the lead singer and his supporters. It was called *avatāraṇā.* The third step, known as *ārambha,* consisted of sounding the tonic for all the singing and playing to be done in the play. The tonic was appended by a brief '*ālāpa.*' In the fourth step, the instruments were tuned to this vocal ground and an instrumental composition was played to test this tuning called *āśrāvaṇā.* The fifth step, called *vaktrapāṇī,* was to play only the strings to test their mutual coordination. *Parighaṭṭanā,* was the next step, it was again an instrumental composition in which the fingering and the strokes were displayed by the players. In the seventh step, *saṅghoṭanā,* the three *pāṇis* (three ways of making vocal combinations with instruments) were shown. In the eighth step called *mārgāsārita,* the drums were combined with the instruments. And finally a long composition was played as the ninth step named *āsārita,* in which the divisions of *tāla* were demonstrated and counted. With this much accomplished, the *yavanikā* was taken aside (*NŚ* 5:17-21). All this could only be heard by the audience as it all happened behind the curtain.

After the curtain was flicked away, the first visual was a presentation of song and dance (*gītavidhi*) in praise of gods. A *vardhamānaka dhruvā* was now presented to which many danseuses provided gestural accompaniment in groups. *Gītavidhi* was first of the ten steps to be seen by the spectators. Next came the cardinal ritual of *pūrvaraṅga,* the entry of the *sūtradhāra* with the *jarjara* pole. At the end of the *sūtradhāra's* prayer to ward off interferences (*vighnas*), the *utthāpinī dhruvā* was sung. This much was called *utthāpanā.* The *sūtradhāra* now encircled the stage many times worshipping the *lokapālas* (guardian deities of the ten directions). As part of this action, a handful of flowers were placed on the *jarjara,* and all the instruments were played while an *avakṛṣṭā dhruvā* was sung. Before this a *parivartanā dhruvā* was sung at the time of encircling the stage. The step was, therefore, called *parivartanā.* The fourth step was the recitation of the well known *nāndī* which was never sung but always recited, as it was not '*geya*' but '*pāṭhya.*' Then, as the fifth action, came the *śuṣkāvakṛṣṭā,* a *dhruvā* song with no poetry but nonsensical syllables accompanied by dance.

Upto this point there was very little *abhinaya* in the *pūrvaraṅga.* Abhinaya was now introduced by the *sūtradhāra* through his recitation of verses in the praise of gods, the king, the brahmins and the *jarjara* pole. As the *sūtradhāra* provided *āṅgika abhinaya* to the verses, this step was called *raṅgadvāra* (door to acting). The *purvaraṅga* then moved on to the seventh step called *cārī* in which an *aḍḍitā dhruvā* was provided. *Cārī* was the enactment of an erotic song narrating the love of Śiva and Pārvatī, says Abhinava. The erotic mood continued in the next step called *mahācārī* in which a *caturaśra dhruvā* was sung. After singing some verses himself the *sūtradhāra* called his aides on to the stage. While they moved in, the musicians (*kutapa*) sang a *narkuṭa dhruvā* in the *māgadhī* dialect. The theme, again, was of love. Then, there was some conversation between the *sūtradhāra* his aides and the *vidūṣaka* in a lighter vein. This 'done by three' or *trigata* was the ninth step. After this, everybody except the *sūtradhāra* retired from the stage. The *sūtradhāra* finally extended an invitation to the spectators to watch the play. In this last step, a counter *sūtradhāra* called *sthāpaka* (according to some commentators the same *sūtradhāra* was called *sthāpaka* at this moment) performed another *cārī* while some suitable *dhruvā* was sung. He then made the announcement, *prastāvanā,* about the play and retired. This concluded the *pūrvaraṅga* (*NŚ 5:17-29*). As we can see, things begin in the *pūrvaraṅga* with music. To this, dance is added, and finally gestures or *abhinaya* are added. It is to be noted that there was a constant spell of sound created by the *kutapa* which sat on the stage throughout the performance. It helped with the singing of *dhruvā* and other songs and gave musical support to the dances that were sometimes inserted. The drummers (*muraja* and *mṛdaṅga* players) provided rhythmic accompaniment to the gait or the steps (*gatipracāra*) of all the actors throughout the play. The drummers were, thus, more active than even the singer or the *vīṇā* player.

With the beginning of the play proper, we find that the visual content introduced in *raṅgadvāra* comes into full bloom.

Abhinaya, or the gestures of the actor, were a complicated affair. All the four *abhinayas* were mixed (*samānīkṛta,* the *NŚ* equivalent of "gesamtkuntswerk"); speech was accompanied by the intricate gestures and psychosomatic expressions of the *naṭa* wearing the prescribed costume (*āhārya*). All acting was divided into six methodologies: *sūcya, vākya, aṅkura, śākhā, nāṭyāyita* and *nivṛtyāṅkura* (*NŚ 22:43*). Whereas the earlier four fold division of *abhinaya* was based on the media of *abhinaya,* this categorization is according to the six ways of mixing the four kinds of *abhinaya* to suit the dramatic needs. That is why Bharata Muni has placed it in the chapter on *samānīkaraṇa* or mixing. Of *vākya abhinaya,* no exposition is needed here. "If through *sāttvika abhinaya* the meaning of the words, yet to be spoken, is communicated (*sūcā*) and then later on the words are rendered, then such acting is called *sūcā*" (*NŚ 22:45*). As we can imagine, this purely gestural *sūcā* would break the continuous exchange of words which is a marked feature of a present day dramatic presentation. And so would *aṅkura,* if it is practiced today. "If the deeper intent in the heart is expressed without words through *āṅgika abhinaya* in a skillful manner, then such a creation of *sūcā* is called *aṅkura*" (*NŚ 22:46*). *Aṅkura,* as we can see, is a kind of *sūcā.* Whereas *sūcā* is restricted to the enactment of the purport of spoken word, *aṅkura* aims to express its deeper but unstated implications. *Aṅkura* is, thus, the actor's interpretation rendered through creative *abhinaya* and is invariably the most vital part of a traditional Indian performance even now. "When a player does *sūcā abhinaya* in response to a sentence uttered by some other actor, then the manner in which a relationship between the sentence and the *sūcā* is established is called *nivṛtyāṅkura*" (*NŚ 22:50*).

The movements of the actors were to cover all the codified gestures of head, chin, neck, etc. which we have described earlier while dealing with *āṅgika abhinaya.* But the hands and legs activity was separately codified as *śākhā.* In reality, it was none other than the *nṛtta hasta* and *cārī* work, to which has been added the *karaṇas* and *aṅgahāras* of pure dance. This provided a total visual of semiotic wealth, which was given another name, *śārīra abhinaya* by Bharata Muni. Mixing the gestures of the different parts of the body was also part of the *samānīkaraṇa* process just as mixing the body movements, speech, *sāttvika abhinaya* and costume was also *samānikaraṇa.* "Where head, hand, breast, shins, thighs and *karaṇa* are balanced in their movements, the activity is called *sāmānya.* By the graceful movements of hands and soft motions of the body, the experts should perform acting according to the demands to *rasa* and *bhāva*" (*NŚ 22:73-74*). Acting on the ancient stage was done though embellished gestures and not in the bare mode of realism. (Some critics of eminence still believe that naturalism had a place there and was called *lokadharmī*, but it was not so. Even *lokadharmī* made use of codified gestures as we shall show later). To assert that *saṃyuta hastas* and *grīvākarma* like gestures were used in acting, some critics have quoted the medieval commentary (*circa* 16th cent.) of Rāghavabhaṭṭa on *Abhijñānaśākuntalam*. Elaborating on the stage directions, the commentator writes, "then she enacts the watering of trees, the *abhinaya* for this is: hands to be held in *nalinīpadmakoṣa* gesture, shoulders to be bent, the head to be put in *avadhūta* position and while looking down the whole body should be bent" (Act I, verse 16). Similarly, in Act II, Duṣyanta enacts erotic fever. On this Rāghavabhaṭṭa says, "it is to be indicated by *lolita* posture of head, *dolā* hands, and *śūnya dṛṣṭi*." But in addition to the countless verses of the *Nāṭyaśāstra*, which describe the application (*viniyoga*, *karma* or *prayoga*) of various kinds of *abhinaya*, there is a whole chapter on *citrābhinaya*. If the gestures were not for dramatic purposes why would their application be advocated? It may be noted that Rāghavabhaṭṭa has given the *abhinaya* for only the stage directions; for the dialogue he takes it for granted that there would be gestural acting. The *citrābhinaya* chapter (the twenty-fifth), describes acting for those situations and actions which have not been covered in the earlier chapters. For example, it begins by saying that to indicate the morning, the skies, the seasons, deep woods and waters, the *uttāna* hand posture followed by *svastika*, is to be used in combination with the appropriate eye movements. For greeting elders or teachers, *svastika* and *tripatāka hastas* should be used to enact folded hands. *Khaṭakāmukha hasta* should be used for holding the whip" (*NŚ 25:169*). "Small birds like parrots and bigger ones like peacock, crane and swan are to be indicated by body postures (*aṅgahāras* and *recakas*)" (*NŚ 25:69*). Leg movements and gaits are prescribed for denoting ghosts, *yakṣas* and demons. A verse says that people are to be denoted by *aṅgahāras* as well as by naming. The supposedly invisible characters, like the gods, should be denoted only by *aṅgahāras*. Actions like running, fainting, praying etc., are also given in this chapter along with the way of acting asides, soliloquy, and so forth. The *NŚ* says that for all this depiction, there are three guides to *anukaraṇa*: the actions of the people (*loka*), the arts and sciences (*veda*) and personal experience (*ādhyātma,* or '*svasaṃvedana*' as Abhinava renaınes it). *Loka* or rather, *trailoka* (the three worlds, upper of gods, middle of men and lower of demons) is the subject of *nāṭya. Veda* is the art of *nāṭya* consisting of all the techniques of *abhinayas, rasa* etc. which have been given in the *NŚ*. However, the way in which these prescribed codes are to be used are endless. Also, by the evidence of *loka* and concepts of *nāṭya,* new prescriptions can be made on the basis of *ādhyātma.* The codes of *nāṭya,* then, are not as said earlier, closed signifiers but are open and variable.

> How is that the meaning of the attributes of *nāṭya,* which is patterned after pity and love and such like feelings, is made available to perception? By the media of *āṅgika* and other *abhinayas,* these *āṅgika* and other *abhinayas* are neither to be taken as *liṅga* nor as *saṅket.* " *Evaṃ dayā ratyādi rūpānusaraṇabhuto nāṭyalakṣaṇa arthaḥ kathaṃ pratītigocarī bhavati iti āha—aṅgādi iti. Ye abhinayāḥ āṅgikādayaḥ na ca te liṅga-saṅketādirūpāḥ, apitu pratyakṣasākṣātkārakalpā pratītiḥ.*" *(NŚ, Ab. 1:119)*

Liṅga in logic means the invariable mark which proves the existence of anything in an object ("as in the proposition: 'There is fire because there is smoke,' smoke is the *liṅga*" (Monier Williams 901). Now if the *hastas* and other gestures were *liṅgas,* there would be an invariable or fixed relationship between them and the meaning they convey; their meaning could be easily and indisputably deciphered, or inferred as fire is from smoke. A *patākā* would have only one meaning, let us presume the sword. Seeing *patākā hasta* one would invariably infer the sword. But it is not so. As the *NŚ* says, *patākā* can be employed to represent many things. Similarly, *abhinaya* is not a *saṅket* or a " preconcerted sign or signal or gesture" (Monier Williams 1126). Tradition and stage convention does introduce a certain amount of preconception in a *hasta* but it does not limit the meaning to one sense. A *hasta* for a ball can also mean other rotund things like breasts or oranges and which particular meaning is implied at a given moment has to be discovered from the context. That is why Abhinava says that the *nāṭya* experience is '*pratyakṣasākṣtkārakalpā pratītiḥ* an experience or perception (*pratītiḥ*) which is based on the direct report of the senses. The meaning of *nāṭya* is known from what is happening right in front of the eyes. It is not inferred from *abhinayas* as *liṅga* or *saṅket*, for this kind of knowledge is neither true nor false nor real in worldly terms ("*ato na laukikasamyaṅmithyājñānādirūpāḥ*," *NŚ Ab. 1:119*). As Abhinava further clarifies:

> The erotic and other *bhāvas* of this experience (*nāṭya pratīti*) are synonymous with an unparalleled tasting (*vilakṣaṇa āsvāda*) of which the helpers are *rati* and like feelings. Therefore, by the reason of being communicated from (something) in front of a person the communication is denoted by the word *abhinaya*, a word not current in common parlance or other *śāstras* (disciplines). "*Tasyaiva bhāvāḥ śṛṅgārādayo vilakṣaṇāsvādaparyāyapratītyupayoginaḥ ratyādayaḥ. Ata evābhimukhyanayanahetutvādanyalokaśāstrāprasiddhenābhinayaśabdena vyapadeṣyāḥ*." (*NŚ Ab. 1:119*)

Abhinaya, then, is interpreted by Abhinava as not only a system of unfixed signs or what has been called "denotational flexibility" in modern semiotics (Elam 12), but also as a system which not only signifies things that are worldly, but creates something non-worldly (*alaukika*) also. At the end of his commentary to the chapter on *citrābhinaya*, Abhinava gives about fifty verses of his own in which *hastas* are prescribed to depict Viṣhṇu, Sarasvatī, Gaṅgā, Vindhyās, Jain saints, birds, horses, armies, etc. To clinch his point on the floating signification in *abhinaya* and to demonstrate its improvisational potential he says:

> That which is created by one's own imagination is called *citrābhinaya* ("*tasya svabudhyā ghaṭanaṃ citrābhinayaṃ viduḥ*"), and adds, "...even Vācaspati cannot exhaust its variety, what to say of one like

me". (*NŚ Ab.* 25:124)

It is clear from the above citations that acting on the ancient Indian stage consisted of semiotized gestures called *hastas, recakas, aṅgahāras* etc. But were these employed uniformly in all plays irrespective of differences in dramatic genres? It was not so. *Sukumāra* and *āviddha* (gentle or embellished and bold or energetic) were the two main modes of production. *Nāṭaka, prakaraṇa, bhāṇa, vīthī* and *utsṛṣṭkāṅka* were *sukumāra*, whereas *ḍima, samavakāra, īhāmṛga, vyāyoga* and *prahasana* were *āviddha* (*NŚ* 26:26-30). This general dichotomy observed the concept of *vṛttis* which were employed according to the dramatic themes. The *sukumāra* group had erotic themes, the *āviddha* ones were on war. Genres like *nāṭakas* and *prakaraṇas* were done in the *kaiśikī vṛtti* with full use of *aṇgahāras* and *recakas* as a high degree of embellishment in gestures constituted the *kaiśikī vṛtti*. *Bhāṇa* and *vīthī* were less sophisticated. Their production was much subdued in ornamentation. But even in the *āviddha* mode used for *ḍima* and such agonal genres the gestures, were the same, though not embellished. It should not be believed that to represent the heroic temper and austerity of emotion, acting was made devoid of codified gestures, or was done in a statuesque style. The *hastas* and *aṅgahāras* were fully employed but were done with a vigour and brashness to depict heroic feelings. The use of *cārīs* and *nyāyas* (fighting postures) was made in abundance here.

This brings us to the question: what role did dancing play in these plays? Pure dance (*nṛtta*) constituted a good deal of the *pūrvaraṅga*. All the *dhruvā* songs inserted here were danced and the chief danseuse was made to perform them. Her status was great as she had received special blessings from the *nāṭyācārya* at *raṅgapūjana*. Besides their inclusion in *pūrvaraṅga*, the *dhruvā* songs were employed throughout the play. The playwright (*kavi*) did not compose them, but they were inserted by the producer at five episodic situations: entry and exit of every persona, on fainting, as an interruption, and to soothe the audience after some highly exciting episode. The *dhruvās* were enacted while the *kutapa* sang their verses in *prākṛta*. The enactment was presumably meant to incorporate pure dancing in the gestural *abhinaya*. However, in the episodic action, *nṛtta* was rare, except on occasions like Mālavikā dancing before Agnimitra. It is also clear that the whole range of codified gestures was the same for both dramatic acting (*nāṭya*) and pure dance (*nṛtta*). In *nṛtta* these *aṅgahāras* etc. conveyed a mood or complex emotion but no story. The addition of a story, or the episodic element, was enough to push *nṛtta* towards *nāṭya*. In *nṛtta*, gestures were subsidiary to the moving about of limbs (*gātravikṣepa*); but in *nāṭya* they became meaningful (*arthabhāvakam*). To the modern Eurocentered spectator ancient drama would have seemed burdened with dance, a sort of ballet overladen with music and choreography, just as to those who envy the freedom of modern Western dance, traditional classical Indian dances seem "manacled to a descriptive, narrative and episodic text..." (Chaitanya:8). Modern reactions are only reflective of the splintering of dance and drama that simply did not exist in ancient times.

As regards the exact appearance of the dancing/acting postures of Bharata Muni's times, we have to be content with speculation. But we are here on more definitive grounds than in the case of ancient Greek gestures. A few names (like *hallīsaka* from *Harivaṃśa*) of specific dance genres have come down but with descriptions of little worth. However, what has been uniquely preserved in India, is an unbroken tradition of keeping alive in practice the choreology that Bharata Muni had compiled. The evidence from sculpture, right from the Mauryan times down to the late medieval, corroborates this continuity which is also evidenced by dance manuals. Regading *karaṇas* which could be called the spine of the choreology, a profound scholar, V. Raghavan maintains:

> This is the essence of dance, and although the old names of those poses had become obsolete in later times the material as such, as I have noted elsewhere, has not changed and either in whole or in part, under diverse later and local nomenclature, these poses or parts of them persisted and could still be

recognized in the surviving dance forms. (Preface to *Nṛttaratnāvalī 85*)

So it can be safely presumed that the basic structure of not only *karaṇas* but all *abhinaya* codes and *hastas* and *cārīs* included, has not changed much in spite of regional modifications and local developments. The system of Bharata Muni had come to be called '*mārgī*' from the seventh century onwards. The repertoire inherited from tradition was called '*mārgī*' and the newer additions and innovations were given the name of '*deśī*'. It is sometimes believed that *deśī* was based on concepts different from the ancient ones. But nothing could be further from the truth. The medieval *grāmarāgas, bhāṣārāgas, tālas* of music, and the *deśī karaṇas* were structured on the same ancient conceptual basis. Just as the ten characteristics (*aṃśa, graha* etc.) of singing a *jāti* of Bharata Muni's time were used to render *grāmarāgas* and later *rāgas*, and are observed even today, similarly, the *deśī karaṇas* and *aṅgahāras* were remodellings, often only in nomenclature, of the ancient *karaṇas*. It is worthwhile to bear in mind V. Raghavan's observation:

> A complete *mārgī-deśī* co-ordination is to be undertaken to show the actual additions and the cases of overlapping and the same old movement coming up under new Sanskrit or *prākṛta* or other local nomenclature. Such a co-ordination would show that it would be difficult to draw a line, in the flowing current of development of the art, to show where exactly *Mārga* ends and *Deśī* begins or to pick out of the mass or movements what exactly is *Mārga* and what is *Deśī*. The very concept of *Mārga* and *Deśī* would become fluid with a lot of overlapping. The rough and ready definition of *Deśī* supplied by Kallinatha, that it is what Bharata did not speak of, but Kohala and others spoke about, would have to be taken with adjustments in many cases. (Preface to *Nṛttaratnāvalī 118*).

The inclusion of *deśī*, therefore, does not pose any serious threat to the continuity of Bharata Muni's system.

In fact, the system had been evolved into a standardized form by the time Bharata Muni came to compile it and has had the resilience to persist under the Indian system of teaching and preservation. As a result, even though we are in no position to recapture the exact choreographic shape of ancient *nāṭya* productions, we are certainly in a position to reconstruct an extremely close likeness to them with the clear and definitive knowledge of the grammar of dance/*nāṭya* still extant. What is more, those *karaṇas, nṛtta-hastas, cāris* and *sthānas* which are today lost or forgotten can be reconstructed from the *NŚ* with certitude. In brief, unlike the reconstruction of Greek drama, that of Indian drama is well within reach. What is lacking is only the will to achieve it.

10

The Aural Content

THE aural in theatre can be divided into two parts; the spoken word and the sung word (with or without instrumental accompaniment). The spoken word in the form of natural conversational speech was not much used in ancient theatre. It was always a studied pitch variation, ranging from intoned speech to fully embellished song. There was also a variety of usage between the intoned word and the song. On the contrary, in Naturalist theatre there has always been a gap between the spoken dialogue and the song. As there was no such gap in those times, the ancient theatre theorists were not concerned with the distinction between the spoken word and the sung word. Instead, what was more important to them, was the distinction between the linguistic content of the word and its musical content. Sound was considered to generate meaning in two ways; by ***lexis*** and ***melopoiia.*** In Indian terms, by *vāk* and *gāna*. Language, ***lexis*** or *vāk* was transformed into dramatic discourse through intonation, pitch variation, or song, and all these three ways combined to make up the ancient actor's dialogue.

Lexis

As is well known, Aristotle has counted ***lexis*** and ***melopoiia*** among the six cardinal elements of tragedy (all drama by extention). However, they both have been given a short srift in the *Poetics*. On ***lexis,*** Aristotle says:

> Next, as regards Diction. One branch of the inquiry treats Modes of Utterance. But this province of knowledge belongs to the art of Delivery and to the masters of that science. It includes, for instance, what is a command, a prayer, a statement, a threat, a question, an answer, and so forth. To know or not to know these things involves no serious censure upon the poet's art... We, may therefore, pass this over as an inquiry that belongs to another art, not to poetry. (*Poetics XIX, 4-5*)

This exclusion of Modes of Utterance from inquiry, reveals that Aristotle looked at diction only in terms of phonology, grammar and figures of speech, and not at its conversion into dramatic discourse. If a dramatist need not know what is a command, a threat, etc., then who else should? It is no wonder that after the above quoted observation Aristotle proceeds to consider only the functional aspects of language such as letters, syllables and so forth. This part of ***lexis*** is factual and we need not go into it. Instead we may go on to see what he has to say on a playwright's linguistic style. Here, Artistotle seems to recommend a balance between the clarity produced by usage of current words and the loftiness achieved by extraordinary usage which avoids obscurity or eccentricity:

> The perfection of style is to be clear without being mean... That diction, on the other hand, is lofty and raised above the common-place which employs unusual words. By unusual, I mean strange (or rare) words, metaphorical, lengthened—anything, in short, that differs from the normal idiom, yet a style wholly composed of such words is either a riddle or a jargon;...For by deviating in exceptional cases from the normal idiom, the language will gain distinction, while at the same time, the partial conformity with usage will give perspicuity. (*Poetics XXII, 1-5*)

Some examples of style that he takes up from the dramatic poets suggest that loftiness was much admired by him. But on the possible ways in which language, or rather the total verbal content may have been rendered on the Greek stage, the *Poetics* is of little help.

Rhythm and Tone

As asserted earlier, the gap between speech and song was not so wide in ancient theatres as it is in our theatres today. For the ancients this gap was partially filled by the very nature of their languages which would rather seem musical to us. In Greek and Sanskrit (and other Prākṛts as well) words were made up of long and short syllables of measured quantity. The short was roughly half of the long. (Some have speculated that stress was used in ancient Greek, but there is little proof of it in the writings of classical authors (Stanford 65).[1] The speakers of these languages would have been more aware of the effects of rhythm than those people whose languages were not so rhythmically well measured. For the Greeks and the Indians all utterances, whether in prose, poetry on song, were in measured rhythms. Although, this exactness of the measure of long and short syllables may have been difficult to maintain in daily speech, in formal speech, recitation or song, it could have been achieved without any special effort. Moreover, the effects of rhythm would have been consciously enjoyed. For the same reason it must have been easy to compose music for poetry, as rhythm was the common basis for speech, metre and song. (Basis, is a cardinal word in this context: in Sanskrit the word used for rhythm is '*tala*' (basis), ('*tala pratiṣṭhākaraṇe*'). As regards the Greek practice Stanford notes:

> Classical writers recognized speech, especially when pronounced with resonant and rhythmical way that orators and actors used, had all the properties of song, though to a less perceptible degree. Both were regarded as forms of ***mousike*** and both were produced by the same instrument (63).

The 'instrument' here is the human voice as speech or song, both considered parts of ***mousike***. Rhythm is the connecting element, which was also a method of ***psuchagogia*** or emotional arousal. "The emotional effects of rhythm were a subject of serious study in Greece since the fifth century. Thrasymachos, the early expert in appeals of pity, was particularly interested in them. Subsequently moralists like Plato, as well as rhetoricians continued to examine their ethical qualities" (Stanford 65). As Plutarch has observed, "use of successive long syllables express caution, calmness or melancholy, and successive short syllables eagerness, agitation and excitement..." (Stanford 66). Moreover, rhythm like melody was a vibration of sound and could produce or generate the emotions which were regarded as movements in the psyche. "Rhythm could have a stronger effect then melody, since the heart beat is essentially rhythmical. The Greek physicians Herophuos and Galen compared the rhythm of the heart, with its systole and diastole, to that of a metrical foot" (66). The choice of a particular metre for a given dramatic utterance was based on this principle. Many instances from classical plays are cited by Stanford and Aylen to illustrate the use of metres for creating specific rhythmic effects. A theoretical support is found in Aristotle as well, who though passing over the topic in the *Poetics,* comments upon it in the *Rhetoric.* As Stanford reports:

> That orator who wishes to arouse emotion must know how to use rhythm, volume and voice melody ('the sharp, low and middle tone') for that purpose. He adds that those (actors) who use these properly nearly always won the prizes in the dramatic contests. (Stanford 71)

Here, besides rhythm, the sharp, low and middle tones of speech are said to be useful for emotional communication. In day to day speech, voice modulation or the rise and fall of pitch, is sure indication of changes in emotional states. The shrill tones of joy , the gutteral pitch of sadness or the quivering tones of fear or excitement are universal. In music, the ascent and descent of tones upto three registers is based on this same natural law. Likewise dramatic dialogue, the application of voice modulation, creates predictable effects. In fact, its ample use bridges the gap between speech and song.

In the Greek theatre there was no use of prose at all. The constant use of poetic metre imposed a rhythm that was always far removed from the intonation of conversational speech. It would be ridiculous to presume that the Greek actor ever tried to reduce metrical rhythm to conversational stacatto as is sometimes done in modern Shakespearean productions. The Greek view was simple; why go through the pain of composing in metre if it is to be rendered as unmeasured speech. Besides, in the theatre only fraction of the verse was not sung. "The only part of tragedy or comedy that were spoken are the passages in iambic trimetre, the metre of dialogue verse, which it used to be natural to translate into English black verse, and for which in modern English verse there is no obvious equivalent" (Aylen 104). This spoken portion, even if it was not chanted must have used the "sharp, low and middle tones" that Aristotle has mentioned. Regarding iambic trimetre and delivery in general, Pickard-Cambridge sums it up as follows:

> The practice of Greek actors included speech unaccompanied by music, speech accompanied by instrument (what is often called recitative and song). The first was normally employed for the portions of a play written in iambic trimetre (these metres being closest to speech) whether in dialogue or in monologue, the second for delivery of tetrametres and of iambics inserted in the midst of lyric systems, the third for lyrics. The texts which give direct evidence of this are few and except as regards recitative raise no difficulty. (*Dramatic Festivals of Athens 156*)

Even the whole of the text composed in iambic trimetre was not invariably spoken. Much of the iambic trimetre was recited with flute accompaniment when it formed part of the lyric system. As Pickard-Cambridge further explains:

> The word (recitative) does appear to apply to iambics delivered to an accompaniment, but it has already been noticed that there can be no certainty what exactly were those accompanied iambics adopted by the tragic poets from Archilochus, or those described

by Atheneaus. In fact a large proportion of the iambic trimetres associated with lyrics form part of the symmetrical epirrhematic structures in which the lyrics, strophe and antistrophe are each followed by the same number of iambic lines, two, three, four, five or more rarely by a single line; it seems at least possible that these lines in iambic were recited, and the contrast between these recited iambics and sung lyrics may be what is referred to as ***pathetikon*** in Aristotelian *Problems XIX 6.* (*162-63*)

This leaves very little spoken dialogue in Greek theatre, even if we presume that it was rendered in conversational cadence. The Greek actor, then, spent most of his time reciting or singing. On the nature of the recitative, ***parakataloge***, Leo Aylen has more decisive views:

> ***Parakataloge*** is the term applied to all sequences in between speech and song. I assume that it mostly implied a chant with many syllables on one note, or a very primitive tune of only a very few notes. But it seems that it may well have covered the entire range between speech and song, from something very near speech but against a musical accompaniment, to something almost song. On occasions its use seems very like recitative in some opera; often it is like liturgical chant; sometimes it seems to be a kind of colored and heightened declamation. (Aylen *104-105*)

A cardinal question that may be raised to decipher the nature of ***parakataloge*** is, did the actor use the same notes as the accompanying flute and how many notes were employed in a single line of verse. If the number of notes was two or three the ***parakataloge*** would have sounded like a chant, if it was five or six it would have been like singing. However, just the number of notes is not sufficient to make a line into a chant or song. As is known even chants can be with a few notes or with many. The examples of the oldest known chants, the Vedic, are sufficient to demonstrate this. The *Ṛk* uses as few as three notes and the *Sāman* as many as seven. Actually, it is not the number of notes but their ornamental usage that turns a line into song. But we shall never really know how exactly the Greeks used ***parakataloge***. All the same, seeing that the flute was invariably used for accompanying ***parakataloge***, the over all effect should have been that of a song and not of a chant. Even today, recitation of the *Koran* or the *Vedas* is without instrumental support and if (risking an outcry from the orthodox) that is added, the *āyats* or the *mantras* would sound like song. Perhaps such was the effect of the *Sāman* chants in the most distant past when the 'hundred stringed' harp accompanied the recitation. May be that is why the Vedic chants were called '*gāna*' and the ***parakataloge*** may have sounded somewhat like the very ancient Vedic singing. Not only the actor but the chorus also used ***parakataloge*** particularly when it entered the orchestra.

About the lyric systems (***strophe, antistrophe*** and ***epode***) there are no two opinions. "All ancient Greek lyrics were sung, and none were ever written except to be sung, since what the grammarians refer to as lyric metres are patterns that dictate exactly the rhythm of the song" (Aylen 106). It is also suggested that like the metrical structure the musical score in antistrophe was an exact repetition of the music in ***strophe***. Aylen has argued that even the choreography was an exact repetition. This, as I have said, may be doubted, but the music could have been repeated to provide the essential balance. The chorus members were made to sing in unison and their only accompanist was the ***aulodos***. The discourse between the chorus and the actor was usually the recitative answered by a song. In this way, musical rendition dominated the aural content of this theatre.

In Greek theatre practice, the transition from speech to recitation, or to chant, or to song (and vice-versa), was facilitated by a constant manipulation of rhythm and tones. There the meaning of words was never feared to be obstructed by music. On the contrary, rhythm and tones were supposed to reinforce the meaning. In the choral singing of the classical period, clarity of words was well maintained. Excessive employment of notes did not submerge the poetry which was enunciated with clarity. But this balance between poetry and music seems to have been given up in the favour of tonal elaborations by the later dramatists:

> But what seemed to the orthodox to be corruption set in when a new school of poets, and above all Timotheos, introduced for the first time into dithyramb and nomoi, music of much more elaborate and florid type, abandoning strophic responsion...This style was adopted in tragedy by Agathon and Euripides, who are mocked by Aristophanes for their innovations—their notes running hither and thither, compared with the tiny, tortuous galleries of an ant hill and probably setting of a single syllable to several notes...such things could hardly fail to rob the words of the required precision in utterances. (*Dramatic Festivals of Athens 261*)

The disturbance in the balance that obtained earlier was the beginning of the divorce between poetry and music.

Melopoiia: The Greek Musical System

It is not coincidental that a musical system developed in Europe just about the same time as a new dramatic system, which clouded the understanding of ancient theatre. The new musical system also made the understanding of the ancient musical system impossible. The new polyphonic harmony set to tempered scale where an octave is divided into twelve equal intervals, was an entirely European innovation. This system, in which many instruments play the same tune or its parts in different chords to create a symphony was a marvellous creation. But it also engendered a musical opaqueness; those with ears attuned to it are prevented from enjoying the monophonic music of other lands, ancient or modern. Before the innovation of European polyphony only the monophonic line was recognized as the base for constructing the play patterns of notes. Any number of instruments or voices followed the same line. (The later music of Greek ***pantomimi*** plays which used many instruments may have sounded the same as the present day ventures of Indian composers with orchestral music). The music score of Greek classical theatre has hardly survived except for a single fragment revealing a line from Euripedes' *Oresteia*. And so, "we are virtually without any evidence, and are dependent upon a few passages to the subject of the writers who just refer to it" (Pickard-Cambridge 257). But the records on Greek musical grammar have survived and it can be presumed safely that even though what is available to us today was put down on paper centuries later by Aristoxenus (a disciple of Aristotle) it was more or less the same system as was practised by the Greek dramatists of the fifth century B.C.

The Greek scales were derived from the notes as placed on harps like ***kithara*** and ***phorminx***. Here, one string (chord) was fixed for one note (***tonos***). The scales (***sustema***) were constructed from a building block of four notes (tetrachords) which were brought together in conjunct or disjunct manners. The conjunct system (***sunafe***) had the same common note at the end of the first tetrachord and the beginning of the second tetrachord such as E F G A + A Bb C D = E F G A Bb C D. Its interval division was S T T S T T, although the exact interval (***diesis***) value is difficult to ascertain today. The disjunct system (***diazenksis***) was made by inserting a tone between two tetrachords to make an octave thus: E F G C + B C D E with intervals of S T T T S T T. By joining the tetrachords thus, three major systems were derived. The Lesser Perfect, which was made of three conjunct tetrachords to which a note (***proslambanomenos***) was added at the bottom to give a sequence of one plus ten tones. The Greater Perfect System consisted of ***proslambanomenos*** and four tetrachords grouped in conjunct pairs to yield a sequence of one plus fourteen notes. The two systems were combined to make the Immutable system.

The famous so called modes of the Greek music were lifted out of the Perfect system. A mode was actually an octave beginning with the first, or the second, or the third (and so forth) note of the system. In all, there were seven modes (***harmoniai*** or ***eide tou dia pasoon***) called Mixolydian,

Lydian, Phrygian, Dorian, Hypolydian, Hypophrygian, and Hypodorian. All the ***harmoniai*** could be played in high or low pitch. There were thirteen such pitches or ***tonoi***. This was done obviously to facilitate different instruments and voices. There was no standard pitch for notes then as is the practice in European music today. Like the Indians do even now, the ancient Greeks, it seems, varied the pitch of their tonic all the time.

A given tetrachord was divided into three, diatonic, chromatic and enharmonic, according to the position of tones on it. Each kind was called a ***genos***. The first and the last tones of a tetrachord were fixed, the middle two shifted their positions to make the ***genos***. Each of the ***genos*** was further varied by a change of position of notes. The diatonic had two positions, high and soft, chromatic had three, tonic, hemiolic and soft, and the enharmonic had just one position. The variations of genera were called colours (***chroai***).

Among the many puzzles of the ancient musical system is the position of the tonic. Its position in a System or the ***harmoniai*** is different to ascertain today. In a given mode change of tonic from one note to another would have changed the melody. We cannot be sure today if such modulation was practised. Another puzzle is the existence of seven note scale or ***heptachordon*** which was also called ***harmoniai,*** as is mentioned by Aristoxenus. Perhaps Plato was referring to the ***heptachordon harmoniai*** tradition which for him had names such as Ionian and Syntonolydian and which are not to be found in the list of Aristoxenus.

From the variation of scales, ***harmoniai*** and ***genos-chroai*** one can see that the wealth of melodic intonation available to the Greeks was immense. The ***chroai*** can be found as paralleled only in the Indian system of *śruti* variation and it must have provided for the expression of a very wide and subtle range of emotions. Of the relationship between ***harmoniai*** and emotions a few celebrated sayings have survived which indicate for sure the Greek belief that music was regarded as the most effective means of emotional arousal and character formation. "Theophrastos, Aristotle's nephew explained them on the grounds that both music and emotions were the result of movements, music being caused by physical vibrations, emotion by vibrations in the ***psuche***. They also believed that the main sources of music were grief, joy and ***enthousiasmos*** (Plutarch, *Moralia 623A*)" (Satanford 50). Also as Aristotle observed, "In the rhythms and melodies we have the most realistic imitations of anger and mildness as well as courage, temperance and all their opposites" (*Politics V (viii) 5. 1340a 18 qtd. Butcher 129*). Also, "Melody even apart from words has ethical quality" (*Problems xix 27. 929b qtd Butcher 131*). Regarding the ***harmoniai*** and their association to specific emotions there is no description in Aristoxenus but Plato has called the Dorian as manly and heroic, and the Phyrgian as ecstatic. Mixolydian and Syntonolydian, he felt were mournful, and Lydian and Ionian were fit for revelry. On the whole there seems to have been three categories Lydian, Phrygian and Dorian for the pathetic, ecstatic and heroic feelings respectively, and the mixed forms such as Ionian and Mixolydian were ramifications of the first, Hypophrygian of the second and Hypodorian of the third. The ***genera*** and their ***chroai*** by interval variation further amplified the range of these ***harmoniai***.

Application in Theatre

The Greek chorus and the actors had the liberty to use all the prevalent musical forms as there was no restriction for ritual reasons. The immense variety of tunes and melodies with the subtle nuances of tone colour could have provided a vast area of cultural reference. Tone colour, on which monophonic music depends entirely, is not so much a matter of universal laws as of cultural associations with given melodies. For instance, in Indian music we believe in the association of certain tone colours with seasons or specific emotional states. But this association is taken for granted by trained listeners only. In fact, the association is perceived only as a result of training. The Greek dramatists must have used the same ploy. Giving an example of cultural memory used by the composer, Stanford says, "If a dramatist wished to evoke poignant memories from the political past of Athens he could introduce a tune from the popular drinking songs (***skolia***) that went back to the time of tyranny of Peistratids..."(52). But other than particular jingles or tunes, the modes and their melodies must have been used to introduce new choric tunes. "According to 'Plutarch' (*Moralia* 1136C-E) and Aristoxenos, Aristotle believed that Sappho invented the emotional Mixolydian type and that the tragedians took it from her and used it with the Dorian" (Standord 51). This is an obvious example of the efforts made by dramatists to widen their range. "Aristoxenos is also the source of a statement in the anonymous *Life of Sophocles* (23) that Sophocles introduced the Phrygian mode into tragedy. And according to Psellos, Sophocles also brought in the Lydian mode" (Stanford 51). Such statements indicate that the great playwrights improved drama by not only providing fresh scripts of high literary value, they were composers of music and dance as well. As the famous saying goes, Phrenikos invented "as many dance steps as the waves of the sea." The value of music was pivotal in tragedy; recognizing which Nietzche observed that, as the genius of music had fled from tragedy in modern times, tragedy is, strictly speaking dead.

As regards the actual sounding of ancient Greek music, particularly in theatre, I am tempted to imagine that it may not have been too far removed from the attempts of Indian composers at choral singing. Group singing has not been a major tradition in India and the present day attempts are inspired by the West. The Indian composers are unable to employ European methods of harmonization based on tempered scale as the *śruti* intervals of the *rāgas* are disfigured if tempered or harmonized. As a result, composers are forced to use a polyphony which is no more than many voices or instruments playing the same melodic line in unison. The Greek ***chroai*** would have been disfigured like the *śrutis*.[2] Therefore, Leo Aylen is perhaps not too off the mark when he says :

But if an Indian composer were to set a Sophocles

> chorus to the *rāga* appropriate to the mood of the piece, making use of the exact rhythm score that Sophocles has left and using only a unison tune accompanied in unison by a rough reed instrument, then for his audience he would have got very near indeed to the music of Sophocles. (109)

This, of course, would only be a demonstration of the structure of Greek choral music, not its reconstruction or reproduction. The music of a people is not only a matter of scales and systems, its identity is shaped by the way notes are put to embellishment and the manner in which the voice is used. Those subtle ways can never be written down and so can never be reconstructed. Perhaps after the Greek modes have been reliably decoded, a score can be made for the production of a passage from plays. A composer could set that melody score using a *rāga* of the same scale as the decoded mode. Instead of using the Indian tonal ornamentations like *'meenḍ'* and *'gamak'*, he could employ European quivers and glassando to create an effect less Indian and more Eurasian. This would be a more convincing likeness to the ancient sounds that once filled the Greek theatres.

The Vāgabhinaya Concept

While explaining the concept of *abhinaya* earlier, I had emphasized that in *abhinaya* all the four channels of gesture (*āṅgika*), speech (*vācikas*), subtly gesture (*sāttvika*) and costume (*āhārya*) were mixed together. It is a common fallacy that all other channels are meant to express the context of the spoken word (*vācika*). At the time of explaining the concept of mixing of the channels (*sādhāraṇīkaraṇa*), I had argued that it is not so. Sometimes the verse which defines *abhinaya*, is quoted to indicate the dominant status of the verbal. "That which takes the meaning of words (from the actor to the spectator) is called *abhinaya*" ("*yasmāt padārthān nayati tasmādabhinayaḥ smṛtaḥ*" *NŚ 8:7*). However, it should be noted that the correct reading of this verse is, "*yasmātprayogaṃ nayati*," that is, that which takes the performance to the audience is called *abhinaya*. The unprivileged status of the verbal, its non-dominant position and its equality with other channels is the chief feature of hieropraxis. All the same, the *NŚ* has not undervalued the verbal nor has attempted to keep it away from theatre as was the attempt of Artaud. The value of ***muthos*** or *itivṛtta* is given its due here. Abhinava says that *itivṛtta* is contained in the verbal content ("*sarvakāratve ca vacaḥ itivṛttaṃ tu nāṭyasya śarīraṃ parikīrtitam*" *NŚ Ab., 14:3*). He only says in advance, what Bharata Muni states four chapters later. Explaining further, Abhinava uses an extended metaphor, and says:

> Just as on a land, walls are raised to make a palace, similarly, for the palace of the literary content of a play, the use of words in metre is the land; choosing a specific metre is measuring that land; giving it a suitability of composition is raising the walls; using the ten genres is making windows and ventillators, the figures of speech are the painting on the walls; voice, melody and intonation are setting the space for living use. (*NŚ Ab, 15:227*)

"The verbal content is to be executed with great care by the poet while writing and by the actor while performing" (..."*yatnastu kartavyaḥ iti kavinā nirmāṇakāle naṭena prayogakāle*" *NŚ Ab, 14:2*). However, while it is recognized that the word content of the 'body of *nāṭya*', *(nāṭyatanu)* "is the base for the employment of instruments, song, and other *abhinayas,*" it is also true that, in itself, the verbal is only one form of *abhinaya*. Its special worth, however, lies in the fact that unlike other *abhinayas,* the word content can be stored. For this, and for no other reason, it has been called the basis of a play.

The *vācika* or the *vāgabhinaya,* as one of the four *abhinayas*, does not cover the whole of aural content in the Indian theatre. It is restricted to the actor's speech and was called *pāṭhya*. It does not include the vocal or instrumental music which was known as *gāndharva* used for *gāna* and *gīta*. The total aural content comprised of *vāgabhinaya, svara, ātodya, gāna* and *gīta*. Besides *paṭhya,* I shall discuss here, *svara* or the rise and fall of voice as intonation in speech and as notes in music. *Gāna,* or *dhruvā* songs will be dealt with briefly. The Indian musical system, *gāndharva,* which has been described in great detail by Bharata Muni and which was used in the *dhruvā* songs, shall be taken up later to make a sketchy comparison with the Greek system. The dramatic *gītas* and the theory of musical instruments as given in the *NŚ*, has been left out for shortage of space.

Pāṭhya

The extant plays seem to follow the injunctions of the *NŚ* regarding the choice of language and prosody. It is prescribed that the speech of a character should be either in Sanskrit or in the various forms of *Prākṛta (NŚ 14:5).* Only twenty-five per cent of the total usage could be in Sanskrit. In that case, is it justified to call ancient Indian drama as 'Sanskrit drama'? In that age drama was meant to be multilingual and this unique feature has no parallel in the history of world theatre. I shall not go into the controversy whether *Prākṛta* was introduced into Sanskrit plays as a concession to non-Aryans, or whether Sanskrit was assimilated into the *Prakṛta* content of the originally pre-Aryan practices of *nāṭya.* Setting aside such historically unverifiable possibilities, I am inclined to accept that the choice of language was determined by the nature of characters to be represented and that this multilinguism was based on the concept of *anukaraṇa* which had been accepted as a practical reality for a long time in the history of Indian drama. With no prejudice or loyalty for particular languages, as it exists today in modern nation states or regions of India, the producers, audience and actors, in ancient times treated language purely as a medium of communication and used it according to the conventions of a given art form. It is true that in medieval times, when the living theatre had vanished, the pundit-playwrights 'wrote' *Prākṛta* dialogues transliterated from Sanskrit according to the rules of grammar laid down in the *NŚ*. But this was not the case in the age of performances. The *Prākṛtas,* then, must have been enjoyed by the bulk of the audience which consisted of women, children and common folks. It is a fallacy that all classical drama was a harem affair, as has been very strongly argued by Indu Shekhar (144-45). Although, some harem performances were held frequently, there would have been no raison de'etre for *Prākṛtas* to be used if harem performances were the rule and not the exception.

The Sanskrit content was said to be of two kinds, *atibhāṣā* and *āryabhāṣā*. The first was to be spoken by the gods. Abhinava adds that it was distinct from refined Sanskrit because it drew in abundance upon the vedic vocabulary ("*vaidikaśabda bāhulyāt āryabhāṣāto vilakṣaṇatvaṃ asyā iti*"). However, he cites no examples and *atibhāṣā* is difficult to find in the extant plays. Perhaps it was used in very early plays which do not survive. *Āryabhāṣā* was the refined and scholarly Sanskrit, of royal persons. Even the *Prākṛta* used by the protagonist was supposed to be *āryabhāṣā*. Here, in the *NŚ*, it denotes the language used by the upper classes. Normally the protagonist was supposed to speak Sanskrit, but where poverty or lack of education prevailed, some *Prākṛta* was used. The arrogantly wealthy, the poor, the prodigals, the uneducated, fake-mendicants, Buddhists and Jain monks, ascetics, outcastes, women, the lower classes, and hermaphrodites spoke in *Prākṛta*. The monks of Vedic tradition, Buddhists of *Śākya* orders, high monks, *kṣatriyas*, the sophisticated, *Śaiva* ascetics, royal women, prostitutes, artists, the creative and the refined (*kalāvasthāntarakṛta*) spoke in Sanskrit (*NŚ 17:28-39*).

The *Prākṛta* for respectable castes (*śuddhāṣu jātiṣu*) was *Śaurasenī*. Others were to use a variety of *jātibhāṣā*, that is a dialect or a regional Indian language (*'bhāratam varṣaṃ āśritā*) which could even be ill-pronounced. *Māgadhī, Avantijā Prācyā, Śaurasenī, Ardhamāgadhī, Bāhlīkā* and *Dākṣiṇātyā* are the seven *Prākṛtas* mentioned. The last category of linguistic usage, besides *ati, ārya* and *jāti* is, *yonyantarī bhāṣā*, which seems to be a classification consisting of the dialects of *śakāra, ābhīra, cāṇḍāla, śabara, dramila* tribes, forest dwellers and such liminal peoples. The *NŚ* recommends the association of certain dialects with some artisans and it also gives details of the dominance of certain vowels and consonants in the languages of some regions (*NŚ 17:45-64*). Such dominance is not easy to verify today.

Prose-Verse Dialogue in Indian Drama

From the earliest plays to the late medieval scripts all dialogue in classical drama was made upon of an alteration between prose (*cūrṇapada*) and verse (*nibaddha pada*) (*NŚ 14:40-43*). The speech of all characters, whether of high or low status, conforms to this pattern. Verse in other theatres, such as in Elizabethan drama, was used for the sake of sublimity of thought or raising the dignity of a character. The lower-rank characters used blank verse for parody. But in Indian theatre, even the lowest characters spoke in verse set to various metres. For instance, in the play *Mṛcchakaṭikam* Darduraka, a quarrelling street gambler shouts in verse while bashing up another gambler called Saṃvāhaka. As the name suggests, Darduraka, should be a drum player and a *śūdra*. It seems that changing over to verse from prose had some plausible reasons: the need to use a conceit, to express a strongly felt emotion (real or affected), to describe a wonderful sight, and very often, an attempt to reveal the beauty of objects, persons or Nature. In Indian plays, verse was certainly not meant to elevate conversational speech into a formal rendering or to create theatric sonorousness, as was the case with English theatre from Marlowe to Dryden. In Indian plays, the episodic action was moved forward only by prose dialogue. The verse content was invariably an intellectual reflection upon things or happenings. A character usually stopped action for a moment and made a ruminative statement in verse, and then having read his *śloka*, proceeded on with the action. The *śloka* could have been dropped, very often, with little damage to the course of action. A similar function was performed by the lyrics in Greek plays where the chorus commented upon the plight of the persona, on things or on life in general. The chorus was a reflector as well as a participator in action. Similarly, the Indian actor acted and reflected in alteration. But this action-reflection diad should not be seen as action in jerks, nor as an ornamental concession to poetry. Instead, it should be recognized as part of the total action in which not only the agonal (conflictive) but the contemplative and emotional action was a major content. These intellectual and emotional reflections were not discursive or ideological, or reformist in content. Rather, they were comments upon the peculiarity (*vilakṣaṇatā*) of things. Impressed by the strangeness of even ordinary things, a character repeatedly forgets himself and his immediate concerns, and gets lost in the goodness or strangeness of things which he describes in verse. For example, Cārudatta is awakened by the servant-girl to come and see the opening in the wall made by the burglar. The protagonist (*dhīrapraśānta nāyaka*) instead of showing any anxiety for the safety of his property, at once beings to admire the finesse with which the burglar had done his job. He speaks a verse in praise of the opening. His next verse expresses the regret at having disappointed the thief. He reflects upon poverty that makes a man so helpless that he is unable to gratify a visiting thief. Expressive of the speaker's ethos, such thoughts also have a universal appeal. They can be easily taken out of context and be read as proverbs, paradigms, descriptions and ruminations. Yet they are reflections born out of dramatic action. The action-reflection diad transforms the momentary and the particular into a deeply felt and correctly evaluated reality. The purpose here is not merely to philosophize or to uphold the doctrine of *karma* (supposed by many to be the objective of ancient drama). It employs poetry to elevate action into universality, regardless of its philosophical premises (of Hinduism or otherwise) by which this universality may be defined. Action is de-temporalised here, it is dislocated from the immediate to become universal and hieropraxic. The function of poetry in all those hundreds of metres over which Bharata Muni has spent two lengthy chapters, is to elevate action to this dimension, and not merely to magnify delivery. The *NŚ* nowhere mentions whether the verse portions of dialogue should be spoken, intoned, recited or sung. But things are not as mysterious here as they are with the Greek ***parakataloge***.

In my opinion, the verse dialogue in ancient drama was not sung as it has been classified by Bharata Muni as *pāṭhya* and not as *gāna*. On the analogy of some surviving traditional theatrical genres like Nauṭankī and Bhavai, it is sometimes wrongly imagined that verses were sung in ancient theatre. But it was not always so. The *pāṭhya* verses were not given any instrumental support, though the gait of the actors was supported by drum beats (*pāṭākṣaras*). The following analysis will help us find some clues to the nature of theatrical utterances of ancient Indian drama.

Elements of Dialogue or Pāṭhya

Speech and song are both produced by a rise and fall in the vocal pitch. Pitch alterations are related to emotional states and the relationship between the two is not merely a matter of culturally governed behaviour patterns. The shrill tones of terror, the fallen pitch of sadness, the lively normal pitch of delight are a universal phenomenon. Along with pitch variations, changes in the rhythm of delivery according to the states of emotion also follow a degree of universality. In excitement words come fast, in pain slowly, and in comfortable states they are steady and measured. Bharata Muni analyses the phenomenon of voice fluctuation by dividing it into six elements (*pāṭhyaguṇāni*). The seven notes *ṣaḍja* etc., are the first element; the three voice registers (*sthānas*), upper, middle and lower make up the second element; the four accents (*varṇas*) *udātta, anudātta, svarita* and *kampita*, are the third element; two kinds of *kāku* (voice alterations) is the fourth; the six *alaṅkāras* or ways of tonal fluctuations within one register make up the fifth element; and finally the six *aṅgas* or the ways of producing tonal fluctuation in all the three registers with pauses and rhythmic control are the sixth element. It is suggested by Abhinavagupta that although *kāku* is defined here as one of the six elements, in reality the total phenomenon of the rise and fall of voice and all its changes should be called by the name of *kāku*. Any slight change in voice, intentional or otherwise, is *kāku* ("*kaka laulye, laulyaṃ ca sākāṅkṣe yayā svaravaicitryaṃ lakṣayate vācyabhūmiḥ sampadyate sā kākuḥ. Īṣadarthe kuśabdasya kādeśaḥ. Kākurvājihvyā tadvyāpāra sampadyatvāt kākuḥ." NŚ Ab. 17:106*). The vocal chords govern the tonal quality of voice, but the tongue makes it into phonemes. Thus it also governs *kāku.*

But Abhinava warns that the mention of the seven notes and *kāku* as pitch alteration, should not mislead us to conclude that there is no difference between song and speech as both use tonal fluctuations. If speech is also to use notes and registers, how is *pāṭhya,* then, distinct from *gāna?* Abhinava points out:

> Whereas in *gāna* there is in notes and accents the quality of sonorousness (*anuraṇana*), which is extrememly pleasing (*raktipradhāna*), in *pāṭhya* this quality is not present; instead the high, low and middle tones are barely touched upon. If sweetness or colour (*rakti*) of tones is made dominant then the usage becomes song and is no longer speech. If it is argued that in speech all the seven notes are not used as they are in music (*gāna*) and hence omission of notes leads to speech, then it may be pointed out that there is omission of notes in *rāgas* also. (*NŚ Ab. 17:102*)

Abhinava has made a most valid distinction. It is the exact usage of notes, in their proper intervals, employed along with embellishments which makes up the shape of a melody. In speech, notes are used barely or roughly and there is no dwelling upon their consonances. While speaking or intoning, the pitch fluctuations may be the same as in a melody; but there is no purity of notes, as notes are not used with exactitude.

The tonal fluctuations in speech, however, are meant not only to shape the words which have specific meaning but also to convey, signify and alter the specific meaning of words in many ways. As Abhinava explains:

> Some people question the importance of *kāku.* Words, they say, are sufficient to convey meaning...But we have to submit that the prime reality called *spanda* (vibration) which is produced by the play of (*prāṇa*)

> breadth and which may be without phonemes is pure sound. It is capable of conveying to our ears the feelings (of happiness and sorrow) of the conveyer, the acquiescence and negation of his intentions inferred from the sound itself. The reactions of fear or anger that is seen in people who have heard the sounds made by a deer, a dog or another creature, is on account of the intention of the creature that is inferred from the sound. Now, words are woven together like strings of sounds and are capable of being employed in ways (to render meaning) different from what is customary (*prācyaprayatna*), that is, words can be made to express something quite different from the usual meaning. They are indeterminate. But sound (its tonal effect) is produced by the speaker or crier in the same instant when he experiences an emotion, and this sound is accompanied by a change in facial colour, horripilation, or such things that cannot be contrary to what is actually felt. It, sound or tone, can even obstruct the usual meaning of words or contradict their intention...In *pāṭhya*, therefore, *kāku* or pitch variation is most vital. (*NŚ Ab. 17:103*)

If nothing in *pāṭhya* was to be sung, then why at all does Bharata Muni make the seven notes as one of the six elements of *pāṭhya*? As said earlier, voice fluctuation is related to emotional fluctuation; this relationship works the same in music as in *pāṭhya,* only that in music pitch fluctuation takes the form of exact notes whereas in *pāṭhya* the notes remain approximations. To guide the speaker, (in theatre it is the trained actor) the musical notes of a particular scale can be given as approximate locations around which he may inflect his voice. The recommendations of Bharata Muni are, "when the emotional contents of words are related to humour or love, *madhyama* or *pañcama* should be made '*svara*' (or employed as tonic); for the heroic, wonderous and terrible emotions, the notes are *ṣadja* and *ṛṣabha*; *gāndhāra* and *niṣāda* are to be used for pity and *dhaivata* for fear and disgust" (*NŚ 17:103*). What could have 'making *svara*' ('*svarau kāryau*') meant? This is one of the major conundrums of ancient music. Abhinava suggests that it implies using the *aṃśa* notes of the *Jātis* (ancient melodic scales, like *rāgas* today) in *pāṭhya*. For example, for erotic passages, the *aṃśa* of *Madhyamā Jātī* is to be used. If it is accepted that '*aṃśa*', 'making *svara*,' '*sthāyī svara*' and tonic mean the same thing, then in such a case, *pāṭhya* with erotic content is to be spoken making the tonic of *Madhyamā Jāti* (the note *madhyama*) as the central tone around which all fluctuations in the delivery of dialogue would take place. Similarly, for the heroic and wonderous feelings, the tonics of *Ṣāḍjī* and *Ārṣabhī Jātis* are required. For the sentiments of pity, the tonics of *Gāndhārī* and *Naiṣādī Jātis* will be needed. What is the point in using tonics of the *Jātis*? If the inflexion itself is not to approximate the tune of a *Jāti*, then why just take its tonic? If the tune of a *Jāti* is to be followed then, in that case, the speech of a character becomes tuneful intonation, more or less like the Greek ***parakataloge.*** In any case, there is little clarity on the method of employing tonics in dialogue.

For the raising and lowering of voice, or *kāku* activity, the three *sthānas* (voice registers—*mandra, madhya* and *tāra*) are prescribed. They are the same for the singer and speaker. It is in this context that Abhinava repeats that, in speech the voice does not touch the position of notes as in music. For calling somebody afar or shouting, the high register should be used; for talking to people nearby the medium one and for intimate conversation the low register is appropriate (*NŚ 17:106*). Within one register or while changing from one register to another, the voice undergoes only minor pitch fluctuations. These are called accents or *varṇas*. In song, the changes of register are very frequent, in speech they are not so rapid. *Udātta* (high), *anudātta* (low), *svarita* (circumflex) and *kampita* (shaking) are the four accents. The erotic and the humorous passages should be rendered with *svarita* and *udātta*; the heroic, the terrible and the wonderous in *udātta* and *kampita;* for the pathetic, the tearful and the horrible *udātta, svarita* and *kampita* are required. The *kampita* is really an improvization on the *svarita*.

After dealing with notes, registers and accents, Bharata Muni defines *kāku* as the fourth element of *pāthya*. As I have said earlier all tonal fluctuation is *kāku*, yet one of the six elements of *pāṭhya* is also given the name of *kāku*. This is of two kinds, *sākāṅkṣa* and *nirākāṅkṣa*. When, in addition to the obvious meaning (of a sentence), there is also another intention (*ākāṅkṣā*) indicated by tonal inflection, the usage is called *sākāṅkṣa kāku*. The meaning of such a sentence remains ambiguous (*aniyukta*). When the meaning is unambiguous (*niyukta*), the same as stated, when nothing additional, different or contradictory is implied by tonal inflection, when the inflection of tone reinforces the stated meaning, the *kāku* is called *nirākaṅkṣa*. This particular feature of *pāṭhya* is dependent upon the capacity of tonal changes or pure sounds which alter and modify the lexical meaning. Abhinava, as we have quoted earlier, greatly emphasised this power of sound (*spanda*). The name that Bharata Muni gives to this interplay between the lexical and the tonal meaning is *kāku*. This interplay is most vital to any expressive speech and most of all to the dramatic. *Kāku* is used in six different ways, called *alaṅkāras; ucca, dīpta, mandra, nīca, druta,* and *vilambita*. *Ucca* is the high pitch in the highest register. It is used for talking to somebody very far away, for showing wonder, for controversy, intimidating and pain etc. *Dīpta* is still higher, the uppermost periphery of the highest register used for wrangling, shrieking, angry exchanges, shouting and war cries. *Mandra* is the usage of lower register, i.e., of the deeper tones for peaceful utterances, regrets, anxieties, hopefulness, lament, play and so on. *Nīca* is the lowest periphery of the lowest register used in acute pain, groans, deep peace, fear and fainting. *Druta* is the middle register usage of which the upper portion is used for quick speech, cooing to children, feverishness, and prayers. Use of the lower end of the middle register for utterances of erotic, pathetic, thoughtful and reflective nature is called *vilambita* (*NŚ 17:115-29*). The *alaṅkāras* are divisions of the three voice registers into six parts. When the pitch fluctuation in speech works in the upper or lower portion of a register, it is given the separate name of an *alaṅkāra.*

Now we come to the so called six *aṅgas* which are ways of controlling the volume of sound, of going from one register to another, of pausing and changing the rhythm of dialogue. These are *viccheda, arpaṇa, visarga, anubandha, dīpana* and *praśamana*. Soft, joyous, vibrant and loud enough tone ('pervading the auditorium') is *arpaṇa*. When a sentence in dialogue is not given importance, that is, it is barely run through (*nyāsa*), the rendering is called *visarga*. Pause, in between a sentence, for exclamation or sighing, or for other reasons, is called *anubandha*. Going through all the three registers is *dīpana*. And finally, coming down from the highest register to the lowest without allowing the voice to falter is *praśamana*. The *NŚ* defines the emotional states which can be best expressed through these *alaṅkāras*. As for the rhythms, they are the usual three, fast, middle and slow. The *NŚ* has given special attention to the technique of *virāma* (pause). " All pause in delivery should be according to the dictates of meaning and those of metre" (*NŚ 17:131*). This is indication enough that verse was delivered in the same way as prose passages, that it was not sung or intoned. But here, by *virāma*, Bharata Muni means something more than the pauses natural to the flow of speech. *Virāma* is also the pause artificially made to accommodate the very intricate gestures of *āṅgika abhinaya*, particularly those of the hands. The *sūcā, nivṛtyāṅkura* and *aṅkura abhinaya* discussed earlier, have to be accommodated by *virāma*. And most so when there are unequal and scanty syllables in a passage ("*Sūcāsu ca aṅkuragate ca tathopacāreṣu alpa akṣarāṇi hi pādāni bhavanti kavye*" *NŚ 17:132*). Moreover, as I have repeatedly said, in this theatre of *sāmānīkaraṇa* unified channels of verbal, gestural, subtly gestural and costumic *abhinayas*, the words have to be combined with the rhythm of the gestures and not vice-versa. In the dialogue privileged logocentric theatre of Europe, the flow of speech intermittently accommodates the movements of the body. But in hieropraxic theatre, each word has to keep pace with the accompanying gesture. Moreover, long spells of silences (*virāma*) are necessary when purely gestural *sūcā* (done to indicate the meaning of words yet to be spoken) and *aṅkura* (done to express the deeper intention through gestures which is not stated in words of the dialogue) are performed. *Virāma* is the most essential feature of traditional Indian acting. Giving an example from the practice of his times Abhinava says:

> While acting out the line, "what with the moon when her face is so charming and gracious" ("*tasyāstan-mukhamasti saumyasubhagaṃ kiṃ pārvaṇendunā*"?) the word, 'her' requires *sūcā* acting in which the reminiscence of this rare beloved's actions is to be shown. And through *nivṛtyāṅkura* gestures, her supposed waiting, listening, and hiding is also to be portrayed. Then, after speaking the word 'face,' the actor should show the anxiety to kiss that face and the acute desire to meet the beloved. (*NŚ Ab. 17:132*)

Reviewing the tonal methodology of *kāku prayoga* or voice modulation in dialogue, we may conclude: prose and verse were rendered alike; there was no singing or intoned recitation of the verse; the dialogue was not of course rendered conversationally; it was an aritifical theatrical (*nāṭyadharmī*) rendering in which the voice rose and fell through three registers, changing rhythm and tone colour from moment to moment according to the emotional content of the speech. Above all, it was controlled to match the gestural action which was always necessary for full theatrical effect, except at the time of following the *bhāratī vṛtti*.

Gāna or Dhruvā Songs

If all dialogue, even in verse, was not sung, how much room, then, was left for song in the performance script of this drama? In the context of *pūrvaraṅga*, I have described the first nine steps of aural purification in which the instruments were tuned and played without any vocal support. The tenth step was *gītavidhi*, a long composition in the praise of gods, which was also the first song of the performance. The successive eight steps have been sketched by me earlier in the context of dance content. These consisted of vocal compositions which were sung and danced. From *gītavidhi* onwards begins a process that runs continuously not only through the rest of *pūrvaraṅga* but through the rest of the dramatic action as well. This was the use of *gāna* or *dhruvā* songs which was as vital to the Indian dramatic performance as was the choral song to Greek theatre. Bharata Muni has a chapter of 428 verses in which he describes in great detail the makeup of *dhruvās* and the method of their employment. At the end of the chapter, it is said, "Song is the couch on which *nāṭya* is seated, and therefore, song deserves the greatest attention. If song and instruments are employed properly there is no risk of failure in drama" (*NŚ 32:426*). Anticipating the question, why should one use song in drama, Bharata Muni says, "That which cannot be said through speech, should be said through song. If the *vākyārtha* (statement) cannot do it one should use similies." To this Abhinavagupta adds, "'That' means a state of feeling which cannot be described. In places where a literary statement is unable to convey (a feeling), statement through song can do the work" (*NŚ Ab. 32:351*). Bharata Muni's concept of *nāṭya* clearly recognizes that where literature ends music can take over, not for its own sake but for the sake of *nāṭya*. Song is capable of intensifying emotions that have been enacted and it can as well create emotional states that are conducive to receive the forthcoming enactment. In any case, the state created by song, and the meaning conveyed by it, is impossible to signify through other means.

Unlike the Greek choral odes, which were part of the literary text composed by the playwright and which are available to us as text today, the verbal content of *dhruvās* was not composed by the playwright. It seems that they existed as independent songs which were inserted into the play script at the appropriate places by producers. Such places were five in number. Before or during the entry of a persona (*prāveśikī*), on exit or the end of an act (*naiṣkrāmikī*), for calming down after a violent disturbance (*prāsādikī*), on a sudden entry or unexpected change of mood (*ākṣepikī*), and to be sung when somebody has fainted or is deeply dejected (*antarā*). All these *dhruvās* were sung by the vocalists sitting on the prescribed platform at centre back-stage. Sometimes the actor sang the *dhruvā* or enacted it through dance. Enacting of a *dhruvā* was known as *nāṭyāyita*. "Done at the (proper) moment, the enactment of a *dhruvā* full of joy, bereavement, etc., is known by the name *nāṭyāyita*. It is done for the sake of *bhāva* and *rasa*" (*NŚ 22:49*). Instrumental support was always provided.

The verbal content of the *dhruvā* songs was not directly related to the dramatic action. It was neither a commentary on the dramatic events, nor was it a description of the qualities of any dramatic character. In itself, a *dhruvā* was a literary composition on the sun, the moon, the stars, the clouds, the sea, elephants, swans, cuckoo, bees and the like. A single *dhruvā* was about one thing at a time, be it a cloud or a swan or a bee, describing how sad, love-lorn, frightened, happy or excited the creature was. This description was meant to reflect upon the emotional state of the person (the dramatic persona) in reference to whom the song had been sung. For instance, before the enactment of a scene where a prince is to be shown anxiously waiting for his beloved, even before the entry of the prince, a *dhruvā* was sung describing how splendidly the moon shone through the clouds. By implied similitude, the audience was prepared to watch a forthcoming scene of a prince in love. The *dhruvā* may have been enacted by the very actor who would, a minute later, enact the prince. The *NŚ* does not clearly mention who performed the *dhruvā abhinaya* called *nāṭyāyita*. It could have been the cast or additional actors who came for *dhruvā abhinaya* only.

The verses giving directions to the producer regarding the use of *dhruvā* songs, are as follows: "One should bear in mind the situation (entry, exit, etc.), the place (like, forest or house), time (day or night), season (spring or rains), the character (prince, brahmin or worker), emotional state (love, pathos, fear or wonder and so on) and gestures (sitting, weeping, etc.) while employing a *dhruvā*" (*NŚ 32:328*). This is enough to indicate that *dhruvās* reflected upon each action and its consequent emotional impact in the play. From the point of view of the votaries of Naturalism, such songs are musical interferences in dramatic action. Modern productions of 'Sanskrit Drama' have felt no need for them. So far they have never been tried, not at least in publicised productions; very few scholars and hardly any producers are aware of their presence in ancient dramaturgy. But those who wish to reconstruct classical performances must realise that *dhruvās* were the "couch of *nāṭya*." I will cite two examples from the *Nāṭyaśāstra*:

> Pulling at the trees, so good at shrieking, never going straight, breaking against the mountain sides, raising storms of red and yellow dust, this uncontrolled wind blows across the sky. (*NŚ 32:166*)

Destructive wind can indicate a furious ascetic or a *kṣatriya* prince setting out for combat. The above verse, can be suitably used for Bhīma's entry at the time of his seeking Duryodhana hiding in the lotus pond, in *Veṇīsaṃhāra*. This *prāveśikī dhruvā* can be set to a fast tempo and to the *Ārṣabhī Jāti* if the ancient musical scales are to be used. For indicating the entry of a mediocre character, the following may suffice:

> This lady swan, full of desire, is anxious to leave these woods to wander in sport with her companion. (*NŚ 32:98*)

For using this stanza as a *dhruvā*, a suitable episode could be the setting out (*abhisāra*) of Vasantasenā to meet Cārudatta. This could be the *naiṣkrāmikī dhruvā* in the last Act of Bhāsa's *Cārudatta* or for the same situation in Śūdraka's *Mṛcchakaṭikam*. The *aḍḍitā* portion would be required as the song of *sṛṅgāra* in the *dhruvā*. For music, the *Madhyamā Jāti* set to medium tempo would be the most appropriate.

We may take one more *dhruvā* for the low status character:

> The owl mauled by crows leaves the open grounds of the woods and takes refuge in a tree. Chased so hard, this red-eyed wanderer hastily gets into the hollow of a tree. (*NŚ 32:281*)

The flight of Saṃvāhaka from the gamblers, Māthura

and Darduraka, who have been clobbering him, and his consequent refuge in Vasantasenā's house, could be an apt situation for this *dhruvā* text. The *dhruvā* could be made into a *prāveśikī*, to be performed before the entry of the fleeing Saṃvāhaka in the second Act or it can be made into an *ākṣepikī dhruvā* during the further mauling of Saṃvāhaka. As a component of the *dhruvā* it would be suitable that the *avakṛṣṭā* portion (which is meant to show incidents of humiliation and sorrow) is used. A quick tempo with notes of *Dhaivatī Jāti* would be the right musical choice.

The *dhruvā* songs were composed in the *śaurasenī* dialect for the sake of wider communciation with the spectators, the bulk of whom were women, children and working folks. For the *dhruvās* called *narkuṭa*, the language was *Māgadhī* (*NŚ 32:384*). Simplicity of language was a great aid in the popularity of the *dhruvās*. They also brought on to the stage the whole world of Nature, as all the simulators (*upamānas*) like the sun, moon, wind, mountains, etc. came from it. This is to be expected, because human and extra-terrestrial characters in Indian drama are often compared to forces of Nature, and objects like mountains, winds and stars are also looked upon as living things having the same existence (*bhāva*) as the humans. It is not as if Man has imposed himself on Nature here, but that Nature, moving (*jaṅgama*) or still (*sthāvara*), is seen as 'melted' (*līna*) in the same *bhāvas* which are neither of Man nor of Nature, but of the cosmos. Man and Nature, are thus, made to reflect the same reality; in reflecting which both enter into a perfect consonance (*saṃvāda*) which is the aim of *nāṭya*.

Gāndharva

Music in the age of the *NŚ* was called *Gāndharva*. It was used for *dhruvā* songs and for all musical accompaniment for dances and the *pūrvaraṅga*. It was a very complicated affair and for this reason Bharata Muni has devoted nine chapters (28 to 36, quantitatively nearly one-fourth of the *NŚ*) to it. Here, I shall state some of its basic principles that postulate a relationship between scales and human emotions.

It seems that in the epic age certain melodic scales, called the *Jātis*, were in vogue all over the country. When a complicated system of music came to be developed, it drew upon this fund of the *Jātis*. "Because of the *Jātis* and *śrutis*, the notes were classified into *Grāmas*" (*Jātibhiḥ śrutibhiścaiva svarāḥ grāmatvamāgatāḥ. NŚ 18:5*). Whereas Greek music had tetrachords as its basic building block, in Indian music trichords, or a set of three tones (*udātta, anudātta* and *svarita*) was the basic block. After their initial use in *Ṛgvedic* chants, the number of tones increased to seven and was later known as a *saptaka* (septette). As was always the case with ancient systems, the series of seven notes began with the 'first note' and was followed by six others in a descending order. The sequence was like this: *udātta, anudātta, svarita* + *udatta, anudātta, svarita* + *udātta.* Later on, names like *madhyama, gāndhāra, ṛṣabha* etc., were introduced and the same sequence came in the order of MA GA RI SA NI DHA PA. Still later, *SA* was made the first note for the generic scale called *Ṣaḍjagrāma* and the sequence was put to the ascending order of *SA RE GA MA PA DHA NI*. Another generic scale was also used and was called *Madhyamagrāma*. Here, *PA* was slightly lowered and *MA* was made the first note of the septette, set as *MA PA DHA NI SA RE GA*. The whole septette of both generic scales was divided into twenty-two microtones or *śrutis*. The details about the nature of these microtones, their measures and qualities have been given elsewhere.[3] Here, it is sufficient to point out that each of the seven notes was said to consist of definite microtones. For instance, the arrangement of *śrutis* for the notes of the *Ṣaḍjagrāma* genre is as follows: *4SA 3RE 2GA 4MA 4PA 3DHA 2NI*. For the *Madhyamagrāma* it is 4MA 3PA 4DHA 2NI 4SA 3RE 2GA. Unlike the contemporary practice in India, in ancient times, for singing or tuning the harps (*vīṇās*) the tonic was fixed at any note of the septette and not essentially at *SA*. This seven note sequence was called '*mūrcchanā*'. Three *mūrcchanās* in a succession provided the three registers for a full range of twenty-one notes. The two *Grāmas* and their *mūrcchanās* (seven in each) seem comparable to the Greek Systems and the **harmoniai**. Just as there was no fixed pitch for the **harmoniai,** similarly, there was none for the *mūrcchanās* either. Like the **harmoniai,** the *mūrcchanās* were supposed to arouse specific emotions. But it is important to bear in mind that just as the mere scale of **harmoniai** was not sufficient to create a melody, similarly, a *mūrcchanā* had to be used in a *Jāti* (comparable to modern *rāgas*), to provide musical expression. There were eighteen *Jātis,* seven pure and eleven mixed, some classified under the *Ṣaḍjagrāma* while others under the *Madhyamagrāma.* The *NŚ* postulates that (when used in a *Jāti*) the notes have their own power of arousing specific emotions.

> *Madhyama* and *pañcama* are to be used for arousing *hāsya* (humour) and *śṛṅgāra* (eros); *ṣaḍja* and *ṛṣabha* for *vīra* (heroic), *raudra* (terrible) and *adbhuta* (wonderous); and *gāndhāra* and *niṣāda* are for *karuṇa* (pathos); and finally *dhaivata* is meant to arouse *bībhatsa* (repulsion) and *bhayānaka* (fear). (*NŚ 29:14*)

The *Jātis* were supposed to arouse emotions according to the power of the notes used. For instance, the *Ṣaḍjodīcyavā* and the *Ṣaḍjamadhyamā Jātis* used *madhyama* and *pañcama* in abundance; thus they were considered to be expressive of the humorous and the erotic sentiments. In the *dhruvā* songs, specific *Jātis* were used to suit the sentiments in different dramatic situations.

As with Greek **genera** and **chroai**, in *Gāndharva*, the *śrutis* (microtonal intervals of the notes) were used to create melodic diversity. The system of flattening and sharpening the notes was called *svarasādhāraṇa* and the melodic colour (*rāga*) was supposed to be governed by it. For instance, prescribing the use of *antaragāndhāra*, a kind of *svarasādhāraṇa*, Bharata Muni says, "*Antaragāndhara* note should be used sparingly in the ascent of a *Jāti* and should never be used in descent. If used in descent, whether abundantly or sparingly, it spoils the colour (*rāga*) of a *Jāti* and its *śruti*" (*NŚ 28:36*). Changes in tonal microtones (*śrutis*) were the surest way of providing a great wealth of subtle intonations to the composer and delicacy and fineness of outline to the melodies. 'Knower of *śrutis*' was the highest praise that could be accorded to a musician. Lava and Kuśa were eulogized as '*jātiśrutiviśāradau*' and the fine singers of Ayodhyā were described as '*śrutiśīlāḥ*' by Vālmīki. The *Yājñavalkya Smṛti* went as far as to grant liberation (*mokṣa*) to the knower of *Jātis* and *śrutis* ('*jātiśrutiviśāradaḥ mokṣamārgaṃniyacchati*'). The word '*rāga*,' which literally means colour, was taken to be the cause of pleasure (*rakti*) in the terminology of *Gāndharva*. This pleasure or *rāga/rakti* resided in microtonal usage or *śruti* variation. The word *rāga* came to denote a whole melodic structure not before the medieval times. The *Jātis* were the only recognized melodic structures in the age of *Gāndharva*. *Grāmarāgas, rāgabhāṣās* were the new melodic structures that came into vogue around the third or the fourth century A.D. and soon after the term '*rāga*' came to suffice for any melodic structure. Looking at the notation and the scales available in the *NŚ* and the *Saṅgītaratnākara*, it is possible to reconstruct the ancient *Jātis*.[4]

The main employment of *Gāndharva* in *nāṭya* was for the sake of *dhruvā* songs. In *pūrvaraṅga*, as I have shown, instrument tuning and drumming was followed by *dhruvā* songs and *lāsya* dances. In the play proper, the dialogue was also delivered in studied pitch variations, infused with a musicality that was highly pronounced and was close to the rise and fall of notes as in *Gāndharva*. *Gāndharva*, was thus, in ever present coordination with *pāṭhya* (dramatic speech) and exceeded it in the total content of the performance script.

Dianoia

Dianoia is an Aristotelian concept which has no parallel in Indian theory, even though the Indian plays contain as many dianoic speeches as in any other drama. Defining ***dianoia*** Aristotle says:

> Third in order is Though—that is, the faculty of saying what is possible and pertinent in given circumstances. In the case of oratory, this is the

> function of political art and the art of rhetoric: and so indeed the older poets make their characters speak the language of civic life: the poets of our time, the language of the rhetoricians. Character is that which reveals moral purpose, showing what kind of things a man chooses or avoids. Speeches, therefore, which do not make this manifest, or in which the speaker does not choose or avoid anything whatever, are not expressive of character. Thought on the other hand, is found where something is proved to be or not to be, or a general maxim is enunciated. (*Poetics VI:16*)

The inner questioning that goes on in the mind of a character and makes him choose one way or another is called ***dianoia***. The ability to choose, the moral fibre or the courage to choose is ***ethos***, but the ferment of thoughts that leads to the point of choice is ***dianoia***. This thought process often becomes part of the dialogue when a character bevails his or her plight and speculates on the nature of things. For this reason Aristotle has called ***dianoia*** an element of tragedy. The general maxims that a character quotes in support of his decision are also called ***dianoia***. It is not just any thinking like plotting, scheming, hoping or wishing that can qualify to be called ***dianoia***, but only a debate which has a moral or philosophical perspective. "The emphasis laid by Aristotle on this dialectical ***dianoia*** is doubtless connected with the decisive influence exercised by political debate and forensic pleading on the Greek theatre, the ***agon*** of ecclesia or of the law-courts being reproduced in the ***agon*** of the drama" (Butcher 343).

Sanskrit plays are also full of ***dianoia*** but not in the agonic form. There are no debates here between characters, but still the inner thoughts or ruminations of a character are expressed in verses all the time. The general fondness of Sanskrit poets for maxims is shared readily by playwrights. There is a marked influence of the '*subhāṣita*' (an intellectual observation well put or a witticism) tradition. In it, the process of debate is not traced, but the result is put forth very succinctly. ***Dianoia,*** then, has as pervasive a range in

Indian drama as in the Greek one, but it comes from a different cultural temperament. Much of the verse content has been mentioned by me earlier in the context of prose-verse diad of the *pāṭhya* or dialogue and it need not be repeated here.

Notes

1. Stanford's view is corroborated by Rosenmeyer. "Ictus or stress, an emphasis in pronunciation which, as some modern metricians believe, is to be placed upon the arsis of every ***metron*** or foot. ...Whether Greek and Latin poetry actually had ictus or not is still controversial." *The Metres of Greek and Latin Poetry* (New York: Bubbs Merrill, 1963) 125.
2. ***Chroai*** and *śrutis* perform an identical function in Greek and Indian music. The fine charm of a *rāga* lies in the *śruti* usage. Varying the *śruti* of a note is to give a different sweetness or "*rañjakatva*" to that note. As the Sanskrit word *rañjakatva* means colour, it should be clear that in both traditions altering or modifying a note is denoted by the metaphor of colour alteration. By the medieval times, a musical scale or the structure of a tune, earlier called '*jāti*', was renamed "*rāga*" or '*colour*' which only indicates that *śruti* alteration, or colour alteration was considered as the finest and the most essential aspect of music. That the Greeks were no less concerned with achieving effectiveness of music through the same technique of fine alteration in note, or colour manipulation, is evident from their theory of ***chroai***.
3. See the *śruti* system of the *NŚ*, in "Music in the *Nāṭyaśāstra*." *Journal of Music Academy Madras* 58 (1987): 91-109, and in *The Nāṭyaśāstra, Chapter 28: Ancient Scales of Indian Music.* With *Sañjīvanam* commentary. trans. to English (Delhi: Bṛahaspati Publications, 1993).
4. The famous musicologist Ācārya K.C. Bṛhaspati was able to reconstruct the *Jātis*. A recording of these is available in the archives of the Sangeet Natak Academy, New Delhi.

11

Dramatic Genres and Play Structures

HERE, I shall study the dramatic genres of tragedy and comedy for the purpose of a comparison with *nāṭakas*, *prakaraṇa* and other *rūpakas*. The study of Greek genres has been a preoccupation of long standing in the history of literary criticism. My purpose here, is only to state the archaic Aristotelian concept in order to compare it with the classical Indian *daśarūpakas*.

The Serious and the Trivial

After stating that ***mimesis*** is natural to man, Aristotle says that the practice of ***mimesis*** took the shape of poetry, and took two directions. The genesis of tragedy and comedy lies in this split:

> Poetry now diverged in two directions, according to individual character of writers. The graver spirits imitated noble actions, and the actions of good men. The more trivial sort imitated the actions of meaner persons, at first composing satires, as the former did hymns to the gods and the praises of famous men. (*Poetics IV: 7-8*)

The deciding factors here are graver writers choosing to mimetize nobler subjects and lighter spirits mimetizing mean people. But as Aristotle says, Homer himself wrote in both kinds, the writer therefore, is not the deciding factor; what decides a genre is the subject of ***mimesis***.

Aristotle's most important statement that tragedy and comedy arose from the actions of those who conducted (***exarkhonton***) the dithyrambs and those who conducted the ***phallika***, is not merely a historical fact (if it was so at all) but also is a part of his theory that the nature of the actions to be imitated determines a genre. The grave dithyrambs led to tragedy and the foul ***phallikoi*** to comedy (satyrikon as a genre, seems to have been taken by Aristotle as a part of comedy). Similarly, in the history of poetry the graver subjects produced the *Iliad* and the *Odyssey*, and lighter thoughts resulted in the *Margites*. Aristotle has given us a sketch of the historical development of tragedy and its six elements. Of comedy, he says, the history is unknown, except for a fact or two and on them he proposes to speak elsewhere. It is only a matter of speculation if the six parts of tragedy, ***muthos, ethos***, etc., would have been considered proper to comedy also. Seeing the comedies that are extant it can be said that this classification can work well for them or for all western drama. In fact, some of these parts have been taken as common to epic by Aristotle and later literatures have used some of them for narratives of all kinds. Therefore, these 'elements' again are not the deciding factor in the making of a genre, but it is the subject of ***mimesis***, as I have said earlier.

But there is more to tragedy and comedy than the choice of mimetic subjects and their elements. Drama is not narration but a form of action; tragedy is "an imitation of an action that is serious, complete, and of certain magnitude" and "through pity and fear effecting the proper purgation of these emotions" (*Poetics V:2-3*). It is "an imitation not only of complete action, but of events inspiring fear and pity" (*Poetics IX:11*). The poet, says Aristotle, should aim to, "imitate actions which excite pity and fear, this being the distinctive mark of tragic imitation" (*Poetics XIII:2*). He is then at pains to show how this can be achieved by acting out the downfall of a specific kind of character not vicious but who greatly misses the mark. By experiment it was found that only some ***muthoi*** were suitable for evoking tragic horror and pity. "At first the poets recounted any legend that came their way. Now, the best tragedies are on the story of a few houses ... and those other who have done or suffered something terrible" (*Poetics XIII:5*). The second rate tragedy, at least as Aristotle would define it, has an "opposite catastrophe" where according to the wishes of the audience the author averts the unhappy ending; the pleasure of such a tragedy is "proper rather to comedy, where, those who in the piece are deadliest enemies — like Orestes and Aegisthus — quit stage as friends and at the close no one slays or is slain" (*Poetics XIII:8*). This is not exactly what is now called 'tragi-comedy' but a moderate form of tragedy.

Aristotle is quite insistent that the actions in a tragedy should "strike us as terrible and pitiful" (*XIV:4*). After examining them he repeats that, "This, then, is why a few families only, as has been already observed, furnish the subject of tragedy" (*XIV:8*). The sublimity of the subject and the arousal of horror and pity, it seems are the chief factors in the making of ancient tragedy. The prescriptions about ***muthos, hamartia*** and ***ethos*** are the means to achieve them.

About comedy, the only significant thing said by Aristotle is that it is "an imitation of characters of a lower type — not however, in the full sense of the word bad, the ludicrous being merely a subdivision of the ugly. It consists of some defect or ugliness which is not painful or destructive" (*Poetics V:1*). Though not stated, humour is the emotion meant for arousal, and perhaps for ***katharsis*** too. From the surviving plays, (those too of only one author) it is obvious that until the classical period, comic humour was meant to be crude and vulgar. Abandon and excess, as opposed to tragic restraint and balance, were its aim. The satyrikon was a "subdivision of the comic." The theme of love, considered now to be the soul of comedy, was not so for the ancient Greeks. Lampooning, it seems, was its prime aim. Gods, writers, administrators and all that was feared and revered was thrown open to ridicule under its special license. Perhaps sexuality was the first subject of ridicule, and the satyrs who were erstwhile sacred to sexual rituals, were made the subject of laughter. This reversal of values or a licence to mock was a momentary freedom from the yoke of sublimity. It has been a universal urge behind all carnivals. The Greeks developed tragedy and comedy to concentrate on two extremes of seriousness and hilarity with little in between.

Daśarūpakas

The *Nāṭyaśāstra* mentions ten dramatic genres (*rūpakas*) which have been accepted with minor additions by all literary theorists till late medieval times. These ten genres, however, can be divided into two groups; *sukumāra* (on erotic themes) and *āviddha* (agon oriented). In the first group some *rūpakas* were to deal with sensitive and profound love, while others were meant for depicting its crude aspects. Of the *āviddha*, too, there were two categories — divine combats and human duels. The most prominent of all ten genres was the *nāṭaka*. It was supposed to be constructed out of a well known story, in which the hero belonged to a royal family, or was a king himself. He bore an *udātta* (elevated) character. In the *nāṭaka*, a supernatural episode was a necessary element, like the disappearance of Śakuntalā in a whirl of light after her rejection by the king. The element of the wondrous was emphasized. The wealth of royalty, their erotic exploits, the cycle of pleasure and pain were fully displayed. The genre consisted of five to ten acts. It was recommended that in a *nāṭaka* or a *prakaraṇa* there should be no more than four to five personae at a time on the stage. Both the genres *nāṭaka* and *prakaraṇa* were to be done in the *kaiśikī vṛtti*, which the other eight genres used sparingly. The playing time for a single act was one day, if '*ekadivasa pravittam*' is taken to mean 'to be performed in one day' and not to mean 'depiction of the actions of one day.' Abhinava seems to interpret it the former way ("*atha aṅkasya proyogakālaparimāṇaṃ iyaṃ iti darśayati ekadivasapravittamiti*" *NŚ Ab. 18:21*). If the first meaning is accepted, then a single play would have taken five to ten days to be performed. Nowadays, it takes only two hours. The ancient productions took time as the performance script was full of songs (*dhruvās*), and gestural communications (*sūcī, aṅkura, śākhā* etc.). Besides, the *pūrvaraṅga* was performed every day, at least in the simple (*śuddha*), if not in the ornamental *citra* form, which was essential on the first day. The *rūpakas* called *samavakāras* were played in 18 *nāḍīs* (7 hrs.).

A *nāṭaka* was usually, but not invariably, a love story (*'pratyakṣacarita sambhoga,' 'riddhivilāsādibhirguṇaiścayutam'*). The most famous *nāṭakas* are romances but others like *Mudrārākṣasa* and *Veṇīsaṃhāra* are not so. Abhinava has noted that in spite of the injuction of the *NŚ* that *nāṭaka* and *prakaraṇa* have to be produced in *kaiśikī vṛtti, Mudrārākṣasa, Kṛtyārāvaṇa* and *Veṇīsaṃhāra* are devoid of *kaiśikī*. Actually, to call these three plays as '*nāṭakas*' is a mistake; they should rather be categorized as *vyāyogas* in multiple acts. Because a *vyāyoga* was supposed to be a one act affair, these plays were fitted into the *nāṭaka* category, overlooking their themes which are not erotic but martial. The classic examples of a *nāṭaka* are *Svapnavāsavadattam, Abhijñānaśākuntalam, Uttararāmacaritam* and *Mālavikāgnimitram*.

A *prakaraṇa* was structured just like a *nāṭaka*, except that it had a set of characters of a lower social status. Also, the story (*vastu*) and the protagonist need not have been from the cultural memory bank but may have been imagined (*autpattikam*) by the playwright. Examples of a *prakaraṇa* are *Mṛcchakaṭikam* and *Puśpadūtikā*. Here the protagonist was either a brahmin, a merchant, a minister, or a big trader. Minor characters were servants, pimps, small traders, courtesans and servant women. The episodes centred upon a household as no travel to other worlds or other regions of India was shown. Normally, the mixing of courtesans and women of the household was not shown. If perchance an episode depicted such an occasion, it was recommended that the conversation be in Sanskrit. A mixed genre which drew upon *nāṭaka* and *prakaraṇa*, though not counted as one of the ten genres, was the *nāṭikā*. It was supposed to be a tale of a king's irresistible and wayward infatuation with some young girl from the royal retinue or a musical trainee under royal patronage. It was supposed to be replete with song and dance, and to contain the usual scenes of courtship, tiffs, jealousies, quarrels and union. *Ratnāvalī* is the best known example.

There were no other genres for depicting man-woman love. The remaining eight genres were either agon-centred or humour-based. The *samavakāra* was supposed to take up only extraterrestrial personages like gods and demons (*devā, asura*). The story could only be a well known one, told in three acts. It was constructed out of the episodes showing upheavals and reversals, each of three kinds. War or flood, whirlwind, elephant attack, and taking siege, were the three types of upheavals (*vidrava*). Intrigue, godly wrath and change of fortune were the three reverses (*kapaṭa*). Three kinds of man-woman relationships could also be shown; for *dharma*, for well being, and for love. It seems that this genre was basically meant for depicting war and women were part of the war booty. There could be as many as twelve protagonists. Obviously, the plot was set on a grand scale, where the two camps collided in an epic struggle. Abhinava's teacher, Bhaṭṭa Tauta thought that in *samavakāraṣ* it was not necessary for the erotic scenes to be done in the *kaiśikī vṛtti* as the erotic desire of terrible heroes could not be depicted in *kaiśikī*. ("*Upāddhyāyāstu āhuḥ na kāmasad-bhāvamātrādeva kaiśikīsambhavaḥ, raudra prakṛtīnāḥ tad abhāvāt*" *NŚ Ab. 8:76*). *Ārabhaṭī, sāttvatī* and *bhāratī vṛttis* were all combined in a *samavakāra*. This genre must have been very popular once, but not a single play-text of this sort has survived. *Amṛtamanthana* was performed as a *samavakāra* by Bharata Muni, when he first put up a play at the banner festival of Indra. The playing time for a *samavakāra* was supposed to be 18 *nāḍīs* (24 min. x 18 = 7.2 hrs). The first act was of 13 *nāḍīs* duration, the second of 6 *nāḍīs* and the third of 2 *nāḍīs*.

The genre *īhāmṛga* had a limited theme. Its characters could only be extra-terrestrial (*divya*), no other than *devatās, yakṣas, kinnaras* or *gandharvas*. It was the story of a single protagonist fighting over a woman (*apsarā* etc.). Like the *vyāyoga*, it was made of one act and was agonal. However, witty conversations, as found in the genre called *vīthī*, were also appropriated by the *īhāmṛga* ("*Susamāhitaḥ kāvyabandha iti anena vīthī aṅgāni atra yojyāni iti darśayati.*" *NŚ Ab. 18:80*).

The general action was of conflict, upheavals and rancour. Breach of faith was supposed to be the main cause of conflict. No ancient example is known of this kind. It is not known whether the story could be imaginary or it had to be from collective memory. Abhinava says that the genre was called so, as it showed the desire (*īhā*) and action (*ceṣṭā*) for a woman, who is like a deer (*mṛga*), (that is, not easy to obtain). But he, too, has cited no play as an example. One may guess what the ancient *īhāmṛgas* were like, from *Rukmaṇīpariṇaya* by the thirteenth century author Vatsarāja who may have had before him some ancient *īhāmṛgas*.

Ḍima, like the *samavakāra* was a grand action genre with a well known story and hero. But here there was no touch of the erotic or the humorous. However, the other six sentiments of *vīra, raudra,* etc. were in plenty here. Its pattern was basically agonal and the events were spun out of war, combats, upheavals, flight, chase, magical warfare (*māyā-indrajāla*) and use of magical models (*pustayoga*). *Devatās*, serpents, *rākṣasas, yakṣas* and *piśāca* characters about sixteen in number were included. There were no human characters in a *ḍima*. The number of acts for a *ḍima* is not mentioned. The three *vṛttis,* other than the *kaiśikī* were employed. No play-text survives of this genre either, except the late exercise, *Tripuradāha* again by Vatsarāja. The *NŚ* mentions that Bharata Muni performed a *ḍima* for Śiva; which was also called '*Tripuradāha.*' The sixth genre called *vyāyoga* also took up a famous story. It had few women characters and the events depicted were supposed to be of a day. The play was a small one-act affair. Here there were no extraterrestrial characters, but only humans. It was meant to show the battles of the smaller warlords. Bhāsa's *Madhyamavyāyoga* is a classic example.

Turning from wrath and spectacle we come to a different genre meant to depict the tragedy of war. The *utsṛṣṭikāṅka* usually took up a well known muthoic episode but sometimes an unknown one. It had only human characters; it was full of the pathos that war brings in its wake. The lament of women was its major feature and it had many speeches of despair and consolation. Unconsoled women where shown, beating their breasts or rolling on the ground. There was not much action but mostly verbal *abhinaya*, and for this reason the *bhāratī vṛtti* was employed. Abhinava says that the genre acquired this name as the subject of death (*utsṛṣṭiḥ*) was depicted (*aṅkita*) in it. There is no surviving example of this genre, though Bhasa's *Urubhaṅgam* is often thought to be one. But if one could, for the sake of illustration, say so, Euripides' *Andromache* should fit into the definition of an *utsṛṣṭikāṅka* par excellence, and so could, his *Daughters of Troy*.

In all the genres from *samavakāra* onwards, the locale had to be *Bhāratavarṣa*, or India; other lands like *Ilā* etc., were not to be shown. Even the gods, *devās, rākṣasas* etc., have to act in India as this region is lovable (*hṛdya*), auspicious-smelling and golden. There is no pain or suffering in other regions but only unalloyed pleasure. Here, there is initiation into *karma* i.e., '*Karmārambha*' (*NŚ 18:100*), and the earthly conflict of pleasure and pain, which alone can provide a theme for drama, is found in abundance.

There are no other categories of agonic plays. Bharata Muni has three genres for the lighter vein, the triad of *prahasana, bhāṇa* and *vīthī*, all of which have low characters and rough humour. For all the three genres the *vṛtti* usually adopted was *bhāratī*, though the *NŚ* does not say so specifically. The sophisticated *prahasana*, used characters like low degree ascetics, mendicants and brahmins who indulged in satyric humour with crude men. Here, there was no vulgarity of action or language. The rough *prahasana* contained a different set of characters like courtesans, pimps and prodigals who were outright vulgar. Out of the two categories of *prahasana*, in one, humour was derived from satyrization of the pseudo-learned and, in the other by a depiction of the depravity and villainy of the show-biz and flesh-trade people. Certain witty dialogue-patterns prescribed for the genre *vīthī*, were employed in the *prahasana* also. It was a one-act affair. Like the *nāṭakas*, examples of *prahasanas* have survived in plenty. Obviously, they were no less popular and if the legend in the *NŚ* is to be believed, they caused a temporary degradation of drama. From Bhāsā's

Dāmaka, upto the works of medieval times, there is a long list of which *Mattavilāsa, Laṭakamelaka*, and *Bhagavadajjukīyam* are the better known ones. A large number of titles are mentioned by classical authors, of which the plays are no longer extant. Of the ten *rūpakas*, the *bhāṇa* was a unique form, and like the ***pantomimus*** was a one man show. Here the actor, *bhāṇa*, dressed as a pimp, and enacted out a series of episodes. He pretended to walk around a town, visiting its pleasure-houses, describing the people, events, episodes and the things he saw. The genre was reserved for a depiction of unrestrained prodigals, their courtesans, gamblers, parasites and cronies. The *bhāṇa* enacted a conversation with others where the dialogue of the other person was prefixed with '*kiṃ bravīṣi*' (what do you say?). The dialogues of others were very brief, only to make the *bhāṇa* speak further. For example:

> What do you say? "I've got to tell you of my problem." What is it? What do you say. "My father has decided to marry me off to a girl." Well, you are damned. Nobody should be struck with such a misfortune. What ill luck that I have to hear such bad news. I feel like raising my hands and crying. Now you got to give up the highway of a courtesan and enter the narrow lane of a respectable wife.
>
> Dear audience, let me tell you something. A wife is no better than a blind person at the time of love making; she makes a pitiable face, hardly utters a word, she is over clad with modesty, she is so stupid that she never opens her thighs herself, she is docile like a roped animal. Such a respectable housewife is a dungeon for a (freeman's) heart. What do you say? "I shall never enter such a dungeon." Good! I am glad, you have learnt something in my company. (*Dhūrtaviṭasaṃvāda 13*)

All talk was accompanied by *āṅgika abhinaya* but the gestures were not in *kaiśikī vṛtti*. They were rather minimal. The genre was called '*sukumāra*' not because of the element of *karaṇas* and *aṅgahāras* in it but only because its subject was of love. *Bhāṇas* are mostly lost, but four excellent examples have survived *Padmaprābhṛtakam, Dhūrtaviṭasaṃvāda, Ubhaisārikā* and *Pādatāḍitakam.*

The genre, called *vīthī*, was enacted by one or two players. It was a one-act performance and like the *bhāṇa* had no set story or episodic development. Characters in a *vīthī* could be low, medium or high and they indulged in "thirteen kinds of witticism and word play." *Bakulavīthī* is a well known example. Abhinava mentions a *Pāṇḍavānanda*, now not extant.

The Four Vṛttis

In the dramatic theory of Bharata Muni the emotional content was related to the modes of production or the four *vṛttis: bhāratī, sāttvatī, kaiśikī* and *ārabhaṭī. Vṛtti* is an expression of emotional intensity (like enthusiasm, love or heroism) manifesting through various activities of speech, mind and body. Rather than having a separate *vṛtti* for every emotion, four general emotional stances are prescribed. Abhinavagupta points out that emotional intensity (*āveśa*) is of two kinds; wordly (*laukika*), which is personal, and non-wordly (*alaukika*) which appears in drama as depersonalized emotion. Only the latter affords aesthetic pleasure. The *vṛttis* were first manifest in Vishṇu's act of killing the demons, an impersonal act performed for others (*NŚ Ab. 20:1*). Of these four modes, which make up certain emotional stances and bodily activity suitable to those stances, the first is called *bhāratī*. Here the verbal content was supposed to be Sanskrit dominated. Consequently it was meant more for male and less for female dramatis personae. In *bhāratī*, body enactment, song and instrument were used sparingly. Thus, it was most appropriate for employing in the prologues (*prarocanās*) of plays, and in *rūpakas* like *vīthī, prahasana, bhāṇa* and *utsṛṣṭikāṅka* (*NŚ 20:26-28*).

Bhāratī was also most suitable for humour, scolding and moralization. As for *sāttvatī*, it is said, "where mental force (*sattva*), and combat movements (*nyāya*) are employed, hope and elation is expressed and sorrow is set aside, such a *vṛtti* is called *sāttvatī*" (*NŚ 20:41*). Here movements of strength and heroism are used for the emotive expressions of heroism (*vīra*) and the wonderous (*adbhuta*); the erotic is set aside as is pathos. Comments, arguments, challenges and verbal duels all are best done in *sāttvatī*. It hardly needs to be pointed out that for all agonic (*āviddha*) forms, *sāttvatī* would be a major constituent. *Kaiśikī* abounds in the use of enchanting costume, feminine characters, dance and music, and to expand the erotic mood. Elegant verses, laughter and tears of lovers, and all the intricate mental states of lovers in union and separation make up *kaiśikī*. The *nāṭaka* and the *prakaraṇa* only are to use *kaiśiki*, there being little room for it in other genres. The *bhāṇa* uses it sparingly.

Ārabhaṭī is the mode for showing heavy fighting and cruel combats, which inspire neither admiration nor wonder. *Ārabhaṭī* is meant for gross combats full of pride, guilt, deceit and false words. Many kinds of backdrops and stage props, such as flying mountains, and trees to name only a few are used. The *vṛtti* is suitable for scenes of fear, exhiliration, flights, upheavals and duels. It is the mode suitable for *samavakāra*, *ḍima* and *īhāmṛga* genres.

A *vṛtti*, sets the tone of a production. In any production all the four *vṛttis* will be used, as in every play the verbal, mental and physical actions are all mixed. There can be no single emotion, or even a set of emotions, which alone can make up *nāṭya*. In the production of *rasa*, one emotion may be dominant (*sthāyī*) but others must be there as subsidiary emotions (*sañcārī*). All combinations of *vṛttis* are known by the name of the *vṛtti* which dominates (among the four) at a given time. The word *vṛtti* also means a profession by which a man conducts himself and projects his image, even though he may have other skills and diversions. For instance, a surgeon may know how to swim or fly planes, but his daily routine and thinking are governed by his profession of surgery. The idea of classifying *daśarūpakas* according to *vṛttis* is based upon the notion that each genre can create a specific emotional effect. A *vṛtti* provides that emotional impact in full force to the production. The inner emotional content envisaged by the dramatist is brought to the audience through a particular *vṛtti*.

Significance of Daśarūpakas

A review of the content of dramatic genres should free us of certain cliches that have prevailed in literary criticism. I quote Sombu Mitra who vocalizes well the view that ancient Indian drama was devoid of conflict:

> It is true that Indian civilization has affinities with ancient Greek civilization, yet the classical dramaturgy of India is fundamentally different from that of Greece. The notion of conflict, basic to Greek drama — and to most other theatres — is not the basis of Indian drama. Underlying this is a difference in respective philosophies of life, which explain the differences between Indian art and the art of Greek civilization — the source of European aesthetics. (*Mitra: 202-03*)

The notion that Indian drama overlooks conflict, which was the basis of Greek and consequentially all Western drama, was floated by early twentieth century critics like A.B. Keith. "Indian drama is thus deprived of a motif which is invaluable to Greek tragedy" .... "hence it is impossible to expect that any drama should be true tragedy" (Keith 277). To this one may add Henry W. Wells' remarks:

> The Eastern thinker marvels that the West can be so troubled by the storm on life's surface. The Western thinker marvels that the East can remain so blandly submerged in contemplation. The Western Dramatist is a general deploying life's forces into a battle, the Eastern dramatist, a choreographer arranging them in a dance. One drama exploits free will, the other, destiny; one exploits tension, the other conspires to eliminate it. (Wells 9-10)

With four genres depicting nothing but combat and upheaval (*saṃpheta, vidrava)* etc., why should Indian drama be considered devoid of conflict. The above quoted views generalize as if all that classical theatre had to offer was the *nāṭaka* full of *kaiśikī vṛtti* and that too of Kālidāsa only. It reduces all Indian drama to *nāṭaka* and *prakaraṇa*. It is true that the verbal content of the *samavakāras* and the *ḍimas* has not survived. Perhaps it was of inferior literary quality and that the producers may have been improvising this verbal content from traditional sources. But this should not permit us to forget that five agonic (*āviddha*) genres were a major part of our dramatic practice. Moreover, a particular approach to the interpretation of Indian philosophy — the very late purāṇic cum vedāntic view of *karmavāda*—has been foisted on ancient Indian theatre. Typical of this view is the observation of R.L. Singal. "Sanskrit drama is conditioned and limited in its scope by Brahmanical view of life, by the belief in divine justice and the triumph of good over evil" (Singal 90). Singal has held that the vedic concept of '*ṛt*' (Truth) is the inspiring philosophy of all ancient Indian playwrights. As a result there is no possibility of unjust suffering or human ***sparagmos***. However, the truth is quite different. The vision of ancient dramatists was not constricted by any ideology. Indian theatre was wedded to the idea of *lokānukṛti*, to show the state of human pleasure and pain and not to uphold varying doctrines that prevailed in India at different times. It is better to have a closer look at the plays themselves to see if any '*karmavāda*' or Vedic optimism has been actually propounded by them. One may notice that in the text of the plays the suffering of characters is hardly ever explained by some ill deed that they might have committed in the past. We do not know why Śakuntalā was cursed by Durvāsā, or why Vasantasenā was brought close to death. There is no attempt in the plays to state, either explicitly or implicitly, that the suffering of Duṣyanta or Vasantasenā was due to some past misdeed, however remote. Śakuntalā accepts her misfortune as her fate when she is not recognized by Duṣyanta "*Aho vidhinā darśitaṃ prabhutvam*"). She neither complains nor asks any questions when she learns of the curse at the end. Fate is accepted as unalterable.[1] It is clear that fate, (*daiva, vidhi, bhavitavyatā, bhāgadheya*—but not *karma* *gati* are mentioned as the forces superior to human will.

This superiority of fate, and its acceptance, does not eliminate the conflict in drama, that is, the conflict a person has to go through from the point of the beginning of his/her desire to the point of its fulfilment, from *ārambha* to *phalāgama*. Very often the proponents of the preciousness of conflict have made out conflict to be a clash between man and God/gods/nature/fate. Greek drama, in particular, has been interpreted as the prototype of this kind of conflict, of man's rebellion against tyrannical gods. But a study of neither the archaic-classical Greek philosophy nor of drama, bears out this interpretation. Fate (***dike***) was equally acceptable to the Greek, as *daiva* was to the Indian. Oedipus was a predetermined defiler, his tragedy was not caused by his mistake. Similarly, Hippolutus had no choice, as Aphrodite had vowed to take revenge on him. If *Oedipus Rex,* then, has more wailing that *Abhijñānaśākuntalam,* that is because as a play it is meant to depict horror, whereas *Śākuntalam* is meant to depict the fulfilment of love. If an *utsṛṣṭakāṅka* had managed to survive — guessing from its attributes (*lakṣaṇas*) as given in the *NŚ* — it would have had plenty of such tragic wails and complaints *('nirveditabhāṣitaḥ')*. One must also notice that the aim of tragedy was to be achieved by the agency of mutability. Death of the hero was not essential. Because of Aristotle's prejudice, *Oedipus Rex* need not be taken as the best and only point of reference. *Iphigenia at Aulis* is equally tragic, even though Iphigenia is saved by a miracle. Besides it should also be remembered that a single play like *Oedipus* or *Bacchae* does not represent the totality of tragic form and experience. The Dionysian festival called for trilogies out of which only one, the *Oresteia*, survives. The ninety odd plays, now extant, are only part of the trilogies, and should not be taken as representative of the tragic view. The *Oresteia* as we see, depicts two murders but avoids the death of Orestes and instead of ending in horror and deprivation arrives at reconciliation and harmony. The play ends with a prayer which sounds surprisingly similar to the concluding benediction of Indian plays. Mutability, then, is sufficient to show suffering. What Aristotle had actually opposed was the contrived happy ending meant to pamper the audience.

Thus, it can be seen that Indian drama is neither devoid of conflict nor is the Greek concept of fate and conflict so diametrically opposed to the Indian as it is often made out to be. There seems to be an acceptance of the irrational superiority of ***dike**/vidhi* in both cultures.

Once we rid ourselves of the notion that the ancient plays are exercises in specific philosophies, though who will assert they are devoid of them, we may be able to appreciate them better as artifacts created to arouse varied emotions for aesthetic pleasure. We will also be able to decipher better their dramaturgic techinques and appreciate them as artistic devices instead of treating them as handmaids of philosophy.

Play Structure

In terms of the total performance script, a play has a very complicated structure which consists of all the speaking, gesturing, dancing, singing and moving that goes on in the performing area. Yet the series of episodes or the story has been regarded as the basic structure of a play even though it is only the ground upon which many complex patterns are raised. As is well known, Aristotle has called ***muthos*** the soul of tragedy, and Bharata Muni says that *itivṛtta* is the body (*śarīra*) of *nāṭya*. Here, one is tempted to speculate what could be the 'body' of drama for Aristotle and the 'soul' for Bharata Muni. Some would hasten to conclude that ***ethos*** was the body and *rasa* was the soul. But this is taking the metaphors too literally. Whatever be the metaphors, both the dramaturgists have looked upon plot as an organic unit and both exhibit a teleological understanding of ***muthos**/itivṛtta*. As I have said earlier, ancient drama was a hieropraxis, the praxity of which consisted not in characterization but in the ***mimesis*** of an action/***praxis*** or *vyāpāra*. There was movement from one state of being to another and that movement has been called ***muthos*** in one text and *itivṛtta* in the other. The structure of plot is seen by the two dramaturgists as an organic whole, for one it is a living animal and for the other a tree. For Aristotle:

> Tragedy is an imitation of an action that is complete, and whole, and of certain magnitude, for there may be a whole that is wanting in magnitude. A whole is that which has a beginning, a middle, and an end... Again, a beautiful object, whether it be a living organism or any whole composed of parts, but must also be of a certain magnitude, for beauty depends on magnitude and order...As, therefore, in the case of animate bodies and organisms a certain magnitude is necessary, and a magnitude which may be easily embraced in the view; so in the plot, a certain length is necessary, and a length which can be easily embraced by memory. (*Poetics VII:3-4*)

Magnitude is in itself the outer structure which is supported by the unity of action "and that a whole, the structural union of the parts being such that, if any one of them is displaced or removed, the whole will be disjointed and disturbed" (*Poetics VIII:4*). To give the poet the liberty to create magnitude and wholeness, Aristotle allows him to make changes in the events. Poetry can modify history, as "it is a more philosophical and higher being than history." Teleology, that is "the unity leading to the end, makes it even higher. The poet can even alter traditional legends as he is maker of plots rather than of verses."

After prescribing an 'air of design,' even in the coincidences of the ***muthos*** to heighten the effect of tragic wonder, Aristotle distinguishes between simple complex plots. The first without ***peripetia*** and ***anagnorisis*** and the second with it. This analysis of the ***muthos*** is not applicable to tragedy alone. Just as magnitude and unity of action would be required in any ***muthos,*** tragic or comic, ***peripetia*** and ***anagnorisis*** are not for tragedy only. ***Peripetia*** can be useful in comedy too, and so can be ***anagnorisis,*** defined as a "change from ignorance to knowledge, producing love or hate between the persons destined by the poet for good or bad fortune." On the whole the system can be employed for both tragic and comic ***muthoi***, and for tragi-comic ones like Euripides' *Helen*, where ***peripetia*** and ***anagnorisis*** clearly work for a happy ending.

But the third part of ***muthos***, the scene of suffering or ***pathos*** ("destructive or painful action, such as death on stage, bodily agony, wounds and the like" *Poetics XI:6*), is required only in the tragedies where there is a reversal from good to bad or a final destruction. There was a view in Aristotle's time that the best tragedies were those in which the final destruction was averted (*Poetics XIII:7*). But for Aristotle that was a second rate tragedy. It is obvious from the *Poetics* that such tragedies were more popular and that poets often succumbed to the wishes of the audience. Perhaps such was the case with *Iphigenia at Aulis*.

The analysis of ***pathos, hamartia*** and tragic ***peripetia*** should not make us think that the unity of action, magnitude and wholeness were only to serve the tragic purpose, of arousal of horror and pity. Magnitude and wholeness would be necessary for the comic plot as well, and so would be the unity of action. These three are actually the basic properties that any plot must have.

Itivṛtta

The analysis of plot in the *Nāṭyaśāstra* is without reference to dramatic genres in particular. Bharata Muni has not discussed the *vastu* of *nāṭaka* or *samavakāra* in particular, as Aristotle had taken up the ***muthos*** for tragedy. His discussion is applicable to all the ten genres, though he does state that some portions of the *sandhis* are not be used in certain genres. In the *NŚ*, *itivṛtta* is shown as having three different aspects, *avasthā*, *arthaprakṛti* and *sandhi*. *Itivṛtta* is basically a series of episodes, and, as in Aristotle, here too, the protagonist and other characters are subservient to it. There is a similarity with Aristotle's view that the unity of action does not come from the hero.

The *itivṛtta* has two strands; the main effects or action that is primary called *ādhikārika* and the incidental events are called *prāsaṅgika* or *ānuṣaṅgika* (*NŚ 19:2*). For example, the primary objective in the story of Rāma is to win back Sītā. Freeing Laṅkā from a tyrant like Rāvaṇa and crowning Vibhīṣaṇa are incidental results. Both are, however, within the main action sequence, they are not plot and subplot which are later defined as *vṛtta* and *patākā*. The action of *itivṛtta* is called *kārya* and it is always geared towards a particular result called fruit (*phala*). Action is like a tree which bears fruit. Just as we plant a tree bearing in mind the kind of fruit we want, similarly, "according to the effort made by the 'poet' (playwright), according to a particular scheme (*vidhi*), according to the timely growth of fruit, according to the effort made by the protagonists, there is the gain of fruit" (*Kaveḥ prayatnānnetṝṇāṃ yuktānāṃ vidhyapāśrayāt/ kalpyate hi phalaprāptiḥ samutkarṣāt phalasya ca. NŚ 19:5*). Two questions may be posed: how can there be fruit without desire, and can there be desire except in a protagonist? Is the fruit not dependent upon the hero or *nāyaka*? No, it is not. As Abhinava has explained, it is the poet who initially decides upon the kind of fruit he wants and in accordance with that he choses the appropriate kind of hero (*uddhata, lalita,* etc.). The poet, of course, has to depend upon the hero to bring about the attainment of fruit. He cannot show it as a fulfilment of his own desire (*yādṛṣi puruṣārthe vyutpattiḥ kartavyā tad ucita nāyaka grahaṇena kaviḥ pravartamāno na svecchayā pravṛtto bhavati iti NŚ Ab. 19:6*). The hero is only a means to the fruit, as Indian drama was not protagonist-centric.

The action (*vyāpāra*) undertaken for the attainment of fruit has five stages (*avasthās*) (*NŚ 19:7*). They are *prārambha* (beginning), *prayatna* (exertion), *prāptisaṃbhava* (hopefulness), *niyatāpti* (reaching out); and, *phalayoga* (fulfilment). About *niyatāpti* there is a controversy; traditional commentators have defined it as the stage when success becomes certain (*niyata*), but Byrski has suggested that the word '*niyata*' means restraint, not certainty of success. He states that a restraint or an obstruction heightens suspense and increases the fun of resolution (109). Without contradicting Byrski, I should like to point out that Bharata Muni has also said that this '*niyata*' or certainty is not actual, but it exists only in the feelings of the *nāyaka*, "*niyataṃ tu phalaprāptiḥ yadā bhāvena paśyati*" (*NŚ 19:12*). *Niyatāpti*, then, means a state of intense determination which drives the hero to counter all odds.

The five *avasthās* in an *itivṛtta* are the different stages of the mental states of the *nāyaka* and his associates. All these are means for the fruit. The teleological intention is stated unequivocally in the *NŚ*: "In these (*avasthās*), which are different in nature, there should be a mutual cohesion inspired by one intention which is called attainment of fruit (*phalahetu*)" (*NŚ19:15*). All plots must have these five *avasthās* (*NŚ 19:14*). That is to say, they may not have all five *sandhis*, but there can be no reduction in the number of *avasthās*.

The nature of the episodes in an *itivṛtta* is given the name *arthaprakṛti*. *Artha* (purpose/end) is the fruit and the episodes are the instruments (*upāya*) or *prakṛti*. They are five; *bīja, bindu, patākā, prakarī* and *kārya*. *Bīja* (seed) is the small beginning; a desire for something, like Duṣyanta's desire for Śakuntalā and vice-versa, which eventually grows into the fruit. *Bindu* is that centrifugal force which maintains a link between all efforts and episodes till the end, and prevents the *itivṛtta* from falling apart. A side plot complete in itself with its own *phala*, but working for the success of the main *phala*, is called *patākā*. For instance, Rāma's friendship with Sugrīva bore the *phala* (result) of Sugrīva's earning the crown of Kiṣkindhā, but this whole effort was instrumental in winning back Sītā. There can be more than one *patākā* in a play. In a *nāṭaka* there can be as many as four (*NŚ 19:30*). Subplots or episodes which have no end of their own but work for the main fulfilment are called *prakarī*. The appearance of Vāsudeva is the *prakarī* in *Veṇīsaṃhāra*. And finally, "the end (*artha*) for which the whole activity (*samārambha*) has been undertaken and for which the experts use the primary story (*vastu*) is called *kārya*" (*NŚ 19:26*). *Kārya* is no other than *phala*. Whereas the four *arthaprakṛtis* are instruments (*upāyas*), *kārya* is the end itself.

If *itivṛtta* is imagined as a body, it can be said to have limbs or *sandhis*. These are five in number: *mukha, pratimukha, garbha, vimarśa,* and *nirvahaṇa.* In a *nāṭaka* or *prakaraṇa* all the five are employed. *Avasthās* and *arthaprakṛtis* are dynamic processes. They are better expressed by the metaphor of a seed growing into a fruit. For *sandhis* the metaphor has changed. *Sandhis* are not processes but the areas of the body (*śarīra*) of *nāṭya* within which all the processes take place. We can see the relationship of the parts (limbs, *sandhis*) to the whole (body, *śarīra*). This '*aṅga-aṅgī bhāva*' (limb-whole pattern) is the basic metaphor adopted by Bharata Muni as a methodology for analysis of a plot. In fact, this methodology is common to other disciplines (*śāstras*) like vedic philosophy, architecture and medicine, to name a few. For the purpose of explaining the nature of plot, Aristotle, too, has described it as a living organism with parts related to each other and to the whole.

Mukha (mouth) is the first *sandhi,* the play-portion where the *bīja,* the wish of the *nāyaka* comes into being and begins to unfold. The portion in which the seed, grows secretly, and is temporarily hidden (like the seed in the earth), is called *pratimukha.* The portion in which the seed, seems lost and needs to be revitalised is called *garbha.* The portion showing the hero's disappointment caused by *garbha* and initial failure is named *vimarśa sandhi.* The part showing the fulfilment of desire, is called *nirvahaṇa.* In the *nāṭaka* and the *prakaraṇa,* the five *sandhis* are used as corresponding to the five *avasthas.* But in the genres where there are only four, three or two *sandhis,* the corresponding *avasthās* are not to be skipped over. All *itivṛttas* must have all the five *avasthās,* whatever be the number of *sandhis* in a *rūpaka.*

Ḍima and *samavakāra* are without *vimarśa.* In *vyāyoga* and *ihāmṛga* there is no *garbha,* as in these genres the heroes are neither very thoughtful nor sensitive. They rush to seek the desired object from the very beginning and do not wait for anybody to create obstruction. *Prahasana, vīthī* and *bhāṇa* are too simple, and their characters too low to go through any vicissitudes, hence only *mukha* and *nirvahaṇa* are enough for them. Bharata Muni has mentioned, sixty-four sub-parts (*anusandhis*) of *sandhis,* which have been left out here for shortage of space as are the examples of *sandhis* from plays.

In the *NŚ* there is no injunction that all plays must have a happy ending. All arrangement of plot was made ("*kalpyate*") according to the fruit that was to be shown as arising from action (*samutkarṣāt phalasya ca, NŚ 19:5*). Where a miserable end was to be shown, as in *Urubhaṅgam,* the seed was likewise. As Abhinava explains while commenting on *mukha sandhi:*

> Where happiness is to be the *phala,* pleasing emotions like *śṛṅgāra* etc., are shown in abundance; where loss and unhappiness are the *phala,* there the feelings of anger, bereavement and misery shall prevail. Both conditions shall have suitable *vyabhicārī bhāvas.* (*NŚ Ab. 19:43*)

The *itivṛtta* with its *arthaprakṛtis sandhis* and *avasthās* should not be made to stand for any wholeness which is more than an artifact or a dramatic device. It was not a symbol of any philosophy that insisted on happiness as its end. *Nāṭya* is an *anukṛti* of worldly situations (*laukikī sukhaduḥkhāvasthā*). Though some schools of Indian philosophy may have asserted that evil is a transistory state of ignorance and knowledge is blissful, the ancient plays, however, do not propagate this view. Bharata Muni does not even admit *śānta rasa* or the virtues of *mukti* as a subject of *nāṭya.* But the foisting of 'Hindu view' on drama continues unabated. For example:

> A drama as a work of art was regarded as a whole, a cycle complete in itself. A drama ending with disastrous consequences would be a mutilated piece from the world of our experience — it would merely mean that the cycle has not been completed, or that it is only a partial view and not the whole ... Thus the five critical situations — *sandhis* — constitute a unity, an epitome of our life as a whole ... Drama is thus the reflection of life as a whole from the Indian point of view and it contains its own philosophy.. (Das Gupta, Preface 81-82)

Wholeness, five *sandhis* and the "Indian view" are all equated. To this, Byrski has added that this kind of optimistic philosophy is derived from the *Vedas.* For him, *nāṭya* is a *yajña*:

> By now we know how true this statement is and where to look for the sources of this philosophy of drama. We know further that the fittest form of the view of life which *Nāṭya* as a whole reflects is expressed by the concept of *Yajña*. Since *Yajña* must reach a positive conclusion, it cannot therefore be overrun by the adverse forces of the *Asuras*, for them the disintegrated body of the Lord of Creatures will not be reconstructed and the whole order of the Universe will be perilously disturbed. *Nāṭya* is supposed to relfect this nature of the world to such an extent that it is itself called a sacrifice so that it cannot disregard this pattern and consequently be an untrue representation of the Three Worlds. (Byrski 137-38)

In equating *yajña* and *nāṭya*, Byrski has depended upon the following evidence. The *NŚ* mentions that *nāṭya* was first performed by Bharata Muni at the banner (*jarjara*) festival of Indra and the play enacted was called *amṛtamanthana*. It was a depiction of gods versus demons conflict. To Byrski, this indicates a history of the origin of *nāṭya* in rituals which were either *yajña* themselves or were performed along with *yajña*. That is why he says that *yajña* and *nāṭya* express the same metaphysics. To prove a common origin, or the continuity of *nāṭya-yajña* ritual he points out that like Indra's use of *jarjara* in *pūrvaraṅga*, in the Vedic *yajñas* enemies were warded-off by a long pole (*dīrghavaṃśena*) from the inner *yajña* chambers (*antaragṛhaṇāt*) as is mentioned in the *Jaimanīya Brāhmaṇa* (*II:150*). The *Śatapatha Brāhmaṇa* also mentions a *daṇḍa* to drive off evil spirits at a *yajña* (*3.2.2.34*). *Pañcaviṃśa Brāhmaṇa* says that this rite was given by Prajāpati to Indra. Thus there was an activity common to *yajña* and *nāṭya*, performed either by Indra or by others in his name. Yajña, contends Byrski, is a *devāsura* conflict. The fight between good and evil is what *yajña* is about and so is *nāṭya*.

Well argued as this may be, Byrski's theory is derived from an extensive European movement which has sought to prove the origin of all myth and drama in ritual. The Cambridge anthropologists from Fraser onwards have applied this theory to Greek and Mediterranean literatures and following their example Byrski does the same to the Indian drama. This theory, however, overlooks a few things. Namely, a particular activity or ritual action may be common to many rituals but this does not mean that all of them have the same purpose. Warding-off by pole may have been a general prohibitory device, like police cordon in our times, which is done at unconnected rituals such as marriages and funerals simply to keep away the crowds. Besides, *yajña* was not disrupted by *asuras* alone. The later epics are full of stories in which one *jāti* (tribe) prevented another from performing a successful *yajña*, worship or meditation. Even men were prevented by *devatās* as were the *asuras* from performing power giving rituals. *Saṃhitās* and *Brāhmaṇas* have many fables about *gandharvas, devas, asuras* and *rākṣasas* as contending for *soma rasa* or *vāk*. The point was simple; for the Indo-Europeans, rituals were ways to power and the opponents thought prevention was a necessary pre-emptive move. If looked upon in this way, *yajña* is a *daivāsura, āsuradaiva* or *mānuṣa-daiva* battle (by the time of epics, *yajña* had been replaced by *tapas* which was a similar target of disruption). But *nāṭya* is not to be looked upon that way. The *asuras* made this mistake — they forgot that *nāṭya* was a play a '*krīḍanīyakam*' — and was to be viewed impersonally. Brahmā reminded them of it and they corrected their mistake. From that time onwards they began protecting *nāṭya* from disruption and were given places in the *raṅga* or the *prekṣāgṛha,* and the sacrificial food at *raṅgapūjana.* The Byrskian reduction of *nāṭya* to *yajña* overlooks the non-agonic genres like *nāṭaka* etc., which have *śṛṅgāra* as their theme. If they too are just viewed as *yajña* in which union of lovers (*kāmapūrti*) is the end and difficulties in the way of lovers are *āsuric* disruptions, then *yajña* is like any human endeavour which has a beginning, its difficulties and fulfilment. *Yajña* then becomes too general a metaphor.

Above all it must not be forgotten that *yajña* and its protection are two differnt things. There is conflict between *deva* and *asura* whether to allow the sacrifice or not, but there is no conflict within the process of *yajña* itself. If the *yajña* can take place undisturbed, its fruits are assured. Similarly, *pūrvaraṅga* is to protect *nāṭya*. If *nāṭya* takes place its results also are assured. But in *nāṭya* there is a conflict within its *itivṛtta,* and it can result in two states — in happiness or misery. *Yajña* can have only one end or no end. *Nāṭya* thus is not to be equated with *yajña* or its world-view. *Nāṭya* should only be seen as a tree which bears fruit according to the seed; the fruit may be bitter or sweet.

Ethos and Nāyakas

In hieropraxis the protagonist is subservient to ***praxis,*** that is, the action or the *karyāvasthā*. Aristotle has said that there can be a tragedy without character but not without plot (which itself is a ***mimesis*** of action). Similarly, Bharata Muni has held that the *nāyaka* is to be chosen by the playwright according to the *phala* (end) he envisages. Besides being subservient to ***praxis***, the protagonist and other characters are shaped according to set patterns. Peculiarity of character, delineation of very personal qualities, or portraiture, is beyond the scope of this drama. In fact, portraiture would deconstruct the patterns of ***ethos*** which have a greater evocative significance than what portraiture can ever achieve.

Ethos

Broadly speaking, characters in a tragedy had to be 'good men' and those in comedy and satire, were 'mean persons.' So all characters fall into the category of either admirable people or ludicrous folks. Aristotle has spoken more about the protagonist of a tragedy. The first requirement was his goodness, which his speeches must reflect in the shape of a moral purpose. This was required of even women and slaves. "The second thing to aim at, is propriety. There is a type of manly valour: but valour in a woman, or unscrupulous cleverness, is inappropriate" (*Poetics XIV: 2*). Aristotle wishes women to be subdued if they are to reflect goodness. "Thirdly, character must be true to life; this is a distinct thing from goodness and propriety, as here described. The fourth point is consistency; for though the subject of the imitation, who suggested the type, be inconsistent, still he must be consistently inconsistent" (*Poetics XV: 3*). Most of all the poet should "make a likeness which is true to life and yet more beautiful .... preserve the type and yet ennoble it" (*Poetics XV: 7*). In all these externals of a character, the most essential thing is ***ethos*** or "that which reveals a moral purpose, showing that kind of thing a man chooses or avoids" (*Poetics VII:17*).

Putting all these into a concrete shape Aristotle has given us a pattern of what the tragic hero should be like. He should be a good man, though not exceptionally good but 'like ourselves.' As he was always supposed to be of royal household he would be valourous too. Moral choices are made by all the protagonists without dithering. It may be a Hippolytus, Antigone, Orestes or Hekabe.

The protagonist does not take too long to decide. He or she gives the reasons for making the choice, deliberately revealing the thought process behind the choice. This willful sharing with the audience was an important feature of dramatic process and was called ***dianoia***. In cultures which do not foster individualism, the protagonist was obliged to explain his conduct to his family, friends, city and the gods. The greatness of ***ethos*** or a character was judged by the courage with which the moral choices were made. A confused procrastinator like Hamlet, unable to make a timely choice, would have been an anti-hero to the Greeks. Reflection upon the nature of things or an analysis of the human condition was not the aim of ***dianoia***. Thinking was for choosing, doing this or that. Action was the culmination of ***ethos***.

But in spite of his best efforts and courageous choice, Man fails. To explain the logic of failure, Aristotle has used the term ***hamartia*** which means hitting off the mark. It is an error of judgement made inadvertently. A large number of Greek tragedies have little room even for ***hamartia***. *Andromache, Supplices, Antigone, Daughters of Troy, Electra,*

Eumenides, are all plays in which misfortune sets in motion even before the protagonist realizes its presence. In the majority of tragedies the events are predetermined, a god has decided to destroy someone as in *Hyppolytus,* or the family duty holds the individual in absolute bondage as in *Oresteia, Electra* or *Antigone.* ***Hamartia,*** then, is a brief appearance in the action sequence of the hero, as an action which at the time of doing does not seem that consequential — such as Oedipus' killing the old man in ignorance, or Hippolytus' rebuking the advances of her mother. The value of ***hamartia*** was highly jacked up in Christian tragedy and modern moralistic tragedy where the downfall of the hero is caused by a cardinal sin or a serious lapse.[2] In such a tragedy, pity for the protagonist and horror at excessive suffering, are both benumbed. In the Greek world, man was not so free. Even by making the right choice he could not avert a calamity or suffering, becuase his suffering was not always caused by any of his weaknesses. It was not the ambition of a Macbeth, the jealousy of an Othello or the arrogance of a Lear, nor the inner sin that destroyed a man, but instead it was the dilemma imposed upon him by forces far beyond his control that caused his destruction. His ***ethos*** lay in his choosing the admirable way to self-annihilation. Here suffering comes from without not from within. This was the Indo-European perception of Man's destiny. It works in the Indian plays as well, though here, suffering does not usually bring the protagonist to the point of destruction if the genre is a *nāṭaka.* But all the same, the suffering is uninvited, undeserved and unjustified.

Nāyakas and Nāyikās

The Indian protaganists and heroines operated under a pre-arranged scheme of the *itivṛtta* which was shaped to achieve a desired emotional effect (*bhāvarasaprakriyā*). Here again, as in Aristotle, goodness is the basic fibre, of not only the hero but of other major characters as well. All dramatis personae are divided into three classifications, namely, noble, medium and low (*'prakṛtistrividhā parikīrtitā uttamamadhymādhamā'* *NŚ 24:1*). Even the lowly are not viscious, they are only degraded in qualities and social status. The malignity or vice that serves no other end but its own is unusual. Ancient drama presents its antagonist or *pratināyaka* as an underserving contender asking for more than he deserves in the face of one who deserves more.

Bharata Muni has given prescriptions for the making of a large number of characters, all of the human category. It is to be presumed that the extra-terrestrial beings, such as *devas* and demons, *gandharvas*, *yakṣas* and *kinnaras* are to be cast long parallel lines. Protagonists *(nāyikās/nāyakas)*, of the noble category should be restrained, knowledgeable, adept in many arts, generous, protective, learned in many *śāstras*, grave and large-hearted. The medium *nāyikās* should be worldly wise, knowlegeable in arts, sweet and clever. And the lowly, whether men or women, should be rough, ill-behaved, irrational, unintelligent, ill-tempered, devious, faithless, lazy, double dealers, greedy and wrong doers.

The protagonists are further shown as possessing any one of the four major temperaments — *dhīroddhata, dhīralalita, dhīrodātta* and *dhīrapraśānta*. This classification has been made to serve the ten genres. The *devas* (gods) are made *dhīroddhata* (aggressive and extrovert) as protagonists in action plays. The kings were *dhīralalita* (restrained and forgiving) and brahmins and merchants were to be *dhīrapraśānta* (contemplative). The *dhīrodātta* had a place in *prakaraṇa* like the contemplative Cārudatta. For *vyāyoga*, human *uddhatas* were needed and for cheaper genres like *bhāṇa, prahasana* and *vīthī*, low characters such as pimps, bawds, parasites and gamblers were employed. In *nāṭaka* or *prakaraṇa* the role of *vidūṣaka* was played by a medium-cum-low character who was a hermit, brahmin, parasite or a disciple (*NŚ 24:4-22*).

The heroines were of four types *dhīrā, lalitā, udāttā* and *nibhṛtā*. Royal women were to be of the first two kinds. The respectable women and the prostitutes could be of the last two types. They were to be matched with appropriate heroes. These are very general recommendations and were often not stuck to by the dramatists. For instance, the Rāma of *Uttararāmacaritam* is not *lalita* but *praśānta*. On the whole these character type are based on the principle that certain emotions are to be enacted by characters of specific social ranks.

Notes

1. C.W. Nuckolls suggests that fate works in three ways or under three 'schemata' in *Abhijñanaśākuntalam*, as omnipresent and unalterable, as selective and malign, and as selective and helpful. "Causal thinking in Sakuntala: A Shema-Theoretic Approach to a Classical Sanskrit Drama." *Philosophy East and West* 37.3 (July 1987): 286-305. Fate is interpreted by Nuckolls as inexorable and unrelenting with little room for human deeds.
2. The extensive use of ***hamartia*** as a dramatic device was encouraged by the stringent moral demands of Christianity, a trait from the Jewish tradition. "The Jehovah religion is an experience of unmistakable demands which the chosen must fulfil." C. Kernyi, *The Religion of the Greeks and Romans* (New York : E.P. Dutton and Co., 1962) 90. Greek religious duty was not so unambiguously defined as Christian allegiance to the ten commandments. The Greek word for religious experience, "***eluabeia,***" "expresses a universal attitude, which it was a duty to observe towards the divine, but no more so than towards any other reality of human life ... ***eulabeia*** as an attitude is determined by the universal rule of life that in every one of life's relationships, one must guard against positive and negative exaggeration, against the too-much and the too-little" (91). Greek culture demands were of maintaining balance, while the Christian demands were of not transgressing. Balance being finer and often imperceptible is easy to lose. And, therefore, it is also not easy to blame the individual — or fix responsibility by clear cut ***hamartia***.

Part III

TRANSFORMATION AND EMOTIONAL AROUSAL

12

Transformation and Emotional Arousal

SO far, I have been comparing the dramatic theories of Aristotle and Bharata Muni as formulated for the art of what I have called hieropraxis. Hieropraxis depended upon semiotized gesture, rhythmic movement, dance, music and codified costume to make up its performance text. In the preceding pages, I have tried to show how each of these elements was used in the two theatres. We may, at this point, ask if this method of using multi-channelled discourse resulted in some identical or similar effects in the two theatres. The answer, to my mind, seems to be in the affirmative. In both theatres there are two common results. One, theatre became essentially a site for transforming reality. Two, theatre provided a deep emotional arousal which was of special psychological consequence and was considered to be the basis of aesthetic pleasure.

In this concluding chapter, I shall deal with the ancient approach to theatrical transformation and emotional arousal. Bharata Muni has defined transformation as of two kinds, *lokadharmī* and *nāṭyadharmi*. Though there is no parallel concept in Aristotle, in actual practice Greek theatrical transformation was in no way less complex and refined than the one achieved on the Indian stage. The second effect, namely that of emotional arousal was supposed to result in a state of mind that one culture analysed as ***katharsis*** and the other defined as *rasa*. It must be noted that transformation made intense emotional arousal possible. The ancient cultures practised what Lotman has called the "aesthetics of identity." Here, there was identity or nearness of the code of the sender with that of the receiver. Thus the initiated were able to follow transformation with ease and respond to it immediately. The aesthetics of identity offers an immediacy and intensity that can be used very well for emotional arousal. It seems that in Greece and India strong emotional arousal was a definite cultural pattern. Hence the concepts of "***psuchagogia***" and "*bhāvavyañjanā* were well formulated. It is befitting that I conclude by comparing them and also by briefly analysing ***katharsis*** and *rasa* which are well known conceptual tools of defining aesthetic pleasure.

Transformation of Reality

Preoccupied with transformation, the theatre of hieropraxis avoided portrayal of characters as complex psychological entities and depiction of social classes and class conflict as a major undertaking. The aim here was not to "reactualize on stage what has happened elsewhere" (Schechner 98), but to create a world of its own in theatre. Music, dance and gesture totally transformed the objects of imitation. While examining the concepts of ***mimesis*** and *anukaraṇa* we have seen that what was required was not a representation of the material characteristics of things, but of their inner nature. While recreating, the object (Nature/*loka*) was totally transformed into a new reality. It was not merely a transformation of signification but of form and shape as well. It was not, as if, an everyday chair was put on the stage and made to signify a throne but that the stage props as well were given a conventionalized shape. Similarly, mask, costume, gesture and gait were given a traditionalized form that transformed the natural characters and situations into a semiotized reality. Transformation succeeded in "creating or incarnating in a theatre place what cannot take place anywhere else" (Schechner 98). These words of Schechner are a repetition of the traditional Indian view that theatre or *nāṭya* is a world, where things happen that are beyond Nature (*alaukika*). This transformational power of theatre is only beginning to be recognized in western criticism. So far, much more weight had been given to realistic representation and conflict. The whole of western theatre, it was believed, rested upon these two factors for its sustenance and Greek theatre was regarded as the progenitor of both realism and conflict. Even Schechner, who draws attention to transformation and declares that "transformation and not conflict is the root of theatre" (90), believes that Greek theatre was geared towards depiction and characterization:

> This transformation is identical in structure to that at the heart of Greek theatre (and its legacy in the West) namely, characterization and presentation of real or possible events. (99)

While one cannot deny the Greek, particularly Aristotelian, emphasis on ***ethos*** and probability, we should not overlook the fact that even in Greek theatre transformation of real behaviour into symbolic behaviour was the dominant element. It was far more semiotised than what Naturalism allowed on European stage, or what the revivers of ancient tragic performances like Rheinhart or Kunst allowed when they performed the Greek tragedies in Epidaurus in the thirties. It must be borne in mind that Aristotle in stating that art imitates nature and that drama should not overlook the probable was not calling for verisimilitude but for choosing for imitation a verifiable world. To the theatrical power of transformation he gave full scope by asserting that theatre should present not the possible particularity of things but the probable and the necessary. In the preceding pages we have seen how the media and conventions of representation in Greek theatre were such that a highly embellished transformation must have taken place.

Bharata Muni has defined theatrical transformation by using the concept of the two *dharmīs*, *lokadharmī* and *nāṭyadharmī*. Where the transformation is simpler and the natural world can be traced in the transformation, the production is called *lokadharmī*, but where the performance succeeds in creating a world of its own through complex transformation, the production is said to be *nāṭyadharmī*. It is worth our while to closely examine the *dharmīs* as they are the oldest conceptualization on the subject of theatrical transformation.

Lokadharmī and Nāṭyadharmī

Even though the *dharmīs* are clearly defined in the *NŚ*, and the commentary of Abhinavagupta brilliantly elaborates the concept for us, still the *dharmis* have been subjected to the gravest misinterpretations by the present day exponents of Indian theatre. It is not the kind of error that results in clouding some marginally functional aspects of performance. The *dharmīs* make up the overall approach to *anukaraṇa* as envisaged by Bharata Muni. It is, therefore, vital to clear up the misunderstandings that prevail.

The three words, *'loka,' 'nāṭya'* and *'dharmī'* have to be viewed first as common Sanskrit words and then as definitive terms used in the text. This, I hope shall emerge from the analysis of some verses that I shall later undertake. But first as to the misunderstandings that prevail about *dharmīs*. There is first of all the modern Hindi meaning of *'loka'* which has caused a change of meaning by replacing the original Sanskrit intent. In Hindi, and a good many other modern Indian languages, *loka* has come to denote *'folk.' 'Loka-kalā,' 'loka-saṅgīta,'* etc. have come to mean folk art and folk music. *Lokadharmī* is thus taken to mean folk mode (of theatre), and *nāṭyadharmī* is interpreted to denote classical theatre. To make matters worse there is no dearth of Indian theorists who have accepted certain European and Orientalist classifications of Indian cultural life into slots of binary opposites like folk versus classical, popular versus elitist, Aryan versus Dravidian, Brahmin versus unvedic, Great Tradition versus Low Tradition and so on. *Lokadharmī* versus *nāṭyadharmī* has been added to this list by drama theorists. What is more, a set of medieval terms, *'mārgī* and *'deśī'*, used in a very different context in manuals on music and dance, have been interpreted to mean folk versus classical. In truth, such a division of art forms or culture could not have existed before the process of industrialization created modern conditions. Was Greek tragedy a classical art form with its poetry in choicest metric forms, or was it folk because a whole city watched it along with slaves? In ancient India too, there seems to have been no difference between the acting styles of the companies that performed in towns and those which performed in the villages. As performance in those days was a caste job, there is little possibility that there was one caste of rural actors and another of urban. Neither the caste rules nor the ancient economy could have allowed it. Certainly the *kuśīlavas, bharatas,* and *naṭas* must have had their schools (*sampradāyas*) but there could have been no classification along rural and urban lines.

There is the vast panorama of popular theatre in India which still retains much of its traditional character. It has acquired a few things from cinema and westernized urban theatre. But still, forms like *Bhavai, Yakṣgāna, Jātra,* etc., have been able to retain an identity which can be safely called traditionally Indian. Nowadays, this kind of theatre is being called folk, hence *lokadharmī* to distinguish it from *aṣṭapadī* dance like *Orrisi, Bharatanāṭyam* and the more dramatic ones like *Kuḍyaṭṭam* and *Kathakali,* which were long ago christened as classical. This spurious distinction has led many to believe that *Jātra,* etc., are rustic art forms different sui generis from *Kuḍiyaṭṭam,* etc. It is conveniently forgotten that these were not rustic until the Industrial revolution in India made them so and till the urban middle class banished them from towns. In terms of performance techniques and methodology there seems to be little difference between *Jātra* theatre and *Kuḍiyaṭṭam.* The elements of *nāṭya,* such as purāṇic stories *abhinaya* as codified gesture, stage conventions and typified characters, all of which are found in rural forms today, are to be found in *aṣṭapadī* dances as well as in the *Nāṭyaśāstra* written for ancient *daśarūpakas.* To call the rural forms of the present times as 'folk' and hence *lokdharmī,* is not correct.

The other major misconception about *lokdharmī* is to interpret it as Realistic histrionics. To a student of theatre history, realistic acting is known as a European phenomenon that appeared for the first time in the eighteenth century. Before that no theatre in the world had any place for it. The twentieth century Indian theatre, revived and nurtured under the shadow of the western stage and cinematic realism, has lost sight of its own non-realistic methodology and taken realism for its own inheritance. It has not been able to establish a link with the ancient Indian or the present day traditional theatre, and it can simply not envisage a production in which dialogue dominant verbosity does not throttle the inherited codes of *āṅgika abhinaya* or body language. The recent efforts of some modern Indian playwrights to include song and dance in plays have resulted in patch-work only. In their productions, neither dance nor music reshapes or succeeds in modifying the realistic mode of acting but, instead, the music and dance remain forced insertions. Realism continues to dominate the vision of playwrights, audiences and scholars alike. That is why even a profound scholar of the *Nāṭyaśāstra* like M.M. Ghosh translated '*lokadharmī*' as 'realistic' in his English translation of the *Nāṭyaśāstra*. His translation, and the support of many others, has given a sanctioned accommodation to realism in our ideas about ancient dramaturgy. Even those who have recognized the non-realistic quality of ancient drama, have defined the concept of *lokadharmī* as realism. In her *Classical Indian Dance in Literature and Arts,* Kapila Vatsyayana says, "The basic approach of this drama is 'idealistic': an elaborate stage convention (*nāṭyadharmī*), meticulous to the last detail, dispenses with the need of realistic presentation (*lokadharmī*) or portraiture" (191). Here, Vatsyayana has admitted that ancient production was far from realism, all the same she conceives of *lokadharmī* as realistic rendering. Eugenio Barba has mistaken *lokadharmī* for something not even of the stage but of the world. He is unable to distinguish between *lokadharma* and *lokadharmī*. "We have two words, Sanjukta Panigrahi says to me, to describe a man's behaviour: one, *lokadharmi,* stands for the behaviour (*dharmī*) of man of daily life (*loka*); the other, *nāṭyadharmī*, for his behaviour in dance (*nāṭya*)" (5-32). Thus Barba calls all off-stage normal movements of the human body as *lokadharmī* and all stage activity as *nāṭyadharmī*. But the *NŚ* has clearly laid down that both the *dharmīs* exist in *nāṭya*, that is in performance. Barba's usage of *lokadharmī* and *nāṭyadharmī* is an obvious case of misinformation. Let us look at the way the *NŚ* defines the terms *lokadharmī* and *nāṭyadharmī*:

> That which shows normal and abnormal behaviour of people rendering their actions as they have been described in the stories transmitted through tradition, without enacting on the stage any embellished movements of the body, is called *lokadharmī*. That which seeks to render through acting (*abhinaya*) the usual ways of various kinds of men and women, such a *nāṭya* is called *lokadharmī*. Where speech, action, nature and expression are all exaggerated, where playfulness, embellished body movements (*aṅgahāras*) are employed, techniques of drama are used, that is *nāṭyadharmī*. Where unusual characters are employed, embellished forms of *svara* (in song and speech) are used, such a drama is called *nāṭyadharmī*. When people (sitting or standing) close by cannot hear each other, but can hear words not spoken that is *nāṭyadharmī*. When mountains, vehicles, air-vehicles, skins, armour and flags are shown symbolically (as stage props) — that is *nāṭyadharmī*. Having acted one role when an actor takes up another role, either because no other actor is available or because one has the skill to do many roles, this (convention) is called *nāṭyadharmī*. When a (socially) uncohabitable woman is made into a cohabitable character or vice-versa such (dramatic freedom) changes are called *nāṭyadharmī*. When one walks dancingly, raising one's feet, employing embellished body movements, this is *nāṭyadharmī*. That which is natural behaviour of people depicting their happy or sorrowful acts, and that which is expressed by intricate gestures is *nāṭyadharmī*.
>
> Traditional stories (*itihāsa*) and the meaning of *Vedas* which has been uttered by Brahmā for the delight

of men and gods, is also *nāṭyadharmī*. *Nāṭya* should always be produced in *nāṭyadharmī*, without body gestures (*aṅgābhinaya*) there is no delight. The spontaneous expression of all (living things) and all acting (*abhinaya*) to express meaning through embellished body movements, is called *nāṭyadharmī*. (*NŚ 13:71-85*)

First of all, it should be noted that there are only two verses about *lokadharmī*. The text gives the impression that it is something obvious, and that it is *nāṭyadharmī* which needs to be explained in detail. Broadly speaking, the representation of "*lokadharma*" (on the stage) or the usual behaviour of the world is *lokadharmī*. The *dharma* of the *naṭa* or the actor which is specifically stage behaviour is *nāṭyadharmī*. It may be asked, why is it necessary to make a classification when all activity in drama is on the stage and is hence *nāṭyadharmī*? It seems that a distinction has to be made primarily to show the difference between the simple and the embellished. It is like the distinction between the raw and the cooked. The raw here is not just providing a realistic or naturalistic representation of worldly behaviour, but it is the choice of keeping to the well-known story, behaviour, characterization and events as they have come down without altering the roles through poetic imagination into '*udātta*' or '*lalita nāyaka*', or embellishing the story with fantastic events. The mode of acting even in *lokadharmī* cannot be realistic. It would have to use the *āṅgika abhinaya* and the *sāttvika* and the *āhārya* as well, but avoid the use of embellished movements that are expressive of intense erotic feelings. Thus it is clear that *lokadharmī* has a specific use and a rather limited one in ancient drama. It is like the raw food at the table, only some of which can go as salad and greens, the rest of which needs to be cooked and seasoned. It is also to be noted that no production can be exclusively *lokadharmī* or *nāṭyadharmī*. Certain movements, some characters and some situations, very often the low and the comic ones, would incline towards *lokadharmī*. But in a good many situations, particularly in *nāṭaka* and *prakaraṇa*, one must follow the *nāṭyadharmī* mode. Wherever there is a need for *kaiśikī vṛtti,* only the intense and fanciful world of *nāṭyadharmī* would suffice. Again, it is clear from the text that all stage conventions are a make-believe and a "*dharma*" of *nāṭya.* Even pictures or models of mountains, air-vehicles and the total paraphernalia of costume (*āhārya*) is a theatrical fiction. To represent animals, furniture and buildings made out of the usual material of gum, wax, cloth etc., was not a *lokadharmī* device, as some scholars have suggested. It was a *nāṭyadharmī* technique.

It is the belief of some specialists that anything placed on the stage is *lokadharmī* if it is inanimate and physical. For instance, the model of a chariot of any kind, realistic or symbolic, is *lokadharmī,* but if a chariot is suggested through hand-gestures and body movements, then the production should be called *nāṭyadharmī.* The text of the *NŚ*, however, does not bear out this view. The verse quoted is explicit (78). A cardboard mountain or other models are *nāṭyadharmī.* Such a model is not realistic but symbolic for Bharata Muni. Stone is the "*dharma*" for the worldly mountain and hence the piling of stone on stage could be called *lokadharmī,* but a cardboard mountain is *nāṭyadharmī.* In the Indian theory of drama, the unreality of the dramatic world is taken for granted. Here, there has been no need to first make things look real, and then to indulge in a willing suspension of disbelief. *Nāṭya* was meant to be a play (*kriḍanīyakam*), which cannot but be "unreal." Hence, even *lokadharmī* cannot claim to be real or realistic. It is transmutation of the worldly things (*lokadharma*) into stage phenomenon. But once put on stage only a fraction of the worldly (*lokadharma*) survives. The rest gets converted into *lokadharmī* (if it retains simplicity and similarity to the original) or into the *dharma* of *nāṭya, nāṭyadharmī* (if it is highly embellished and ornate). That is what Bharata Muni implies in verse 81 when he says that the happy and sorrowful actions of men, when shown on stage through body movements of *abhinaya,* become *naṭyadharmī.* It is the basis, the *lokadharma,* on which the edifice of embellishment is raised. Let us now turn to Abhinava for his analysis:

Although there is no *dharma* except that of the world

(*loka*), for the sake of entertainment, the worldly actions are made to undergo exaggeration and embellishment by the poet and the actor. These are called *nāṭyadharmī*. *Dharmī* has been earlier defined as of two kinds. By 'earlier,' the place indicated is the chapter on *rasa* and *bhāvas*. By saying, '*svabhāvopagatam*,' it is meant that *lokadharma* is primary, that it is like the wall on which embellishment is done like carvings. Some *dharmīs* are of the *loka* kind, some are *nāṭya* kind.

Whatever happens to be the '*svabhāva*' (natural habit), it should be made to reveal itself, *sthāyī* and *vyabhicāris bhāvas* included. What is the right way to include them? The right way to include them is by showing the normal actions. '*Lokavārtā*' is the story that is well known. Now, when the actions of the story are represented in their purity, without change and acted upon the stage in that way then that is called *lokadharmī*. Here, no distinction should be made between *nāṭya* which is the *dharma* (of the stage) and *dharmī* (that which follows this *dharma*). The embellished gestures should be avoided here. But even in *lokadharmī*, natural actions like falling, striking and quarrelling etc., should be shown by gestures like '*patākā*'. For feminine roles women should do the acting and for masculine, men only (in *lokadharmī*) should act. Thus, where there is no acting (of the opposite sex) through gestures — acquired by training — to express the opposite sex, but an expression of gestures natural to one's own sex, that mode is called *lokadharmī*.

All this means — if the poet only describes the story barely as it has come down (as myth), and the actor enacts it, without embellishing according to his own imagination, then, that much part of the play, being dependent upon *loka* is *lokadharmī*. (*NŚ Ab. 13:85*)

The thrust of Abhinava's argument is that the unembellished stands for *lokadharmī*. When the story is left unaltered, when acting is done by men for masculine roles and by women for feminine roles, the poetic and histrionic imagination is given no scope, then the production is called *lokadharmī*; and only that much of the play in which this occurs, is so called. Also, acting in *lokadharmī* cannot be done without the semiotic code of *nṛtta hastas* like '*patākā*' etc.

About *nāṭyadharmī* there is little disagreement. The problem here is not of its definition but of its execution. It was easy for modern producers to call *lokadharmī* realism and follow the dictates of the European practice, all the while believing that this had *śāstrīya* sanction. But once it is realized that *nāṭyadharmī* stands for all kinds of very intricate and embellished acting, a modern producer is faced with a nearly insoluble problem. Some of the conventions of the ancient stage like '*janāntika*' are easy to recreate, nor is it difficult to design ornate costume. But the total creation of a performance script in a non-realistic mode demands a knowledge of various body stances (*karaṇas*), ways of walking (*cārīs* and *gatipracāra*), hand gestures (*nṛtta hastas*), speech inflexion (*kāku*), facial expressions (*uttamāṅga abhinaya*), and finally the most difficult to surmount, the problem of recreating the ancient system of music for the sake of dramatic songs (*dhruvās*) and the instruments. The interrelatedness of all these elements in a performance was once a matter of living practice. But now the 'deep structure' of this performance can only be theoretically reconstructed from the *Nāṭyaśāstra*. Some of the surviving traditional modes can provide a few clues. From the *aṣṭapadī* dances we can take *āṅgika abhinaya* consisting of the various *karaṇas, nṛtta hastas, cārīs* and facial expessions. From theatres like *Kuḍīyaṭṭam* and *Yakṣagāna*, some clues may be gathered about use of stage space (*kakṣyā vidhāna*).

Nāṭyadharmī as exaggeration (*atibhāvakam*) of the given normal actions (of *lokadharma*), comes most naturally at the moments of erotic passion. It engenders a peculiar change in the body movements which has been called '*aṅgalīlā*.' The *kaiśikī vṛtti* is an expression of that. Nevertheless, it would be a mistake to presume that *nāṭyadharmī* is made up of *kaiśiki* only. Exaggerated and imaginative movements can also be in the service of sentiments other than *śṛṅgāra*. They can be employed for the heroic, the terrible or the wonderous. Let us once more turn to *Abhinavabhāratī* for an elucidation of *nāṭyadharmī*. Commenting on the verse 72, it is said:

> Now, *nāṭyadharmī* is defined as '*ativākyakriyopetam,*' that is, provided with exaggerated episodes. '*Vākya*' means the story that has come down to us; when the story is improvised for the purpose of greater delight, this effort of changing is called '*kriyā*'. For instance, the poet Rājaśekhara has done the *kriyā* of adding to the episode of Rāma's banishment, a *rākṣasa* who takes the form of Daśaratha. '*Sattva*' means normal behaviour and '*bhāva*' in this verse means normal feelings. These are here, superimposed upon by the actions and feelings as imagined by the poet (in *nāṭyadharmī*). For instance, the normally fickle and shallow character of the *vidūṣaka* has been turned into a serious and thoughtful counsellor, such as Vasantaka, in the play *Tāpasavatsarāja* and the normally *prakṛta* speaking queen is also made to utter Sanskrit. (*NŚ Ab, 13:85*)

The inner wishes of characters are sometimes made to appear on the stage in personified forms (as described in *NŚ 13:75*). Abhinava gives the example, of, "then enters the Curse of Brahmin," from the play *Māyāpuṣpaka* (*yathā māyāpuṣpake tataḥ praviśati brahmaśāpa iti*). This is a curious example of *nāṭyadharmī*.

At another place in the *Abhinavabhāratī*, the great commentator has pointed out that both *lokadharmī* and *nāṭyadharmī* are of two kinds each. This division has not been stated by Bharata Muni. But while analyzing the nature of *abhinaya* as representation of external objects and as expression of inner feelings, he says:

> *Abhinaya* is to be performed in two ways, *lokadharmī* and *nāṭyadharmī*. The first is of two kinds, internal

> and external. There (in *lokadharmī*) the gestures expressive of the mental states may be shown. For example, placing *patāka hasta* on the forehead shows inner pride. Or it can be an *abhinaya* of purely external nature, such as *padmakoṣa hasta* trying to denote an object. So is *nāṭyadharmī* of two kinds. It can be for the purpose of employing the *kaiśikī vṛtti*, which is instrumental in producing out of the world (*alaukika*) beauty in *nāṭya*. This is done by using four kinds of *karaṇas* (dance stances) such as *āveṣṭita* etc. The second kind of use of *nāṭyadharmī* is by taking support of things which are to be found in the world. For example, by imitating the position of a hand engaged in painting. *(NŚ Ab, 9:2)*

By insisting that even *nāṭyadharmī* is of two kinds Abhinava reveals that the truth about the process of dramatic mimesis is not so easy to grasp. He has made a fine point about the transition from reality to art. Of the two kinds of *nāṭyadharmī*, one he shows, is purely an artifact, *alaukika*, out of the world, not based upon an attempt to indicate anything of the world. It is *aṅgalīlā* or fantasy purely self-made. The other kind of *nāṭyadharmī* is that which draws upon worldly things and achieves ornate mimesis. The latter kind depends for its sustenance ('*upajīvatī*') on *lokadharma*. The process here is the same as we had noticed earlier. *Nāṭyadharmī* transforms the *dharma* of the world (*loka*) into the illusion of *nāṭya*. To summarise, the way of the world is *lokadharma*; this is the unembellished state of normal behaviour, normal action and the prevalent story. It makes up the material that theatre draws upon. When it is presented on the stage as it is, the mode is called *lokadharmī*. But, the production is neither realistic nor 'folk.' It is achieved through the channels of *nāṭya* codes. As for *nāṭyadharmī*, it is the furthest take-off into imagination and adornment, through intricate gestures to create for *nāṭya* a world of its own.

Through the methods of *lokādharmī* and *nāṭyadharmī*, a complex web of theatrical transformation was woven on the Indian stage. These two terms, though of Indian origin, can be used to define the nature of transformation on any stage. For instance, on the Greek stage, choral characters such as the supplicant women or the crowd of elders could be called *lokadharmī*. So are the majority of dramatis personae, except for the gods and satyrs, and so are the bulk of plots that are enacted. But the costume of all actors, particularly their mask, their dance movements, parakatalogic and choral dialogue is purely *nāṭyadharmī*, because such things do not exist beyond theatre. A total performance script is always a combination of the two *dharmīs*. Transformation of the objective world into the stage world, is in parts simple, and in parts very ornate. Some cultures will go for ornate transformation and some will be content with simpler change. Within one culture some dramatic genres are more ornate than others. Bharata Muni had explicitly prescribed that *nāṭaka* and *prakaraṇa* will be totally *nāṭyadharmī* while *bhāṇa, prahasana* and *utsṛṣṭikāṅka* will have more of a *lokadharmī* content. As compared to modern European theatre all ancient performances were highly ornate.

The high point of ornateness, or the transformation of reality into *nāṭyadharmī* did not mean that theatrical representation on ancient stage had lost all connection with earthly reality. On the Indian stage especially, details of personal behaviour, mannerisms, ways of dressing, and speech were brought out with meticulous care. The variety of life was not reduced by transformation into a few symbolic characters in ritual costume as it happened in the case of Noh. Even while stylizing life's variety into stage semiotics, the Indian theatre covered a wider section of life than the Greek theatre. On the Indian stage besides a wider range of characters, Nature and its seasons provided a constant backdrop to all human feelings. Its presence was all the time reinforced by profuse descriptions of seasons, birds and animals to which the characters related their emotions. The *druvā* songs fulfilled the same purpose. This kind of particularity, even of Nature, was avoided by the Greeks. They preferred to keep Nature, as a sacred grove or a hill, symbolic of the cosmic forces of the gods. This maintained a higher degree of ornateness in their transformation.

Transformation for Emotional Arousal

As I have said earlier, transformation on the classical Greek and Indian stage was accompanied by intense emotional arousal because the response of the spectators in this theatre was immediate. In tradition bound societies where theatre takes up so many acts and enactments from rituals, where ***muthoi*** and the characters are well known, where dance and music enhance the intensity of feeling, there is a natural nearness or identity of the code of the sender with that of the receiver. It takes little time to follow what is being said as the audience are trained to feel the depth of what is being said and suggested. Moreover, the ancient audience went to theatre with a desire to be moved by emotion and to revel in it. They were not content to sit back, analyse, speculate or intellectually assess acting, dramatic themes and social problems. They wished to go through an experience which they wanted to be total and moving, so that when they returned from the playhouse they felt different. They did not want to have a different perspective on the problems of the year, but to have an experience they could recall for a year until the next Dionysia or the next *vasantotsava*. Emotionally arousing the audience was, therefore, a primary objective of ancient theatre which unlike the modern European theatre depended most for effectiveness on emotional communication. This emotional arousal was not only for the audience, it was to be felt as much by the actors to be to put across to the spectators.

It would be useful to give an account of the emotional states and attitudes that predominated Greek and Indian drama and which in themselves make up the basis for aesthetic enjoyment.

Emotional Arousal in Greek Theory

In 'the *Poetics*, Aristotle does not explicitly state that the purpose of the dramatist's art should be to create emotional exitement. He seems to take that for granted. But he does say this much; the pleasure proper to tragedy "comes from pity and fear through imitation" (*Poetics XIV:3*). The accounts of ancient authors are sufficient to indicate that the production of Greek plays, particularly tragedy, was geared towards strong emotional arousal. "Even the best of us when we listen to a passage from Homer or from a tragedy... we delight in surrendering ourselves" (*Republic 605c-d*). Herodotus has recorded that when "Phyrnichos in 494 BC produced his tragedy on the recent capture of Miletos by the Persians the Athenian audience 'fell to weeping' so distressingly that the magistrates fined the dramatist heavily and banned further performances of the play" (Stanford 5). The actors prided themelves if they were able to fill the seats with weeping multitudes. In what sounds like a gross exaggeration today but may very well have been true, "in the beginning of his *Eumenides* the spectators were so shocked by the frightful appearance of the Furies that children fainted and women had miscarriages" (Stanford 6). The account of a rhapsode reciting poetry, as given by Plato (*Ion 535C*) shows that his hair stood on end. The reciter while delivering epic poetry was filled with ***enthousia*** and the audience felt it immeidately. Dionysios of Halicarnassos mentions this kind of audience response and admits that even reading to himself the speech of Demosthenes resulted in the same effect:

> But whenever I take up any of the speeches of Demosthenes I get possessed with a kind of ecstasy (enthousia) and I am led this way and that, changing one emotion for another, doubt, agony, fear, scorn, hate, pity, benevolence, anger, spite, taking in turn all the emotions that have the natural power to master the human mind. And it seems to me that there is no difference between me in this condition and the people who are being initiated into the rites of the Great Mother and the Corybantes and other rites of that kind. (*Demosthenes* 22 qtd. Stanford 9)

It may be presumed that the actors who cultivated their art much in the same manner as the rhapsode reciters would have commanded the same response in spectators. There was also some writing on the art of emotional arousal, which is borne by the fact that the author of the treatise commonly known as *On the Sublime* wrote a monograph on pathos, which is lost. The term used by him and by other writers for the power of arousing and controlling emotions was "***psuchagogia,***" which literally means, 'leading the psuche' (Stanford 5). The *Poetics* while taking ***psuchagogia*** for granted does not give any system for its employment in drama. However, Aristotle has quite a few things to say on emotional manipulation in his *Rhetoric* besides the observation in *On the Psuche* (403a 4ff) that " The emotions (pathe) all involve physical symptoms and that some observable bodily effect result from all of them" (Stanford 22). In the first eleven chapters of the second book of *Rhetoric* it is shown that an orator can arouse anger, affection, friendliness, enmity, hatred, fear, shame, pity, indignation and many other emotions.

The supreme emotion on which tragedy depends most is pity (***eleos*** or ***oiktos***). The English word pity, Stanford thinks, is not an appropriate translation of ***eleos*** as the one who pities tends to be regarded as superior to the person who is pitied. "Compassionate grief," he suggests, is a better rendering of the meaning of the term as in this there is sympathy for the sorrow that is witnessed. The Sanskrit word '*karuṇā*' carries the same import. In *Rhetoric,* ***eleos*** is defined as "a kind of pain (***lupe***) felt at the sight of a painful or destructive event happening to someone who does not deserve it — an evil and fearful event close at hand which one might expect to happen to oneself or to a relative or friend, ***philos***" (Stanford 24). Situations in life that can arouse ***eleos*** are all too well-known and the tragic authors knew them well too. However, situations like loss of a child, a father's murder, abduction of a wife, horror at unjust sexual compulsions and innumerable others that arouse ***eleos*** can become tragic or provide 'pleasure proper to tragedy' only if ***eleos*** is placed with the framework of cosmic helplessness. The might or a force greater than man should be obvious for eliciting compasison. Close to ***eleos*** was another feeling which was often employed particularly in tragedy. This was ***philanthropia,*** a compassionate reaching out to human values. Prometheus, in the play by Aeschylus, is an excellent example of one who stands for ***philanthropia*** and thus commands our admiration.

The other major tragic emotion is fear (***phobos***) which seems to imply an instinct to run away. Stanford suggests that terror is a better translation of ***phobos*** as the intensity of the emotion is often very great. Anxiety and apprehension are also named as ***merima, tarbos*** and ***prontis*** (28). "The symptoms of fear as described by rhetoricians and dramatists are — in ascending order of intensity — paleness, chilliness, fast pulse, shivering, shuddering, shrieking, hair standing on end, prostration" (Stanford 28). When fright was sudden or so acute that it caused stupefaction, it was called as ***ekplexis*** The Sanskrit word '*stambha,*' a *sāttvika bhāva,* is an exact equivalent of it in Bharata Muni's theory. When a deed is done in ignorance and later it is discovered that great harm has been caused to a dear one, the shock caused is ***ekplexis.*** Not only may fear cause this state but intense ***eros*** may also bring about ***ekplexis*** as was the case with Phaidra.

In the scheme of Aristotle in *Rhetoric,* anger (***menis*** or ***cholos***) is given the greatest prominence. For orators it is often expedient to provoke the crowds, but even in drama it is the most natural emotion for agonal plots. After all, the prime Greek poem is about the wrath of Achilles. A milder form of ***cholos*** is ***orge,*** the desire for revenge when harm has been done to a ***philos.*** This feeling impels one to defend one's honour, makes the blood boil, and burn the heart with rage. Closely allied with anger, is hatred. Whereas anger cannot last for long and is cured by time, hatred can be everlasting and incurable. Anger if placated may turn into pity specially on seeing how a terrible act in anger has reduced the sufferer to a pitiful condition. But hatred (***misos***) may often result in self-annihilation, as was the case of Clytemnestra, Cassandra and Hekabe. One form of hatred is revulsion or loathing (***stugos***), shown on the stage by spitting and similar actions. When there was justified anger (what we call moral indignation) it was known by the name of ***nemesis***. In *Rhetoric* it is called ***phthonos*** (Stanford 34). "***Nemesis***, connected with a verb meaning 'to apportion' was embodied at the highest religious level in the dread goddess of the temple at Rhamnous in Attica, who struck down those who exceeded the limits of appropriate behaviour, as in *Philoctates*, line 518" (Stanford 34).

Among other important emotions that are discussed in the *Rhetoric* are ***aischune*** and ***aidos***. The first is shame felt before or after a dishonourable deed, such as throwing one's shield in battle or illicit intercourse. ***Aidos*** is the reverence that the virtuous feel for good principles and which is intensified by the thought of not having lived up to high standards. ***Aidos*** led to Phaida's suicide and to Jocasta's, and prevented Hippolytus from breaking his oath.

Next to anger, if not as strong, is the sexual emotion ***eros***. As classical Greek comedy was not emotionally refined but instead was expressly vulgar, there was little room in it for erotic depth and sublety. But in tragedy there was ample room for psychological probing. However, the nature of ***eros*** in tragedy is that of a passion which leads astray, a kind of madness of mind and body, a compulsion that overrides social constraints, in brief, something which is lamentable rather than commendable. It is often depicted as a sickness that strikes women more strongly than men or at least makes them the agency of destruction.

Of the less dominant emotions found in Greek theatre there are filial affection (***storge***), gratitude (***charis***) and general affection or friendship (***philia***). So is love of the native city or land (***philopatria***). For all these emotions mentioned above, Stanford makes two categories; visceral and sentimental:

> Of all the emotions....the strongest and most visceral are terror, anger, passionate desire, hate and grief. Terror and grief are mainly passive and self-centred, the others are dynamic and extrovert. Grief is the least dynamic and most introverted of all, tending, as it does, to inhibit external action. On the other

hand its symptoms and gestures in tragedy can be as violent as any. Some other feelings mentioned tend to become sentiments or mental conditions rather than emotions when they occur in their quieter forms — ***philanthropia, storge, philia, epichairekakia, pothos, tarache*** and ***zelos.*** (45)

This kind of division into visceral and sentimental, or any other based on relationships between emotions, or one set of emotions to another, does not exist in Aristotle. His ***psuchagogia*** is descriptive not analytical.

Indian System of Emotional Arousal

Bharata Muni is the system-maker, if not the originator of a very complex method of employing emotions in drama. He also constructed a theory about the nature of emotions and their mutual relationship, which has been accepted in India, not only by theatre people but by makers of all arts. His word for emotion, '*bhāva*' in Sanskrit usage means; a state of being, becoming, a way of feeling or thinking, sentiment, purport or intention. Though Bharata Muni has used '*bhāva*' primarily to denote emotion, other connotations are not ruled out. There can be many kinds of thoughts or intentions in a given state of being but for the purpose of *nāṭya* (and art in general), the state is denoted by feelings. While defining *bhāvas*, the Muni says:

> How is it that they are called *bhāvas*? Is it because they are (*bhavanti*) existent that they are called so, or because they expand and communicate (*bhāvayanti*) that they are called *bhāvas*? It is said: because with the agencies of verbal, gestural and subtle actions, they communicate (*bhāvayanti*) the meaning of *kāvya* (drama), they are called *bhāvas*...And *bhāva*, desire (*vāsanā*) and completed action (*kṛtam*), all mean the same thing. In common usage, the verb from *bhāva, bhāvitam* is used to indicate impregnation. As in the sentence, "Indeed, this perfume, this flavour has impregnated everything here." (*NŚ 7:1*)

In this system, emotions are looked upon as forces that bring out the total inner intention or the communicable content. The term *bhāva* is supposed to stand for all that. The later-day European cleavage between thought and feeling, emotion and intellect is nowhere to be seen here. "The meaning (intellectual and emotional) affects the body like fire pervades dry wood; it can vibrate from one heart to another (or in many hearts simultaneously) and this becoming (*bhāva*) of meaning leads to the birth of *rasa*" (*NŚ* 7:7).This affirms that the intensity of inner state was considered necessary in Bharata Muni's theory of communication.

Thoughts, or intellectual concepts, may vary or differ with time, but emotional states are an unchanging part of human nature. *Bhāvas*, though freshly felt in new situations and ideas, remain the same in terms of emotional content. They can, thus, be classified as permanent categories. Bharata Muni divides them into three groups: *sthāyī* (dominant), *vyābhicāri* (transient) and *sāttvika* (psychosomatic). Though it is not so stated, it is implied that certain emotions by their very nature are more deeply seated in the human heart. Therefore, they can be expanded upon for a longer time in dramatic action. They can also be felt just by themselves; and one or another of them is always present in the human psyche. Such states are called *sthāyī* by the Muni, and they are eight in number: *rati* or intense pleasure (sexual or otherwise), *hāsa* or humour, *śoka* or grief, *krodha* or anger, *utsāha* or confidence, *bhaya* or fear, *jugupsā* or revulsion, and finally *vismaya* or wonder. The prominence of these among other feelings is indicated by Bharata Muni through similies. The *sthāyīs,* he says, are kings among men, or teachers among students. The transient or *vyabhicārī* emotional states are thirty six: *nirveda* (dejection), *glāni* (guilt), *śaṅkā* (doubt), *asūyā* (envy), *mada* (intoxication), *śrama* (fatigue), *ālasya* (indolence), *dainya* (obsequity),' *cintā* (worry), *moha* (fondness) and so on. One can readily grant that the sentiments in the later category are neither as strong nor as visceral as anger, fear, sexuality and others of the *sthāyī* variety. It is also axiomatic that they cannot be sustained in isolation from the *sthāyīs*. Envy, indeed, overpowered Othello, yet, it was caused by anger and frustrated sex. According to the Indian system, the *sthāyī* in *Othello* are *krodha* and *rati* whereas *asūyā*, *moha* and *cintā* are the *vyabhicārīs*. The third category of *satvika bhāvas* (eight in all) has been discussed in the context of the medium of imitation. Strictly speaking, the *sāttvika bhāvas* are manifestations in the body (***soma***) of the conditions of the mind (***psuche***) excited by *sthāyī bhāvas*. They are overpowering, and are therefore, called *sāttvika* or psychomatic.

Vibhāvas and Anubhāvas

While discussing the medium of imitation, we analysed the four channels of communication that carry the meaning of a performance to the spectators. The actors, the dramatic situations, the environmental and seasonal background in which these channels are employed, are called *vibhāvas*. "Now what is this *vibhāva*? It is said that a *vibhāva* is for making things known. *Vibhāva, karaṇa* (instrument, *nimitta* (medium) and *hetu* (cause) are all synonyms." "That which makes known many kinds of meaning (*bhāvas* or *arthas*) with the help of verbal and bodily *abhinaya* is called a *vibhāva*" (*NŚ 7:4*). It may be asked, why is a category like *vibhava* necessary when there is already the categorization of different channels of *abhinaya*? The answer is simple. The single term *vibhāva* is able to denote all the instruments of signification and this comes in very handy in any analysis of the phenomenon of theatrical communication. The history of theatrical and literary criticism in India is ample proof of the utility of the term *vibhāva*. Though the *NŚ* does not make the distinction, later theorists further sub-divided *vibhāvas* into two, *ālambana* (supportive) and *uddīpana*. The actor was called *ālambana* (supportive) and the seasonal descriptions (of rain or spring) were called *uddīpana* (excitive). If *vibhāvas* are the carriers (*āśrayāḥ*) of the channels of communication, the channels themselves are called *anubhāvas*. "The verbal and body *abhinayas* including the gestures of limbs, torso, head, etc., by which the meaning (of drama) is experienced (*anubhāvyate*), is called *anubhāva* (*NŚ 7:5*). There has always been a debate in Sanskrit literary theory about who experiences meaning, is it the spectator, the actor or both? I have quoted the *NŚ* earlier to show that the actor must become the character giving up his own self like a soul reborn. He is, therefore, supposed to experience the meaning himself, the effect of the emotion to be enacted should be complete on him and it should show on his body and voice. This effect on the body is 'experience' or *anubhāva*. The spectator also experiences the meaning but his response is different as he is not a performer. *Anubhāvas* are a direct result, as well the proof, of strong emotional arousal. If the sentiments felt were cerebral there would have been no theory of *anubhāvas* nor any stress on *sāttvika abhinaya.*

Katharsis and Hedone

As a result of an exclusive reading of Aristotle's famous definition of tragedy (*Poetics VI:2*), ***katharsis*** has been regarded as the sole aim of tragedy. But it is obvious, that for Aristotle, whatever may have been the function of tragedy, and however essential ***katharsis*** may have been to it, ***katharsis*** alone was not the purpose of tragedy. Besides mentioning ***katharsis***, Aristotle has mentioned at three places in the *Poetics*, a 'pleasure which is proper only to tragedy' and which presumably is not to be found in comedy or any other literary form. Are "proper pleasure" (***oikeia hedone***) and ***katharsis*** mutually exclusive, synonymous or intertwined? There are three places in the *Poetics* where pleasure is talked about. In the first place, Aristotle says that tragedy cannot afford every kind of pleasure but only that which is proper to it, and this comes about from pity and fear through imitation (14:3). In the second place, pleasure is said to be derived from completeness and wholeness of action in a plot (23:1). In the third instance, pleasure is said to be a result of music and spectacular effects (26:4). As the famous definition has it:

Tragedy, then, is an imitation of an action that is

> serious, complete, and of a certain magnitude: in language embellished with each kind of artistic ornament, the several kinds being found in separate parts of the play in the form of action, not of narrative: through pity and fear effecting the purgation (***katharsis***) of these emotions. (Butcher 23)

From this it is clear that ***hedone*** and ***katharsis*** are not mutually exclusive as both are caused by an imitation of pity and fear. Music causes pleasure and so does ***katharsis***, as it is said in the *Politics*. Pleasure is also caused by completeness of action which in itself is meant to arouse pity and fear. Thus, even though, ***hedone*** and ***katharsis*** are seen to be intertwined they should be recognized as distinct from each other. In no case, should ***katharsis*** alone be regarded as the end of tragedy, as is often done by literary critics. About the nature of ***hedone***, Aristotle has taken the position that every activity has its own proper pleasure. Thus, comic, tragic, satyric, epic and nomoic pleasures will all be different. Aristotle does not propose that underlying all these delights there may be a common denominator, a literary or a poetic ***hedone***. There has been a sustained attempt to postulate that ***katharsis*** could be that common and basic aesthetic experience. But the very meaning of ***katharsis*** has been a source of conflicting interpretations.

In the nineteenth century one major way of looking at ***katharsis*** was to take it as a medical term transferred to poetic criticism. "***Kenosis*** in the Hippocratic writings denotes the entire removal of healthy but surplus humours: ***katharsis*** is the removal of ***ta lupounta*** and the like — of qualitatively alien matter" (Butcher 253). This doctrine of imbalance of vital forces (later on called humours), as the primary cause of disease, is of purely Indian origin. As demonstrated by Filliozat, the science was well formulated in India as early as the *Atharvaveda*. It was later recodified in the *Āyurveda* of Caraka and travelled to Greece through the Persians. An imbalance in the three (*vāta*, *pitta* and *kapha*) elements (*dhātus*) brought all and every disease. The cure lay in subduing the overswollen element. Both the systems strove to bring about a balance (***summetria*** or *samatava*) between the elements.

Besides this well stated medicinal doctrine, there was also the practice of curing madness through musical ***katharsis***. The patients were made to listen to certain melodies which made them "fall back into their normal state, as if they had undergone a medical or purgative (kathartic) treatment" (*Politics* V.viii.7. 1342 a 15 qtd. in Butcher 249). It is further added that not only is ***katharsis*** achieved musically but that "those who are liable to pity and fear, and in general, persons of emotional temperament pass through a like experience;...they all undergo a ***katharsis*** of some kind and feel a pleasurable relief" (Butcher 251). The nature of ***katharsis*** described in the *Politics* should be true for the *Poetics*, as Aristotle himself has stated that his observations are of a general nature in the former treatise but shall be more detailed in a later work. Therefore, those who presumed that tragic ***katharsis*** like musical ***katharsis*** restores normally healthy emotional state, were not so wrong.

But this rather clinical definition of ***katharsis*** does not satisfy literary theorists. As early as Butcher it was felt there was more to it. "But the word, as taken up by Aristotle into his terminology of art, has probably a further meaning. It expresses not only a fact of psychology or of pathology, but a principle of art" (253). The tragic pity and fear he postulated..."in real life contain a morbid and disturbing element.,.As the tragic action progresses, the lower forms of emotion are found to have been transmuted into more refined forms" (254). He further postulated that this purification is also a change of the personal emotion to the universal. Purged of the "petty interest of the self" (261) emotion now becomes a representation of the universal, so that the "net result is a noble emotional satisfaction" (267). It is not difficult to discern that ***katharsis*** is equated with aesthetic pleasure in which noble emotional satisfaction is an essential feature. "But whatever may have been the indirect effect of the repeated operation of ***katharsis***, we may confidently say that Aristotle in his definition of tragedy is thinking, not only of any remote result, but of the immediate end of the art, of the aesthetic function it fulfils"

(Butcher 269). In my opinion, to raise the balancing function of ***katharsis*** to the level of universalisation is to stretch the concept too far. Certainly, the restorative function of ***katharsis*** may bring a relief such as a sick person feels upon recovery. But it is a presumption on the part of Butcher that universalization takes place because the element purged from the dramatic emotion is that of personal "petty interest of the self" (261). The Aristotelian ***katharsis***, or for that matter the whole tradition of ***katharsis***, by music or Dionysian orgies, has personal cure or satisfaction as its end. Inner restoration, but not the enjoyment of a new aesthetic element, can at best be the purpose of ***katharsis***. The factors of enjoyment, of ***oikeia hedone***, are different as stated earlier.

Other than regarding it as purgational, there has been another major way of interpreting ***katharsis***. The dual concept of purity and impurity which pervaded the physical, moral, religious and spiritual life of the Greeks was the most deep-seated factor governing their daily activities. The duality of ***miasma*** and ***katharsis*** was part of the Indo-European belief system. In India, it was called "*śaucāśaucavicāra*" and was well defined in the codes of conduct written by Manu and Yājñavalkya etc. We find that in Greek plays, all tragic action is dependent on acts of transgression such as the murder of a kin, sexual defilement, affronts to deities, and so on. These acts brought ***miasma*** (pollution) upon the protagonist and the people around him. In Greek religion there were prescriptions for expiation of such crimes, just as in the Indian *Smṛti* codes *prāyaścits* were given for purging of pollution. In tragedies, the very ritual of expiation was often enacted, as in the *Oresteia*. In most plays, the protagonist was expelled from the community by death or banishment; there has expulsion (***kenosis***) of the sinner and purification (***katharsis***) of a given location, city, grove or household. Whereas in some plays, as in the *Oresteia*, this cycle was shown in its completeness, in other plays it was shown partially. In some other plays as in *Hekabe* or *Women of Troy*, there is only ***miasma*** and no ***katharsis***. Looked at in this way, tragedy was a depiction of the cycle of ***miasma*** and ***katharsis***.

To my mind, the annual enactment of tragedy was to reaffirm the ***miasma-katharsis*** diad, a major cultural value of ancient Greek society. In all ancient societies the purpose of retelling the ***muthoi***, particularly on festive occasions, was many-fold; it was to preserve and transmit the stories, to re-state the beliefs they enshrined, and to relive the behaviour patterns sanctified by tradition. The retelling always had a ritual significance even if it took the form of dramatic enactment for the purpose of entertainment. As I have explained earlier, entertainment and ritual were intertwined in hieropraxis. In this manner, tragedy was a reliving of the pollution-purity cycle by both the actors and the spectators. The community, the protagonist, his acts, and the aroused emotions of the audience, all underwent a ***katharsis***.

In his analysis of ***katharsis,*** Gerald Else has rightly grasped the spiritual significance that ***katharsis*** had for the Greeks, but he restricts the scope of purgation to the acts of the protagonist. For Else, remorse makes the hero eligible to spectators' pity, and this pity along with the hero's remorse proves that the act of transgression was actually a pure (***katharos***) act. Thus ***katharsis*** is the process of proving purity. As Else puts it:

> The filthiness inheres in a conscious intention to kill a person who is close kin. An unconscious intention to do so, i.e., in intention to do so without being aware of the kinship — as Oedipus did not know that he killed his father — would therefore be "pure;" ***katharos***. But purity must be proved to our satisfaction. Catharsis would then be the process of proving that the act was pure in that sense. How is such a thing proved? According to *Nicomachean Ethics* 3,2, 1110b19 and 1111a20, by the remorse of the dear, which shows that if he had known the facts he would not have done the deed. In *Oedipus*, the thing which establishes this to our satisfaction is Oedipus' self blinding. It, then, effects a "purification" of the tragic deed and so makes Oedipus

eligible to our pity. (Else 98)

From this interpretation it seems that Else does not believe that ***katharsis*** benefits the audience and their emotions in anyway. In his reading of the famous passage in the *Poetics*, ***katharsis*** is purification of the tragic deed and not of the emotions of the spectators. This goes against all other instances of ***katharsis*** as mentioned by Plato and Aristotle. The examples they have given indicate a change in the mental state of the spectators or music listeners. Besides, it is nowhere indicated by Aristotle that pity in tragedy was aroused for the purpose of regenerating and purifying the sin and the sinner. He is more concerned with showing how we can feel pity for the protagonist. This feeling in us is more capable of providing ***katharsis*** to us rather than just providing that the act of the hero was ***katharos***.

If the concept of ***katharsis*** is to have any general utility, it must be persumed that the cycle of ***miasma*** and ***katharsis*** effects an emotional ***katharsis*** in the audience as well. A harmonious view of ***katharsis*** which combines its spiritual, clinical and aesthetic effects is more in keeping with the unified approach of the ancients.

The Rasa Concept

There is no word in the history of Indian aesthetics which has acquired a greater significance than *rasa*. To go into the entire idealization or denigration of *rasa*, as done over many centuries, would need a separate volume. Here, I merely wish to recapitulate the concept as stated by Bharata Muni along with the four classical interpretations and conclude with some comments on ***katharsis*** and *rasa* from the standpoint of comparison.

From Vedic to classical Sanskrit usage, *rasa* has had two primary meanings. Literally it means 'juice,' or 'fluid'. The secondary meaning is an 'extract'. In Ayurvedic terminology, the word *rasa* was used to denote the vital juice that the digestive system extracts from food and which is later converted into blood, flesh, bones, marrow, fat and sperm

(*Suśruta Saṃhitā. XIV*) The sense in which Bharata Muni uses the word is again that of extract. "*Rasa*, what does this word mean?" Or translated otherwise: "*Rasa*, what is this substance so called?" After raising the question, Bharata Muni gives the answer. "It is so called because it is worthy of being tasted" (*rasa ko padārthaḥ, ucyate āsvādyatvāt NŚ 6:31*). In the context of drama, *rasa* is an extract. It is one element out of the eleven elements that *nāṭya* consists of. But it is extracted from ten other elements (*bhāva, abhinaya, dharmīs, vṛtti, pravṛttis, siddhis, svara, ātodya, gāna* and *raṅga*) of *nāṭya*. It is perhaps called *rasa* or extract because it cannot exist by itself, but, as it were, only in other elements. The ten other elements are condensed into *bhāva, vibhāva* and *anubhāva*; and again the famous *rasa sūtra*, it seems, implies that *rasa* is extracted from these. The term used in the *rasa sūtra* is '*niṣpatti*,' which implies falling down. This again suggests the dripping of an extract. The main *sūtra* and the illustrative (*dṛṣṭānta*) *sūtra* may be translated as follows:

(1) By a union of *vibhāva, anubhāva* and *vyabhicārī* there is emergence of *rasa*.

(2) Is there any example? It is thus. Just as in (eating) a mixture of various foods, spices and herbs, there is the emergence of *rasa*, similarly, in (watching) a union of various *bhāvas*, there is emergence of *rasa*. Just as by mixing sugar and such edibles with foods, spices and herbs, the six *rasas* (sweet, sour, bitter, pungent, salt and astringent) are tasted, similarly by, combining with different *bhāvas*, the *sthāyī bhāvas* are transformed into the state of *rasa*. What thing is this *rasa*? That which is capable of being tasted is *rasa*. How is *rasa* tasted? When appreciative gourmets (*sumanasaḥ puruṣāḥ*) eat foods laced with seasonings and taste *rasa* (the six *rasas*, sweet, bitter, etc.) they experience joy (*harṣa*); in the same way appreciative spectators taste *sthāyī bhāvas* laced with verbal, gestural and *sāttvika abhinayas* of various *bhāvas* and thus experience joy (*harṣa*). (*NŚ 6:31*)

The example of eating and tasting may seem rather crude to those who regard aesthetic pleasure as something too sublime for such gross similes. But Bharata Muni could have hardly chosen a different example. By his time, *rasa* was inextricably connected with eating and mastication. Comparison of *sthāyī bhāvas, anubhāvas* and *bhāvas* (*sañcārī* or *vyabhicārī* with foods, spices and herbs was natural and so was the comparison of the pleasure of eating with the pleasure of watching a play. In *sūtra* (1), the emergence of *rasa* is attributed to a union of the three elements, namely *vibhāva, anubhāva* and *vyabhicārī bhāvas* only. Here, *sthāyī bhāva* is not mentioned as a constituent element. In *sūtra* (2), *vibhāvas* are left out of the simile. Does this mean that according to the *sūtra* (2), *vibhāvas* are not necessary in the emergence of *rasa*? It is not so. The two *sūtras* are not mutually contradictory, nor do they imply that *rasa* emerges from a union of some elements at one time and by a union of some other elements at another time. The *vibhāvas* and *anubhāvas*, acting and gestures, are inspired not only by *vyabhicārī bhāvas*. They are inspired by *sthāyī bhāvas* much more. Therefore, it can be said that the first *sūtra* covers in its ambit the *sthāyī* as well. The second *sūtra* explicitly states that *sthāyī bhāvas* are transformed into *rasa* when they are combined with various *bhāvas* which are expressed through the *abhinaya* of verbal, gestural and *sāttvika* kinds (*nānābhāvābhinayavyañjitān vāgaṅgasattvopetān sthāyībhāvānāsvādayanti sumanasaḥ prekṣakāḥ...*). *Abhinaya,* in its totality is constituted by *vibhāvas*. Therefore, it can be presumed that the second *sūtra* covers *vibhāvas* in its ambit. The mixture or union that leads to the emergence of *rasa* consists of four things; *vibhāvas, anubhāvas, vyabhicārīs* and *sthāyī bhāvas*. Reducing the terminology to a plainer language, it can be said, that dominant emotions like sexual passion, attachment, anger, fear and others are transformed into *rasa,* or are tasted as *rasa*, when they are mixed with transitory emotions like dejection, guilt, doubt, intoxication and so forth. This occurs when they are communicated through verbal and physical acting. On these *sūtras* of Bharata Muni, there must have been innumerable commentaries over the ages. But only those written in the last millennium have survived. They all attempt to make a close analysis of what exactly is the cause of *rasa* emergence (*niṣpatti*). There are some basic questions that have occupied the analysts. Are the constitutent agents *vibhāvas*, *anubhāvas vyabhicārīs* and *sthāyīs*, all capable of transforming into *rasa* or are they catalysts in the presence of which, something new takes its birth? Who experiences *rasa*? The poet, the actor, the spectator, or all of them together? Is the experience of all these people the same or does each have his own distinctive experience? How long does *rasa* last? Does it change the inner psyche of the spectator? And so on. Right from *Abhinavabhāratī*, the earliest of the extant commentaries on the *rasa sūtras*, to the writings of modern experts (*nāṭyaśāstrīs*), there have been many answers to these questions. It would require a lot of space to deal with the various views expressed. For the sake of brevity, I shall take up only the four traditional interpretations given by Lollaṭa, Śaṅkuka, Bhaṭṭanāyaka and Abhinavagupta. The views of these four are so seminal that they often anticipate the positions that can be usually taken in analyzing the *sūtras*. In stating these four views, I have depended upon the *Abhinavabhāratī* only and not upon other later works which also have quoted these views. It is best to depend upon the oldest source because it is doubtful if the original writings of Lollaṭa, Śaṅkuka and Bhaṭṭanāyaka were available to later commentators like Mammaṭa and Viśvanātha.

Lollaṭa's Analysis

It is best to put Lollaṭa's views in his own words:

> When there is union (*saṃyoga*) of *vibhāvas* and others with *sthāyī*, then there is emergence of *rasa*. Here *vibhāva* is the cause of the birth of a mental state which is full of *sthāyī bhāvas*. Here (in this *sūtra*), it is indicated that *anubhāvas* are not the cause of *rasa* (that is, *anubhāvas* do not get converted into *rasa*). They do not deserve to be counted among the causes, of *rasa* emergence. Only *bhāvas* deserve that. Because

> of the very nature of mind (*cittavṛtyātmakatvāt*) *anubhāvas* and *vyabhicārīs* are not such that they can be of identical make up (*sahabhāvinaḥ*); however, the nature of *sthāyī bhāvas*, as deep-rooted desires (*vāsanātmakatā*), is clarified here. In the illustrative *sūtra* as well, out of the different constituent foods and spices, some are said to be like deep seated desires (*sthāyīs*) and others like superficial desires (*vyabhicārīs*). The *sthāyī*, when it combines with (*upacita*) *vibhāvas* and *anubhāvas* becomes *rasa*. When this does not happen, it remains *sthāyī*. By the power of concentration (*anusandhān balāt*) this *rasa* can occur in the character (*anukārya* like Rāma) and in the actor (*anukartā* or *naṭa*). (*NŚ*

Lollaṭa has very much stuck to the enunciation by Bharata Muni that *sthāyī bhāvas* become *rasa* when they are combined with *vyabhicāris*. But he makes an observation of his own that *sthāyī bhāvas* are based upon deep rooted desire or instincts that are ever present in the human heart as *vāsanā*. Besides deep rooted emotions, there are modes and attitudes which manifest as superficial emotions and they are the basis for *vyabhicārī bhāvas*. Lollaṭa, thus, takes a step forward in analysing the psychological basis of *sthāyī* and *vyabhicārī bhāvas*. He shifts the attention from the stage to the mind of the spectator. In this way, he can be said to have initiated the enquiry as to who really experiences *rasa*. For him, there is experience of *rasa* by the actor just as there is *rasa* in a character as well. This also starts one thinking about the method of communication needed for *rasa*. All later thinkers who have pursued this enquiry are indebted to Lollaṭa.

Śaṅkuka's Analysis

Again, it is best to quote the commentator himself:

> By the instrument of *vibhāvas* and the actual actions of *anubhāvas*, as well as by the complimentary *vyabhicārīs*, by the artificial efforts made by the actor,

> such efforts as do not seem to be artificial, the *sthāyī bhāva* is inferred (*pratīyamānaḥ*) to be located in the actor by the force of signs *(liṅga balataḥ)* (signs, such as gestures of all kinds); this *sthāyī bhāva* is an imitative rendering (*anukaraṇarūpa*) of the *sthāyī bhāva* present in the hearts of main characters like Rāma and others. By mimetic rendering (*anukaraṇa*), this (*sthāyī bhāva*) is known by the different name, *rasa*. (*NŚ Ab. 6:31*)

Śaṅkuka adds that all acting is done on the basis of a written play or *kāvya*. However, the *sthāyī bhāvas* are not known (understood and felt) merely by reading the words (*sthāyī tu kāvyabalāt api na anusandheyaḥ*). On reading, words yield only their literal meaning. That meaning is fully realized only when communicated through acting (*vibhāvas*). What is more, even through acting or *anukaraṇa* the actual *sthāyī bhāvas* of the characters can never be known. On seeing the acting, the spectator can only infer what the actual *sthāyī bhāvas* of a person may have been. This knowing or inferring the actual *sthāyī bhāva* upon seeing the mimetic action is called, *pratīti* by Śaṅkuka, and this *pratīti* is *rasa*. For Śankuka, the *sthāyī bhāva* does not become *rasa*, but the ***mimesis*** or *anukaraṇa* of *sthāyī bhāva* manifesting as *pratīti* is *rasa*. For this reason, says Śaṅkuka, Bharata Muni has not mentioned *sthāyī bhāva* as one of the constituents that combine to cause emergence of *rasa* in the first *rasa sūtra*. This *pratītī*, adds Śaṅkuka, is a rare phenomenon. It is different from the appearances about which we say "this is real (*samayaka pratītī*), this is false (*mithyā pratīti*), this is real but perhaps false too (*saṃśaya pratīti*), and this is not actually it but is like it (*sādṛśya pratīti*). The appearance of a person (dramatic character) that the actor projects is different (*vilakṣaṇa*), it is beyond reality and unreality. It is a phenomenon of mimetic truth which is full of *rasa*.

Śaṅkuka belongs to the tradition which grants that *rasa* is basically a transmutation of *sthāyī bhāvas*. But unlike Lollaṭa who thought that *sthāyī* transmuted to *rasa* in the actor, Śaṅkuka postulated that an imitation of *sthāyī bhāvas* was what actually occurred in the actor and that the act of mimesis (*anukaraṇa*) or recreation of the *sthāyī bhāvas* was basically responsible for aesthetic pleasure. In the citations of medieval commentators, the analysis of Śaṅkuka came to be known as '*anumitivāda*' because Mammaṭa changed Śaṅkuka's import by quoting him as having said that the *sthāyī bhāvas* of the character or the poet were inferred from (*anumeya*) the actions of the *naṭa*. As a matter of fact, Śaṅkuka's analysis should be called '*anukṛtivāda*' instead, because for him, the *sthāyī bhāva* in the actor appeared (*pratīyamāna*) to be *rasa* as a result of mimesis and was not inferred (*anumeyamāna*) to be *rasa*.

Bhaṭṭanāyaka's Analysis

From Bhaṭṭanāyaka onwards, the focal point in the analysis of *rasa* shifts from what happens on the stage to what is felt by the audience. Lollaṭa and Śaṅkuka both located *rasa* emergence in the actor and they presumed that the audience was able to partake of whatever was experienced by the actor. With Bhaṭṭanāyaka the spectator's psychology becomes a contributory factor in the emergence of *rasa*. He blatantly rejects the earlier views of Lollaṭa and Śaṅkuka. For him there is no birth of *rasa* (*utpatti*) in the actor nor the appearance (*pratīti*) of *rasa*. With great originality, he postulates two phenomena, that of '*bhāvakatva*' and '*bhojakatva*', both of which, according to him, must come into play for the full emergence of *rasa*. He also postulates a third most vital phenomenon of '*sādhāraṇīkaraṇa* or universalization. All the three go together to bring about *rasa* emergence. He begins with *sādhāraṇīkaraṇa*, which he argues, is manifested by the agency of *vibhāvas*. The *vibhāvas* excite such emotions as are quite different from our daily emotional reactions. The reaction to *vibhāvas* are devoid of any personal prejudice or value judgements of good or bad. The spectator keeps away his personal likes or dislikes because *vibhāva* is not something located in the real world which always invites personal reactions. This depersonalized emotion is *sādhāraṇīkaraṇa* which in turn leads to further expansion of emotion. This expansion is known as '*bhāvakatva*' in which our emotional state is distinctly new and different from memory, personal experiences, and personal recollections. This new state subdues or even eliminates the baser passions and vital urges (*tamo* and *rajo guṇas*) from the heart of the spectator; it creates a force of subtler feeling (*sattvodreka*) and peaceful delight which is akin to the joy of knowing the Supreme (as is the experience of *yogīs* in *samādhi*). This *bhāvakatva* or expansive feeling is enjoyed, or is tasted (*bhujayate*) by the spectator, completing the whole process of *rasa* emergence and enjoyment. Mammaṭa, while citing the view of Bhaṭṭanāyaka, adds that it is the *sthāyī bhāva* which undergoes expansion. However, Abhinava's citation of Bhaṭṭanāyaka's views does not make clear as to what exactly undergoes expansion. Seeing that for Bhaṭṭanāyaka, *rasa* is pre-existent (for what else can it be if it is neither born nor perceived as a result of mimesis), it can be said that *bhāvakatva* is really the expansion of *rasa* itself which is dormantly present in the emotions.

Whereas the postulations of expansion and tasting (*bhojakatva* and *bhāvakatva*) have been strongly criticised, Bhaṭṭanāyaka's *sādhāraṇīkaraṇa* has been accepted as a major contribution to the exposition of *rasa*. Depersonalization of emotion has often been thought of as a prerequisite for aesthetic pleasure. Bhaṭṭanāyaka pointed out that depersonalization of emotion can take place only if the baser insticts or the vital passions are subdued and instead a sublimated (*sāttvika*) version of the feelings is made to arise in the hearts of the spectators. The psychology of the *sāṅkhya* school of philosophy has found its place in this interpretation of *rasa*.

Abhinavagupta's Analysis

Though Abhinava's word has been regarded as the final achievement in *rasa sūtra* interpretation, it is obvious that he was drawing most of all on Bhaṭṭanāyaka. He accepts *sādhāraṇīkaraṇa* as the most cardinal of the changes that lead to *rasa*. His first presumption is that only a sensitively appreciative person (*sahṛdaya*) can experience the joy of *rasa*.

Explaining *sādhāraṇīkaraṇa* Abhinava says, that on seeing the deer being chased by Duṣyanta, the spectator knows that the deer is afraid but there is "no earthly reality" ("*viśeṣa rūpa abhāvaḥ*") to which this fear can be related as the "chaser is unreal and the chase is not real in space and time." Therefore, says Abhinava, the spectator is neither afraid himself, nor does he think that the actor is really afraid nor does he think that the 'other' (actor or dramatis persona) is a friend or a foe. Personal reactions to a friend or a foe can detract the spectator from fully feeling the dramtically represented emotion. Such reactions being set aside (or non-existent), the dramatically represented emotion (in this example, that of fear) looms large before the spectator's eyes and goes straight into his heart as '*bhayānaka rasa*,' the *rasa* of fear. At this moment, "the self (*ātmā*) of the spectator is neither assertive nor subdued." In other words, the self of the spectator is not reacting normally. That is to say, dramatic emotion is impersonal and hence felt in a special way; emotional states in daily life can never be felt in such a way as to be stripped of personal reactions.

There is another dimension added by Abhinava to the analysis of *rasa sūtras*. Lollaṭa and Śaṅkuka were content to analyse what went on the stage, Bhaṭṭanāyaka widened the perspective by including the psychology of the spectator. But Abhinava goes even further and suggests that the experience of a single spectator is influenced by the experience of the whole watching community. For Abhinava, *sādhāraṇīkaraṇa* means that the whole community is offered the same perceptive experience (*pratīti*) in the *vibhāva, anubhāava, vyabhicārī* (*naṭasāmagrī*) the resultant *sādhāraṇīkaraṇa* is so strong that all the bonds of time and space are set aside and for the sake of the emergence of *rasa* there is a realization of a single unified experience for all the spectators ("*ata eva sarvasāmājikānāṃ ekaghanatayā eva pratipattiḥ sutarāṃ rasaparipoṣāya*" *NŚ Ab. 6:31*). All the spectators have the same deeply unifying experience, not only because they are moved by the same thing, but also, as Abhinava postulates, because every spectator's consciousness is coloured by the same primordial desire (the seed form of *rati, śoka,* etc.) and because there is a consonance among spectators in experiencing that primordial desire as *rasa*. This consonant experience is without any obstruction, it is a unity and a wonder ("*sarveṣāṃ anādivāsanācitrī-kṛtacetasāṃ vāsanāsaṃvādāt sa ca avighna saṃvit camatkāraḥ*"). Therefore, it may be said that *bhāva* is (known as) *rasa*, when through *nāṭya* experience (*pratīti*) all obstructions (such as personal likes and dislikes have been removed from it ("*sarvathārasanātmakavītavighnapratītigrāhyo bhāva eva rasaḥ*"). Here, *vibhāvas* and others (*anubhāvas* and *sañcārīs*) are the obstruction removers (*tatra vighnāpasārakā vibhāvaprabhṛtayaḥ* (*NŚ Ab. 6:31*).

I have quoted the views of Abhinava as found in the *Abhinavabhāratī*. I have not taken into account what he has to say in the *Dhvanyālokalocana* or what has been presented as his view by Mammaṭa. In the commentaries on non-dramatic literature, while discussing the function of *dhvani*, Abhinava states that "*vyañjakatva vyāpāra*" is the process that promotes *rasa* in poetry (*kāvya*). As in the Indian context, *kāvya* includes drama, critics have concluded that *vyañjanā* plays the role of obstruction remover and have christened Abhinava's analysis as "*vyañjanāvāda*." However, I have tried to keep the *Abhinavabhāratī* and the *Locana* apart and not presumed that *vibhāvas* are "*vyañjakas*." Sticking to *Abhinavabhāratī*, let us note a few things. *Abhinava* does not explicitly state that only *sthāyī bhāvas* are transmuted into *rasa*. Secondly, for him *rasa* in theatre is not personal but communal. The inner reality of *bhāvas* is present in the hearts of all people as *vāsanā* (some critics equate *vāsanā* with *sthāyī bhāvas*). The emergence of *rasa* (*niṣpatti*) is possible because *bhāvas* (which get transmuted into *rasa*) are rooted in *vāsanā* or primordial desire which is universally existent.

Saṃyuktivāda

In the above mentioned classical interpretations and the critical tradition which depends upon them, it is taken for granted that the only element that gets transmuted into *rasa* is the *sthāyī bhāva*. No doubt, such is also the explicit statement of Bharata Muni in the second part of the *rasa sūtra*. However, there is no reason to presume that according to Bharata Muni there was nothing besides *sthāyī bhāva* which was also transmuted into *rasa*. As stated in the first *sūtra*, *vibhāvas, anubhāvas* and *sañcārī bhāvas* also went through this change. The four famous analysts and most commentators have taken for granted that *sthāyī bhāvas* are the elements that undergo change, whereas *vibhāvas* and others (like catalysts) remain as they are. The presence of *vibhāvas, anubhāvas* and *vyabhicāris* has a catalytic function in the transmutation of *sthāyī* into *rasa*. In other words, centuries of criticism has unduly emphasized the function of *sthāyī*. In my opinion, the most cardinal word in the *rasa sūtra* is '*saṃyoga*.' '*Saṃyoga*' has been interpreted as a state leading to the refinement of *sthāyī*. If this approach is abandoned and if it is accepted that *saṃyoga* does not lead to a further state but that *rasa* arises (*niṣpatti*) in *saṃyoga* itself, we shall be able to look at things differently. The refinement of *sthāyī* is a part of *saṃyoga* itself. *Rasa* does not occur in the later transformation of *sthāyī* but in *saṃyoga*. No doubt the connoisseurs (*sahṛdayas*) taste *sthāyī bhāvas*, but they taste *vyabhicārīs* too. The presence of *vyabhicārīs* and *vibhāvānubhāvas* is also essential to keep the spectator encaptured and attuned. Abhinava's interpretation makes *rasa*-arising to be a process taking place finally in the consciouness of the spectator; *nāṭya* is the trigger and spectator the introspective taster. The two analysts, Lollaṭa and Śaṅkuka concentrated on the material, that is, character, *naṭa* and the unique spectacle (*vilakṣaṇa pratīti*). The other two speculated on the consciousness of the spectator. The whole truth, however, is realised by viewing the totality of the phenomenon of the seen and the seer. *Rasa* arises only so long as the two, the seen and the seer are united, i.e., so long there is a *saṃyukti* of the two. The *saṃyoga* of *vibhāvānubhāvas, vyabhicārīs* and *sthāyī* compels the seer to forget all things else. This complete *saṃyukti* with *nāṭya* is *rasa*. *Saṃyukti* occurs not because of introversion, that, by feeling the *sthāyī rasa* which is transmuted by *vyabhicārīs* and *vibhāvānubhāvas* in the spectator's consciousness but it occurs because the spectacle is so encapturing, and the *vibhāvānubhāvas* are so unique (*vilakṣaṇa*) in form. This uniqueness obtains not merely on account of an imitation (*anukṛti*) of the *sthāyī* but because it is so in itself. The *rasa* experience is, therefore, not an introversion but an extreme extroversion, a forgetting, a *saṃyukti*, into the rare form of things created by *nāṭya*.

Katharsis and Rasa

It has been customary to say that ***katharsis*** and *rasa* are worlds apart. Most arguments on the topic boil down to saying: ***katharsis*** is a restorative process; it frees the spectator of emotional unbalance; it is a negative achievement as it merely provides relief from emotional stress. *Rasa*, on the other hand, is a positive achievement, a sense of enjoyment akin to yogic bliss in rapture and intensity. Such a comparison is a simplification. The purgational aspect of aesthetic enjoyment is covered not only by ***katharsis*** but by *rasa* as well. Similarly, the area of pure enjoyment, the declared aim of *rasa*, is interlinked with the concept of ***katharsis***.

As I have shown earlier, ***katharsis*** can be looked upon as a process of emotional relief the final point of which is the pleasure proper to tragedy (***oikeia hedone***). As Aristotle has not dwelt upon the effect of ***hedone*** upon the human psyche, literary criticism has focussed on the purgative aspect of the total process of ***katharsis***. It is necessary not to be misled by this approach. ***Katharsis*** should not be viewed as mere relief, it could better be regarded as restoration to a state of pleasure not generally experienced. It seems to be that the metaphor of ***katharsis*** belongs to philosophies that hold that elimination of evil surely leads to good; redemption from a fallen state leads to Godhead; and elimination of darkness to light. Such philosophies emphasize the fallen state of Man and dwell less elaborately upon the state of bliss.

The doctrine of *rasa* on the other hand, focusses attention on the final state of unmixed delight. By its very definition, *rasa* is purely "that which is capable of being tasted" (*rasa ko padārthaḥ? Āsvādyatvāt*). It contains no other force except the ability to please. But, even though Bharata Muni has not said so in his *rasa sutras*, the classical commentators have explicitly postulated that the process of *rasa* emergence (*rasaniṣpatti*) requires removal of obstructions. Lollaṭa emphasized the removal of ordinary consciousness by the creative power (*anusandhānabala*) of the actor. Śaṇkuka describes mimetic creation as something which is unknown and unseen otherwise (*vilakṣaṇapratīti*) and which wipes out normal perception. Bhaṭṭanāyaka, comes closest to ***katharsis*** when he upholds that *sādhāraṇīkaraṇa* eliminates grosser and vital passions (*tamas* and *rajas*) and creates a condition of emotional refinement (*sattvodreka*) in which *rasa* becomes possible. He is followed by Abhinava who accepts *sādhāraṇīkaraṇa* and further postulates that all artistic representation is nothing but a remover of obstructions (*vighnāpasāraka*). It is meant to purge the spectator's emotions of all personal obstructions such as individual attachments, likes and dislikes, which may stand in the way of feeling the represented emotion in an unbiased manner. For Abhinava, this purged emotion is *rasa*. Aristotle has not defined the psychological changes that constitute purging, but Abhinava has clearly stated them. For him, an emotion divested of all personal attachment is a 'purged' or a universalized one. For Abhinava this purging does not stop at depersonalization but goes on to detemporalization. The immediate emotional experience strikes a consonance with the primordial desires in the spectators. All the audience have their minds coloured by the primordial desires and *rasa* is felt at that deep level. The emotion is thus purged of all temporal bearings. It is not wrong to call this process a kind of ***katharsis***, though such a psychological analysis is far beyond the scope of the Hippocratic ideal of emotional balance. ***Katharsis,*** therefore, may be looked upon as a prerequisite for the manifestation of *rasa*. The Indian concept of *rasa*, as I have shown, includes in its ambit the process of ***katharsis***. At least, the classical commentators, if not Bharata Muni, would have it so. This makes ***katharsis*** and *rasa* two ends of the same spectrum.

Here it may be relevant to point out that the meaning of the terms ***katharsis*** and *rasa* has also been considerably influenced by the nature of the dramatic genres with which these terms have been associated. Because of its connection with tragedy, ***katharsis*** has stood for restoration or piecing together of the spirit torn apart. It has come to stand for temporary relief in an otherwise hopeless world. Because of its association with *nāṭakas* and plays with happy endings, *rasa* has been equated with undisturbed pleasure available in a world where all is well. However, the world views of supposed Olympian pessimism and Vedantic delight should not be allowed to misrepresent the aesthetics of watching drama. It must be remembered that, even though in the final philosophical analysis the world may be a vale of tears, all the same, horror and pity when represented on the stage provide a pleasure, call it kathartic ***hedone*** or *bhayānaka rasa*. According to another approach, the world may be a wheel of pleasure and pain, yet its representation on stage (*lokānukṛti*) is always pleasurable. Whatever the world view, ***katharsis*** and *rasa*, with their separate points of emphasis, both begin with purification and end in delight.

Epilogue

Finally, one may, perhaps venture the speculation that this comparative study can be of some use to theatrical experimentation in the present times. There is now a groping for new dramatic genres and production techniques. In India, there is a growing realization that modern theatre practice, other than the distinctly traditional one now banished to the rural areas, is an unrewarding hybrid groaning under the yoke of European Realism. The yoke is far from being shaken much less shed. Some efforts have been made in recent years to borrow techniques from traditional theatre to break new ground, but so far, such efforts have yielded incongruous results. Reformist realism still sets the tone for most contemporary writing if not for staging of plays; the symbolic and the mythic remain subservient to the habit of creating portraiture, a preoccupation which the Indian writer and the critic is not yet willing to be freed of. On the other hand, apart from commercial productions, experimental drama in Europe and America, has been engaged in such violent and uncontrolled aberrations that, it too, has not been able to evolve a form which can be offered as a stable and distinct alternative to commerical realism. Ever since the explosion of Dada and Surrealism in painting, the area of dramatic innovation has experienced similar stirrings. But for a number of reasons, the ship of experimental theatre which sailed out from the shores of Realism, has not yet anchored in a new haven.

In this welter of confusion, the vision of ancient hieropraxis which represents a balance of various media of theatrical communication, can be extremely useful. The harmonious use of the visual (gestural, symbolic, and kinetic) and the aural (spoken, sung and musical) as achieved in ancient drama, and as exemplified in the dramatic theories of Greece and India, has many a lesson for the present day world theatre. *Śivārpaṇamastu.*

Bibliography

Adkins, Arthur W.H. *Moral Values and Political Behaviour in Ancient Greece: From Homer to the End of the Fifth Century.* New York: Norton, 1972.

Adrados, Francisco R. *Festival, Comedy and Tragedy: The Greek Origins of Theatre.* Leiden: E.J. Brill, 1975.

Aeschylus. *Prometheus Bound, The Suppliants, Seven Against Thebes, The Persians.* Trans. Phillip Vellacot. Penguin, 1961.

—. *The Oresteian Trilogy.* Trans. Philip Vellacott. Penguin, 1956.

Amarasiṅgha. *Amarakoṣa.* Varanasi: Haridas Sanskrit Series, 1964.

Ānandavardhanā. *Dhvanyāloka* with Locana Commentary of Abhinavagupta. 4 vols. Ed. and Trans. into Hindi by R. Tripathi. Delhi: Motilal Banarsidass, 1975.

Anaṅgaharṣa Mātṛrāja. *Tāpasavatsarāja.* Ed. Sampata Kumara Ramanuja. Bangalore, 1927.

Āpastambasūtra. Bombay: Bombay Sanskrit and Prakṛta Series, 1932.

Aristophanes. *Birds, Lysistrata, Thesmophoriazusai, Frogs, Ecclesiazusai, Plautos.* Trans. Patric Dickinson. London: Oxford UP, 1970.

—. *The Knights, Peace, Birds, Thesmophoriazusai, Plautos.* Trans. Alan. H. Sommerstein and David Barett. Penguin, 1977.

Aristotle. *Poetics: Aristotle's Theory of Poetry and Fine Art.* Trans. with notes by S.H. Butcher. Intro. John Gassner. 4th Ed. U.S.A.: Dover Pub. Inc., 1951.

—. *Works of Aristotle.* Trans. W.D. Ross. London: Oxford

UP, 1928.

—. *The Nicomachean Ethics*. Trans. David Ross. Oxford UP, 1980.

Arora, V.P. *Motifs in Indian Mythology and their Greek Parallels*. New Delhi: Indika Publishing House, 1981.

Artaud, A. *The Theatre and its Double*. Trans, from French by Mary Carolina Richards. NY: Grover Press, 1958.

Asthana, Sashi P. *History and Archaeology of India's Contacts with other Countries from Earliest Times to 300 B.C.* New Delhi: BR Pub. Corp., 1976.

Ayangar, N.R. "Curtain in Ancient Theatre." *Annals of BORI* 54(1973): 207-10.

Aylen, Leo. *The Greek Theatre*. London: Fourleigh Dickinson, Univ. Press, 1985.

Bain, David. *Actors and Audience: A Study of Asides and Related Conventions in Greek Drama*. Oxford: UP, 1987.

Barba, Eugenio. "Theatre Anthropology." *The Drama Review* 26.2 (Summer 1982): 5-32.

Beardsley, Monroe C. *Aesthetics From Classical Greece to the Present: a Short History*. Alabama: U of Alabama P, 1932.

Bentley, Eric. *The Playwright as a Thinker*. New York: Harcourt, 1967.

Bharatakoṣa. A dictionary of technical terms with definitions collected from the works on Music and Dramaturgy by Bharata and Others. Compiled by M. Ramakrishna Kavi. Tirupati: Tirupati Devasthanam, 1951.

Bharata Muni. *Nāṭyaśāstram* with *Abhinahavabhāratī*. Ed. Ramakrishna Kavi. 4 vols. *Gaekwad's Oriental Series*. Baroda: Oriental Institute, vol. I (1956), vol. II (1934), vol. III (1954), vol. IV (1964).

—. *Nāṭyaśāstram* with *Abhinavabharati* with commentaries *Madhusūdanī* and *Bālakrīḍā* by Madhusūdan Śāstri. Varanasi: B.H.U., vol. I (1971), vol. II (1975), vol. III (1981).

—. *Nāṭyaśāstra, Chapter 28.* With *Sañjīvanam* and *Sādhana* commentaries by Ācārya K.C. Bṛhaspati. Delhi: Brahaspati Publication, 1986.

—. *Nāṭyaśāstra, Chapter 28: Ancient Scales of Indian Music.* With *Sañjīvanam* commentary by Ācārya Bṛhaspati. Introduced and Trans. by Bharat Gupt. Delhi: Brahaspati

Publications, 1994.

Bhāsa. *Bhāsanāṭakacakra: Complete Plays of Bhāsa.* Varanasi: Chaukhamba Surabhārati Prakashana, 1976.

—. *Svapnavāsavadatam.* Ed. N Kavyatirtha. Bombay: Nirṇaya Sagar Press, 1948.

Bhavabhūti. *Bhavabhūti Granthāvalī: Uttararāmacaritam, Mālatīmādhavam, Mahāvīracaritam.* Ed. and Trans. by Ram Pratap Tripathi. Allahabad: Lokabharati Prakashan, *1973.*

Bṛhaspati, K.C. *Bharata Kā Saṅgīta Siddhānta. Hindi Samiti Granthamala* - 28. Uttar Pradesh: Prakashan Sakha Sūcana Vibhāga, 1959.

Brooke, Iris. *Costume in Greek Classic Drama.* London: Metheun, 1962.

Butcher, S.H. *Aristotle's Theory of Poetry and Fine Art.* Trans. and with notes. Introduction by John Gassner. 4th Ed. USA: Dover Pub. Inc., 1951.

Byrski, Christopher. *Concept of Ancient Indian Theatre.* Delhi: Munshiram Manoharlal, 1974.

Chaitanya, Krishna. "Indian Dance: Native Longings for Winds of Change." *Sangeet Natak 83* (Jan-March 87): 5-13.

Chapekar, N.M. *Ancient India and Greece: A Study of their Cultural Contacts.* Delhi: Ajanta Pub., 1977.

Cole, David. *Theatrical Event, Mythos, a Vocabulary.* Middle Town: Wesleyan U, 1975.

Coomarswamy, A.K. *The Transformation of Nature in Art.* Reprinted. Delhi: Munshiram Manoharlal, 1974.

Damodaragupta. *Kuṭṭanīmatam.* Calcutta: Bibliotheca Indica, 1944.

Das, Sisir Kumar. "Medieval Indian Theatre: A Study in Terminology." *Journal of Comparative Literature.* 24 (1986): 95-123.

Dasgupta, S.N. and De, S.K. *A History of Sanskrit Literature.* Calcutta: U of Calcutta, 1962.

Detienne, Marcel. "Apollo's Slaughterhouse." *Diacritics* (Summer 1986): 46-53.

Devasthali, G.S. *Religion and Philosophy of Brāhmaṇas.* Poona: U of Poona, 1965.

Dhanañjaya. *Daśarupaka.* With *Dhanika's* Commentary. Bombay: Nirnaya Sagar Press, 1928.

Dinnāga. *Kundamālā*. Ed. K.K. Datta. Calcutta: Sanskrit College Research Series, 1964.

Dodds, E.R. *The Greeks and the Irrational*. Berkeley and Los Ang.: U of Cal. P, 1951, rpt. 1968.

Du Bois, Page. *Centaurs and Amazons: Women and Prehistory of the Great Chain of Being*. Ann Arbor: Univ. of Michigan P, 1982.

Eco, Umberto, V.U. Ivanov and Monica Rector. *Carnival*. Ed. Thomas A. Sebeon. New York: Moulton Publishers, 1984.

Elam, Keir. *The Semiotics of Theatre and Drama*. London: Methuen, 1980.

Eliade, Mircea. *Images and Symbols*. New York: Sheed and Ward, 1952.

Else, Gerald F. *Aristotle: Poetics*. Trans. with introduction and notes. Ann Arbor: U of Michigan P, 1967.

Euripides. *Alcestis, Hippolytus, Iphigenia at Tauris*. Trans. Philip Vellacott. Penguin, 1974.

—. *The Bacchae, Ion, Women of Troy, Helen*. Trans. Philip Vellacott. Penguin, 1972.

—. *Media, Hecabe, Electra, Heracles*. Trans. Philip Vellacott. Penguin, 1963.

Euripides. Vol. I Tr. Arthur S. Way. Cambridge, Mass.: Harvard UP, 1912 Rev. 1978.

Farnell, L.R. *Cults of the Greek States*. 4 vols. Oxford, 1896.

Filliozat, J. *The Classical Doctrine of Indian Medicine: Its Origin and its Greek Parallels*. Trans. Dev Raj Chanana. Delhi: Munshiram Manoharlal, 1964.

Fokema, D.W. and Kunne-Ibsch E. *Theories of Literature in the Twentieth Century*. London: Hurst and Company, 1979.

Fontenrose, Joseph. *The Delphic Oracle: Its Responses with a Catalogue of Responses*. Berkeley: U of Cal. Press, 1978.

Frankel, Hermann. *Early Greek Poetry and Philosophy: A history of Greek epic, lyric, and prose to middle of the century*. Trans. by Moses Hades and James Wilis. New York: A Helen and Kurt Wolff Book. Harcourt Brace Novanovich.

Garton, Charles. *Personal Aspects of the Roman Theatre*. Toronto: U of Tornoto, 1972.

Gupt, Bharat. "The Date of the Nāṭyaśāstra." *Journal of Oriental Institute.* Baroda. 36.1-4 (1986-87): 69-86.

—. "Music in the Nāṭyaśāstra." *Journal of Music Academy.* Madras. 56 (1985)-onwards.

—. "Nāṭyaśāstra and Vālmiki's Rāmāyaṇa." *Sangeet Natak.* Journal of Sangeet Natak Academy 81-82 (1986): 63-76.

—. *Nāṭyaśāstra, Chapter 28. Ancient Scales of Indian Music.* With *Sañjīvanam* commentary by Ācārya Bṛhaspati. Introduced and Trans. by Bharat Gupt. Delhi: Brahaspati Publication, 1994.

Graves, Robert. *The Greek Myths.* 2 vols. Penguin, 1955.

Grotowski, Jerzy. *Towards a Poor Theatre.* New York: Simon and Schuster, 1968.

Halliwell, Stephen. *Aristotle's Poetics.* London Duckworth, 1986.

Halporn, J.W., Ostwald, M., Rosenmeyer, T.G. *The Metres of Greek and Latin Poetry.* New York: Bobbs-Merrill Comp. Inc., 1963.

Hanumāna. *Mahānāṭakam.* Ed. Jivananda Bhattacarya. Calcutta, 1890.

Health, Malcolm. *The Poetics of Greek Tragedy.* London: Duckworth, 1987.

Homer. *The Iliad.* Trans. E.V. Rieu. Penguin, 1946.

Hornby, Richard. *Script into Performance: A Structuralist View of Play Production.* Austin: U of Texas P, 1977.

Housten, Mary G. *Ancient Greek, Roman and Byzantine Costume and Decoration.* London: Adam and Charles Black, 1963.

Humphreys, S.C. "'Transcendence' and Intellectual Roles: The Ancient Greek Case." *Daedalus* 104.2 (Spring 1975): 91-118.

Iśvaradatta. *Dhūrtaviṭasaṃvāda* in *Caturbhāṇī.* Ed. and Trans. into Hindi by M. Chandra and V.S. Aggrawal. Bombay: Hindi Granthalaya Ratnakara, 1959.

Izenour, George C. *Theatre Design.* New York: McGraw-Hill, 1977.

Jaideva. *Prasannarāghavam.* Ed. V.L. Pansikara. Bombay: Niranaya Sagar Press, 1922.

Jayasena. *Nṛttaratnāvalī.* Preface and Ed. V. Raghavan. Madras: Govt. Oriental Manuscript Library, 1965.

Kale, Manohar. *Bharatīya Nāṭya Saundarya.* Delhi: Megha Prakashan, 1982.

Kālidāsa. *Abhijnānaśākuntalam* with commentary of Raghava Bhaṭṭa. Ed. N.R. Kavyatirtha. Bombay: Nirnaya Sagar Press, 1958.

—. *Mālavikāgnimitram.* With commentary by Ramashankar Pandeya. Varanasi: Chowkamba Surbharati Prakashan, 1979.

—. *Vikramorvaśīyam.* Ed. R.C. Misra. Varanasi: Chowkhamba Sanskrit Series Office, 1963.

Kane, P.V. *History of Sanskrit Poetics.* Delhi: Motilal Banarsidass, 1961.

Keith, A.B. *History of Sanskrit Literature.* London: Oxford UP, 1920 rep. 1956.

Kersenboom-Story, Saskia C. *Nityasumaṅgalī: Devadāsī Tradition in South India.* Delhi: Motilal Banarsidass, 1987.

Kerenyi, C. *The Religion of the Greeks and Romans.* NY: E.P. Dutton and Co., 1962.

Klein, Richard. "The Metis of Centaurs." *Diacritics (Summer 1986):* 2-20.

Kuluckhohn, Clyde. *Anthropology and the Classics.* Providence: RI Brown UP, 1961.

Kirk, G.S. *The Pre-Socratic Philosophers.* Cambridge: U.P., 1983.

Konow, Sten. *The Indian Drama.* Trans. from German by S.N. Ghosal. Calcutta: General Printers, 1969.

Lawler, L.B. *The Dance in Ancient Greece.* London: Adam and Charles, 1964.

Lotman, Yuri M. *Analysis of the Poetic Text.* Ann Arbor: Michigan UP, 1976.

Mahendravikramavarman. *Mattavilāsaprahasanam.* Trivandrum: T.S.S., 1917.

Mammaṭa. *Kāvyaprakāśa.* Poona: B.O.R.I., 1965.

Manu. *Manusmṛti* with Commentary of Kullukabhatta. Ed. J.L. Sastri. Delhi: Motilal Banarsidass, 1983.

Marasinghe, E.W. *The Sanskrit Theatre and Stagecraft.* Delhi: Sri Satguru Publications, 1989.

Matilal, B.K. *Perception: An Essay on Classical Indian Theories of Knowledge.* Oxford: Clarendon Press, 1986.

Mireaux, Emile. *Daily Life in Times of Homer.* Trans. from

French by Iris Sells. London: George Allen and Unwin, 1959.

Mitra, Sombu. "Building From Tagore." *The Drama Review* 15.3 (TSO) (Spring 1971):202-03.

Momigliano, Arnaldo. "The Fault of the Greeks." *Daedalus* 14.2 (Spring 1975): 9-19.

Monier-Williams, Sir M. *A Sanskrit-English Dictionary.* Reprinted. Delhi: Motilal Banarsidass, 1974.

Morrison, Karl F. *The Mimetic Tradition of Reform in the West.* New Jersey: U of Princeton, 1982.

Nagendra. *Rasa Siddhānta.* Delhi: National Publishing House, 1974.

Nāndikeśvara. *Abhinayadarpaṇam: A Manual of Gestures and Postures in Ancient Indian Dance and Drama.* Trans. M. Gosh. Calcutta: Manisha Granthalaya, 1975.

Napier, David, A. *Masks, Transformation and Paradox.* Los Angles: U of Cal. P., 1986.

Nārāyaṇabhaṭṭa. *Veṇīsaṃhāra.* Ed. R.S. Deshpande. Bombay: 1953.

Neft, R. *The Living Theatre.* New York: The Bobbs-Merill Company, 1970.

Nilsson, M.P. *The Mycenean Origin of Greek Mythology.* Berkeley: U of Cal. Press, 1972.

—. *A History of Greek Religion.* Trans. from Swedish by F.J. Fielden. New York: W.W. Norton and Co., Inc., 1964.

Nuckolls, Charles W. "Causal Thinking in Śakuntalā: A Schema-theoretic Approach to a Classical Sanskrit Drama." *Philosophy East and West.* 37.3 (July 1987): 286-305.

Orians, R.B. *The Origins of European Thought.* Cambridge: Univ. Press, 1951.

Oxford Classical Dictionary. Ed. N.G.L. Hamond and H.H. Scullard. 2nd Ed. Oxford: Clarendon Press, 1970.

Pandey, K.C. *Indian Aesthetics.* 2 vols. Varanasi: Chowkhamba Sanskrit Studies, 1959.

—. *Abhinavagupta: A Historical and Philosophic Study.* 2nd Ed. Varanasi: Chowkhamba Sanskrit Series Office, 1963.

Pāṇini. *Aṣṭādhāyī.* Ed. with Trans. S.C. Vasu. 2 vol. Delhi: Munshiram Manoharlal, 1962.

Patañjali. *Mahābhāṣya.* Bombay: Nirnaya Sagar Press, 1951.

Pendse. S.N. *Oaths and Ordeals in Dharmaśastra*. Baroda : MSU of Baroda, 1985.

Pickard-Cambridge, A. *Dramatic Festivals of Athens*. 2nd Ed. revised by John Gould and D.M. Lewis. Oxford: Clarendon Press, 1973.

—. *The Theatre of Dionysus*. Oxford: Clarendon Press, 1973.

—. *Dithyramb, Tragedy and Comedy*. 2nd Ed. rev. T.B.L. Webster. Oxford: Clarendon Press, 1962.

Plato. *The Dialogues of Plato*. Trans. Benjamin Jowett. 5 vols. 3rd Ed. Oxford, 1893.

—. *The Republic*. Trans, H.D.P. Lee. Penguin, 1955.

—. *Symposium*. Trans. W. Hamilton. Penguin, 1951.

Plautus. *The Rope, The Ghost, A Three Dollar Day, Amphitryo*. Trans. E.F. Watling. Penguin, 1964.

Plautus. *The Pot of Gold, The Prisoners, The Brothers Menaechmus, The Swaggering Soldier, Pseudolus*. Trans. E.F. Walting. Penguin, 1965.

Pronko, Leonard. *Theatre East and West*. Berkeley: U of Cal. Press, 1967.

Prosperi, Mario. "The Masks of Lipari." *The Drama Review* 26.4 (Winter 1982).

Raghavan, V. *The Number of Rasas*. Adyar: The Adyar Library, 1940.

—. *The Social Play in Sanskrit*. Bangalore: IIC, 1952.

Ramacandra Guṇacandra. *Nāṭyadarpaṇam*. Baroda: Oriental Institute, 1959.

Rangacharya, Adya. *The Indian Theatre*. New Delhi: National Book Trust, 1971.

Śaktibhadra. *Āścaryacūḍāmaṇi*. Production Manual from the Tradition of Kutiyattam Sanskrit Drama. Ed. C.F. Jones. Trans. by V. Raghavana. Delhi: Oxford UP, 1984.

Sāmarāja Dīxita. *Dhurtanartakam*. Ed. Babulal Shukla. Delhi: Lal Bahadur Shastri Vidyapitham, 1978.

Sarachchandra, E.R. "The Uses of Tradition." *The Drama Review* 15.3 (Spring 1971): 197-210.

Śāradātanaya. *Bhāvaprakāśana*. Baroda: Oriental Institute, 1930.

Śārṅgadeva. *Saṅgītaratnākara*. With *Kalānidhi* of Kallinatha and *Saṅgītasudhākara* of Siṃhabhūpāla. Ed. Pandit S.S. Sastri in 4 vols. *Adyar Library Series*. Madras: The Adyar Library, Vol. I (1943), Vol. II (1944), Vol. III (1968), Vol. IV (1953).

Schechner, Richard. *Environmental Theatre*. New York: Hawthorn, 1973.

—. *Ritual, Play and Performance*. Ed. R. Schechner and Mady Schuman. New York: Seabury Press, 1976.

—. *Essays on Performance Theory* 1970-76. New York: Drama Book Specialists, 1977.

—. *Between Theatre and Anthropology*. Philadelphia: Univ. of Pennyslvania Press, 1985.

Schwartz, Benjamin I. "The Age of Transcedence." *Daedalus* 104.2 (Spring 1975): 1-7.

Sellin, Eric. *The Dramatic Concepts of Antonin Artaud*. Chicago: UP, 1975.

Seneca. *Thycestes, Phaedra, The Trojan Women, Oedipus, Octavia*. Trans. E.F. Watling. Penguin, 1966.

Singal, R.L. *Aristotle and Bharata: A Comparative Study of their Theories of Drama*. Chandigarh: Singal, 1977.

Sharma, Shyam. *Sanskrit Ke Aitihasik Natak*. Jaipur: Devanagar Prakashan, 1974.

Sharma, M.M. *Vyañjanāprapañcasamīkṣā: A Critique on Comparative Symbolism*. Varanasi: Chaukhamba Orientalia, 1979.

Shastri, Dakshina Ranjan. *Origin and Development of the Rituals of Ancestor Worship in India*. Calcutta: Bookland Private Limited, 1963.

Shastri, Surendra Nath. *The Laws and Practice of Sanskrit Drama*. Vol. I Varanasi: Chowkhamba Sanskrit Series Office, 1961.

Shekhar, Indu. *Sanskrit Drama, Its Origin and Decline*. Lieden: E.J. Brill, 1960. Rep. 2nd Ed. Delhi: Munshiram Manoharlal, 1977.

Sophocles. *King Oedipus, Oedipus at Colonus, Antigone*. Trans. E.F. Watling. Penguin, 1947.

—. *Electra, Ajax, Women of Trachis, Philoctetes*. Trans. B.P. Watling. Penguin, 1953.

Śrīharṣadeva. *Ratnāvalī*. Ed. and Trans. by Vajraratna Bhattacarya. Bombay: Nirnaya Sagar, 1894.

Stanford, W.B. *Greek Tragedy and the Emotions: An Introductory*

Study. London: Routledge and Kegan Paul, 1983.

Srīharṣadeva. *Nagānandam*. Ed. T. Ganapati Sastri. Trivandrum: T.S.S., 1917.

Śūdraka. *Mṛcchakaṭikam*. With commentary of Pṛthvīdhara. Bombay: Nirnaya Sagar Press, 1936.

Suśruta. *Suśrutasaṃhitā*. Eds. V.J. Trikamji and N.R. Kavyatirtha. Bombay: Nirnaya Sagar Press, 1945.

Śudraka. *Padmaprābhṛtakam in Caturbhāṇī*. Bombay: Hindi Grantha Ratnakara Karyalaya, 1959.

Styan, J.L. *Modern Drama in Theory and Practice: Realism and Naturalism*. Cambridge: Univ. Press, 1981.

Śyamilaka. *Pādatāḍita in Caturbhāṇi*. Bombay: Hindi Grantha Ratnakara Karyalaya, 1959.

Tarlekar, G.H. *Studies in Nāṭyaśāstra*. Delhi: Motilal Banarsidass, 1975.

Tola, Fernando and Carmen and Dragonetti. "India and Greece Before Alexander." *Annals of BORI* 67 (1987): 159-94.

Toynbee, Arnold. *Hellenism*. Oxford: Clarendon Press, 1959.

Trivedi, Bhavani Shankar. *Mokṣamyularavaiduṣyam*. Delhi: Arya Bharati, 1981.

Turner, Victor. *The Ritual Process*. Ithaca: Cornell UP, 1969.

—. *Drama, Fields and Metaphors*. Ithaca: Cornell UP, 1974.

Upādhyāya, Ramji. *Madhyakalīn Sanskrit Naṭak*. Sagar: Sanskrit Pariṣad, 1974.

—. *Technical Terms in Nāṭyaśāstra: An Index*. Allahabad: Bhartiya Sanskrit Prakashan, 1980.

Vālmīki. *Rāmāyaṇa*. Gorakhpur: Gita Press, 1960.

Varadpande, M.L. *Traditions of Indian Theatre*. New Delhi: Abhinav Publications, 1979.

Vararuci. *Ubhayasārikā. Chaturbhāṇī*. Ed. and Trans. into Hindi, Moti Chandra and V.S. Aggrawal. Bombay: Hindi Grantha Ratnakara Karyalaya, 1959.

Varma, Mahendra Vikrama. *Mattavilāsaprahasanam* with commentary by Kapiladeva Giri. Varanasi: Chowkhamba Vidyabhavan, 1966.

Vatsarāja. *A Collection of Six Dramas*. Ed. Chiman Lal D. Dalal. Baroda: Oriental Institute, 1972.

Vatsyayan, Kapila. *Classical Indian Dance in Literature and the Arts*. Delhi: Sangeet Natak Academy, 1968.

—. *A Study of Some Tradition of Performing Arts in Eastern India: Mārgī and Desī Polarities*. Gohati: Univ. Dept. of Pub., 1981.

Vātsyāyana Muni. *Kāmasūtra* with *Jayamaṅgalā* commentary of Yaśodhara. 3rd Ed. with Hindi commentary by Devadatta Sastri. *Kashi Sanskrit Granth Mala 29*. Varanasi: Chaukhamba Sanskrit Sansthana, 1982.

Vernant, Jeane Pierre. *The Origins of Greek Thought*. Ithaca: Cornell UP, 1982.

Vickers, Brian. *Towards Greek Tragedy: Drama, Myth and Society*. London: Longman, 1973.

Viśākhadatta. *Mudrārākṣasa*. Ed. M.R. Kale. Bombay: —, 1916.

Vyāsa. *Mahābhārata*. 14 vols. Gorakhpur: Gita Press, 1956.

Webster, T.B.L. *Greek Theatre Production*. London: Methuen, 1956.

—. *The Greek Chorus*. London: Metheun, 1970.

Wells, H.W. *The Classical Drama of India*. Bombay: Asia Publishing House, 1963.

West, M.L. *Early Greek Philosophy and the Orient*. Oxford: 1971.

Wiles, Timothy J. *Theatre Event: Modern Theories of Performance*. Chicago: U of Chicago Press, 1980.

Yājñavalkya. *Yājñavalkyasmṛti*. With *Mitakṣara* of *Vijñāneśvara*. Ed. N.R. Acarya. Bombay: Nirnaya Sagar Press, 1949.

Index

Abhijñānaśākuntalam, 162, 207, 216.
Abhinavabhāratī, 74, 108, 115, 117, 121, 123, 132, 163-5, 182, 188-9, 193, 240, 242-5, 264-5.
Abhinavagupta, 29, 32, 33, 73, 74, 91, 108, 117, 121, 132, 163-4, 182, 193, 209, 241, 244, 267-72.
abhinaya, 86-7, 89, 105, 159, 181, 262.
Ācārya Bṛhaspati, 35.
Achilles, 46, 50, 59.
Adrados, Francisco R., 47, 66-7.
Aeschylus, 46.
aether, 56.
agalma, 65, 153.
Agathon, 176.
Aggrawal, Vasudev, S., 82.
agora, 127-8.
āhārya abhinaya, 8, 89, 106, 116-9, 121, 181, 241.
Alexander, 15.
ākāśikī cārī, 110.
ākṛti, 118.
ākṣepikī, 194.
alātacakra, 122-3.
Amarakośa, 27, 28.
ambrosia, 42.
amṛta, 43.
Amṛtamanthana, 23, 43, 76, 99, 208.
anagnorisis, 116, 218-9.
anamix, 152.
ancestor worship, 48.
Āndhra, 120.
Andromache, 210, 228.
aṅga-aṅgī-bhāva, 222.
aṅgahāra, 89, 112, 162, 164, 211, 239.
āṅgika abhinaya, 89, 106-7, 112, 159, 181, 240.
añjali hasta, 108.
aṅkura, 160-62, 206.
Anthesteria, 48.
Antigone, 45, 46, 227-8.
antistrophe, 146, 156, 175.
anubhāva, 87, 90, 254-5, 261-70.
anudātta, 105, 187, 198.
anukaraṇa, 86-7, 93, 98-101, 105, 163, 183, 234, 265.
anumitivāda, 266.
anuvaṃśya verses, 27.
Aphrodite, 216.
apsarās, 21, 22, 120, 208.
ārabhaṭī vṛtti, 86, 133, 208, 212-3.
Archilochus, 173.
Ardhamāgadhī, 184.
aretee, 53.
Aristophanes, 11, 176.
Aristotle, 85, 95-7, 170.
Aristoxenus, 177, 179-80.
Arjuna, 46.
arthaprakṛti, 219, 221-2.
Arthaśāstra of Bṛhaspati, 27.
Arthaśāstra of Kauṭilya, 28.
āryabhāṣā, 184.
asaṃyuta hasta, 108, 115, 151.
āsārita, 73.
Aṣṭādhyāyī, 29.
Aśvaghoṣa, 20.
Aśvatthāmā, 51.
ate, 43, 44.

Athenaeus, 89, 148, 155.
atibhāṣā, 184.
atikrāntā cārī, 110.
ātodya, 105.
Augustine, St., 7.
aulos player, 129, 136, 146, 175.
Avantijā, 184.
avasthā, 4, 219, 22.
āviddha, 165, 206, 215.
Aylen, Leo, 141, 150, 155-7, 172-5.
Āyurveda, 56, 61, 256.

Bacchae, 155, 216.
bachantes, 155.
Bāhlīkā, 184.
Bakulavīthī, 212.
barbara, 120.
Barba, Eugeno, 238.
bassari, 153.
Beardsley, 94-6.
Bhāgavat, 23.
bhāṇa, 12, 165, 210-2, 213, 222, 246.
bharatamata, 29.
Bharata Muni, 30-2, 85, 105, 168, 187.
Bharatanāṭyam, 5, 237.
bharatas, 31.
Bharataśāstra, 31.
Bharata sūtra, 27.
Bhāratavarṣa, 23, 30, 210.
bhāratī vṛtti, 86, 208.
Bhāsa, 20, 49, 209-10.
Bhaṭṭalollaṭa, 91, 263-4, 266, 268, 270
Bhaṭṭanāyaka, 263, 266-9, 272.
Bhaṭṭa Tauta, 98-9.
bhaumī cārī, 110.
bhāva, 26, 86, 89, 105, 109, 252-3, 261.
Bhavabhūti, 58, 60, 76.
Bhavai, 237.
bhāvakatva, 266-7.
Bhāvaprakāśana, 38.
bhāvavyañjanā, 234.
bhojakatva, 266-7.
bint, 21.
Brahmā, 73, 76, 99-101.
brahmamata, 29.
Brāhmaṇas, 21.
brahmāṇḍa, 45.
Brea, Bernabo Luigi, 131.
Brecht, Bertolt, 11.
Bṛhaspati, K.C., 202.
burial customs, 48-9, 59.
Butcher, S.H., 97, 179, 256-8.
Byrski, Christopher, M., 223-5.

Cārī, 110, 138, 159, 243.
Cārudatta, 50, 186.
Caturbhāṇī, 82.
Centaurs, 23.
cheironomia, 10, 88, 150-1, 154.
choral ode, 146.
choregos, 69.
chorus, tragic, 10, 145.
chorutai, 105.
Christianity, 5.
Christian theology, 7.
chroai, 178-80, 199.
citrā, 21.
citrābhinaya, 162, 164.
comedy, 173, 203-6.
conflict, 235.
Corybantes, 248.
Cratylus, 95.
curetes, 148, 152.
cūrṇapada, 185.

Daimons, 22, 43.
daiva, 53, 215-6.
Dākṣiṇātyā, 184.
Dāmaka, 211.
daśarūpaka, 15, 20, 87, 203, 206, 213-4, 237.
Dasgupta, 223.

Das, Sisir K., 123.
Dattila, 29, 32-3.
Daughters of Troy, 210, 228.
deixeis, 149, 151.
Delphos, 51.
Demosthenes, 248.
devavāṇī, 53.
dharmī, 86-7, 89, 105-6,235-7.
dhīralalita, 229.
dhīrapraśānta, 229.
dhīrodātta, 229.
dhīroddhata, 229.
dhruvā gāna, 165, 183, 193-7, 206, 246.
Dhūrtaviṭasaṃvāda, 211.
dianoia, 86-7, 90, 200-1.
diesis, 177.
dike, 53, 56, 216-7.
ḍima. 20, 33, 165, 209, 213, 222.
Dionysia, 75, 247.
Dionysian festival, 69, 127, 216.
Dionysus, 65, 127, 129, 154.
dithyramb, 10, 148, 154.
divination, 52.
Dodds, E.R., 43, 44.
ḍombikā, 75.
Draviḍa, 120.
dṛṣṭis, 107.

eikon, 95.
ekplexis, 116, 250.
Electra, 147.
Eliade, Mircea, 79, 80.
Elizabethan plays, 10.
Else, G.F., 259-60.
eluabeia, 230.
emmelia, 151, 155.
emotional arousal, 172, 233, 247.
epikrelios, 152.
episode, 146.
epode, 146, 175.
ethos, 10, 86, 111, 201, 204-5, 226-8, 235.
Euripides, 129, 176-7.
European theatre, drama, 5, 9, 119.
exarkhonton, 204.
exodos, 146.

Fate, 215.
festivals of ancient India, 81.
festive drama, 63.
Fifth Veda, 70, 71, 72, 100.
Filliozat, J., 61.
five elements, 56.
funeral rites, 49.

Galen, 172.
gāna, 105, 169, 187, 193.
Gandharva, 21, 25, 43.
Gāndharva, 21, 22, 24, 87, 89, 197, 200.
Garton, Charles, 7, 119.
gatipracāra, 111, 150, 243.
genos, 48, 178, 199.
geranos, 152.
Ghose, Manmohan, 19, 238.
gīta, 24.
gotra, 48.
Graves, Robert, 42, 58-9, 61.
Greek choral music, 181.
Greek choreology, 149-51.
Greek medicine, 61.
Greek musical system, 176.
Greek performance, 145.
Greek-playwright-director, 77.
grīvākarma, 107.
Gupt, Bharat, 15.

Hallīsaka, 75.
hamartia, 46, 205, 219, 227-8, 230.
Hamlet, 4.
Harivarṣa, 138.
harmoniai, 177, 179, 199.

harmony, 103-4.
harps, 20.
harṣa, 91, 261.
Hecuba, 147.
Hekabe, 50, 227, 258.
Helen, 219.
heptachordon, 178.
Herodotos, 248.
Hesiod, 56.
hieromenia, 3, 57.
hieropraxis, 4, 5, 63, 126, 217, 233, 274.
Hippocratic Manuals, 61.
Hippolytus, 52, 216, 227, 251.
Hippolytus, 54, 228.
holy possession, 7.
Homer, 44, 53, 67, 203.
homiosis, 94.
hubris, 46, 47.
hupokrites, 68.
huporkhema, 67, 148-9, 151, 153.

Iambic trimetre, 173.
Ibsen Henrik, 11.
īhāmṛga, 20, 165, 208-9, 213, 222.
ikria, 128.
Ilāvarṣa, 138.
Iliad, 44, 204.
Indo-European, 8, 42.
Indra, 22, 76, 224.
Iphigenia, 50.
Iphigenia at Aulis, 65, 216, 219.
Iphigenia at Tauris, 54.
itivṛtta, 4, 87, 182, 217, 219, 221, 228.
Izenour, George, C., 128.

Jarjara pole, 78, 159, 224.
jāti, 24, 198, 199.
jātibhāṣā, 184.
Jātrā, 237.

Kaiśikī vṛtti, 72, 73, 86, 165, 212-3, 241, 245.
kakṣyā vibhāga, 137.
kāku, 187-89, 243.
kalā, 111.
Kālidāsa, 27, 215.
Kallinātha, 81.
Kāmatantra, 28, 37.
kampita, 187, 191.
karaṇas, 73, 112, 211, 245.
karmārambha, 210.
karmavāda, 56, 215.
Karṇa, 52, 89.
Katagrous, 75.
Kathakali, 5.
katharsis, 42, 90, 91, 205, 233, 255-60, 271-3.
Kauṭilya, 27.
Keith, A.B. 24, 70, 214.
kenosis, 256, 258.
Kernyi, C., 230.
Kersenboom-Storey, Saskia, 64.
khresteria, 53.
kinesis, 149.
kinnars, 22.
kirāta, 120.
kithara, 177.
Kohala, 29, 32, 91.
kommodoi, 76.
komos, 67, 154.
Koran, 175.
kordax, 151, 156.
koros, 46, 47.
koruphaios, 146.
krīḍanīyakam, 88, 100, 136, 224, 241.
Kṛśāśva, 26, 29.
Kṛṣṇa, 24.
Kṛtyārārāvaṇa, 207.
Kudiyaṭṭam, 5, 237.
kumārādhikṛta, 28.
Kuṣāṇa period, 21.
kutapa, 135-40, 143, 160.

Lakṣmīsvayaṃvara, 23.

language, 103-4, 169-71.
Lawler, Lilian, B., 148-52.
Laws, 94.
Lenaia, 75.
lexis, 86-8, 104, 169-70.
Libation Bearers, 147.
Life of Sophocles, 180.
liminal state, 65.
liṅga, 89, 163.
logeion, 129, 130, 141.
lokadharmī, 106, 162, 233-46.
Lollaṭa, 263-4, 266, 268, 270.
Lotman, Yuri, 234.
Lucian, 89, 148.
lute, 20.

Madhyamagrāma, 198.
Madhyamavyāyoga, 209.
maenads, 155, 157.
Māgadhī, 184, 197.
Mahābhārata, 24, 25, 49, 56.
Mahāvīracaritam, 60.
Mālatīmādhavam, 76.
Mālavikāgnimitram, 27, 207.
Mammaṭa, 263, 266-7, 269.
Mānasāra, 143.
maṇḍala, 110.
mantike, 54.
manvantara, 56.
mārga, 81.
Margites, 204.
mask, 7, 8, 130-1.
masque, 9.
Mathurā sculptures, 21.
mattavāraṇīs, 134-7.
Mattavilāsa, 211.
Māyāpuṣpaka, 244.
mechane, 139.
Medea, 95.
melopoic (musical) space, 126, 136, 140.
melopoiia, 86, 88, 104, 169, 176.
Menander, 131.
menos, 43-4.
menteia, 53.
miasma, 42, 45-7, 51, 258, 260.
mimesis, 15, 86-7, 93-5, 99, 103, 105, 203, 217, 226, 234.
Mireaux Emile, 59.
mithexix, 94.
Mitra, Sombu, 214.
moira, 46, 53.
Monier-Williams, M., 163.
monophonic music, 176.
Morrison, K.L., 101.
Moti Chandra, 81.
mousike, 149, 171.
Mṛcchakaṭikam, 50, 185, 196, 207.
Mudrārākṣasa, 207.
mukhaja, 107.
multichannelled theatre, 4.
mūrcchanā, 24, 198-9.
musical instruments, 20.
muthos, 4, 86-8, 182, 204, 217-9, 259.

Nāḍī, 208.
naiṣkrāmikī, 194.
nāndī, 159.
Nāndikeśvara, 29, 31.
Napier, David, A., 8, 9, 118-9, 141.
Nārada, 20, 29.
nāstikadhuryāḥ, 37.
naṭa, 76.
nāṭaka, 12, 165, 203, 206-7, 213, 215, 217, 219, 221, 240, 273.
Naṭasūtra, 29.
Naturalism, 7, 117, 169, 196.
nāṭya, 80, 86, 106, 163, 224.
nāṭyācārya, 77, 78, 165.
nāṭyadharmī, 106, 233, 235-46.
Nāṭyaśāstra, 12, 14, 70, 85, 101.
Nāṭyaveda, 70, 101.

nāṭyaveṣma, 132.
nāṭyāyita, 160, 195.
nāṭyotpatti, 71, 100.
nāyakas, 226, 228.
nāyikās, 228-9.
nepathya, 133, 135.
nepathyagṛha, 137.
Nicomachean Ethics, 116, 259.
niṣpatti, 261, 263, 269.
nivṛtyāṅkura, 160-2, 193.
noos, 44.
nṛtta, 72, 73, 80, 165.
nṛttahastas, 89, 109, 149, 243.
nṛtya, 80.
Nuckolls, C.W., 230.
nyāya (fighting postures), 110.

Oath, 51, 60.
Odysseus, 60.
Odyssey, 67, 204.
Oedipus, 216, 259.
Oedipus Rex, 13, 14, 216, 259.
oekeia hedone, 90, 255-6, 258, 271, 273.
On the Psuche, 249.
On the Sublime, 249.
open theatre (Indian), 139.
opsis, 7, 86, 88, 105.
oracles, 52.
orchestral (dance) space, 126, 128.
oreibasia, 153, 155.
Orestes, 46, 227.
Oresteia, 47, 177, 258.
orsites, 152.

Padmaprābhṛtakam, 212.
paean, 152.
Pahlavas, 120.
Pāṇḍavas, 49.
Pāṇini, 19, 20, 23, 29, 30.
pantomimus, pantomimi, 148, 151, 153-4, 176, 211.
parodoi, 128, 146.
parakataloge, 10, 129, 174-5, 190.
paraplesia, 94.
paraskenia, 130, 134, 141.
Pārśadeva, 32.
pārśvakarma, 109.
parva, 3.
patākā, 108, 163, 220, 240, 245.
Patañjali, 24, 28.
pathos, 219.
pāṭhya, 106, 159, 183, 187-89, 200.
Pelasgians, 41.
Pendse, S.N., 51.
peraṇī, 80.
performance (theatrical) space, 125-7, 133.
peripetia, 218-9.
Phaedrus, 95.
phala, 220-1, 221, 223, 226.
phallika, 66, 154, 204.
phantasma, 95.
phorminx, 177.
phoroi, 10, 149, 151, 158.
Photius, 128.
phratria, 48.
Phrenikos, 180.
Physics, 97, 102.
Pickard-Cambridge, A., 127-30, 146-7, 149, 173, 177.
piṇḍa, 45, 54, 56.
piṇḍībandha, 73, 74, 150.
pitṛṛṇa, 49.
Plato, 93, 94, 115, 127.
Plutarch, 148, 149, 172, 179-80.
Poetics, 12, 14, 85, 169-70. 172, 218.
Politics, 98, 255.
pollution, 42, 46.
polyphonic harmony, 176.
pompee, 127.
portraiture, 10, 11.
Prācyā, 184.

prahasana, 165, 210, 222.
prakaraṇa, 12, 165, 203, 206.
Prākṛta, 165, 171, 183-4.
prakṛti, 118.
prāsādikī, 194.
prastāvanā, 150.
pratīti, 265-6, 268.
prāveśikī, 194, 196.
pravṛtti, 86-7, 89, 105, 107.
praxis, 4, 98, 217, 226.
Problems, 174.
prologue, 145.
Pronko, Leonard, 11.
prorresis, 49.
prosoopon, 118.
Prosperi, Mario, 141.
psuchagogia, 171, 234, 249.
Purāṇas, 19.
purrixe, 152, 153.
Purūravas, 23.
pūrvaraṅga, 74, 76, 137, 158-60, 193, 224.
pusta āhārya, 119.
Pythagoras, 48.

Quintilian, 146-8.

Rāga, 180-1, 199, 202.
Rāghavabhaṭṭa, 162.
rākṣasas, 120.
Rāma, 46.
Rāma Līlā, 69.
Rāmāyaṇa, 15, 21, 23, 24, 64, 76, 118.
Rājaśekhara, 244.
raṅga, 87, 105, 135, 139.
raṅgapīṭha, 133-4, 136, 137.
raṅgapūjana, 78, 165.
raṅgaśīrṣa, 133, 136.
raṅgāvataraṇa, 118.
rasa, 26, 86, 91, 105, 109, 233, 260-273.
Rāsaka, 75.
Realism, 7, 145, 237, 273.
Republic, 94-5, 115, 248.
Renaissance, 5, 6, 98.
Ṛgveda, 22, 36, 55-6, 174, 198.
Rhetoric, 96, 172, 249-51.
rhythm, 103, 171-73.
ritual and drama, 64.
romāñca, 114.
Rukmaṇīpariṇaya, 209.

Sadāśivamata, 29.
sādhāraṇīkaraṇa, 181, 266-9.
Ṣaḍjagrāma, 198-99.
Śailūṣa, 76.
Saindhava, 32.
Śaka, 120, 206.
śakuna, 53.
Sakuntalā, 215.
samāja, 24.
samājotsavaśālinī, 76.
Sāman, 23, 174.
samānīkaraṇa, 120-3, 161.
samavakāra, 20, 33, 35, 165, 207, 208, 213, 222.
sammūrcchita, 24.
saṃpheta, 214.
samudramanthana, 20.
saṃyoga, 263, 270.
saṃyuktivāda, 90, 269-71.
saṃyuta hasta, 108, 114, 151.
sañcārī bhāva, 86-7, 114.
sandhi, 219, 222.
Śāṇḍilya, 29.
saṅgīta, 21.
Saṅgītaratnākara, 27, 75, 80.
saṅgraha, 91.
saṅketa, 89, 163.
Saṅkuka, 96, 98, 263-6. 268, 270.
śānta rasa, 223.
śāpa, 54.
Sappho, 116.
Śāradātanaya, 29, 30-1, 32.
Sārṅgadeva, 27, 32.
śaraṇāgata, 50.
śārīraja, 107.

sarod, 21.
Śatapatha Brāhmaṇa, 21, 30, 224.
śataputrāḥ, 32.
sāttvatī vṛtti, 86, 212-3.
sāttvika abhināya, 89, 106, 112-5, 132, 181.
sāttvika bhāva, 253-4, 261-70.
śauca-aśauca, 42, 51.
Śaurasenī, 184, 197.
Schechner, Richard, 123,234-5.
schemata, 149, 150, 151, 158.
Shastri, Devadatta, 82.
Shaw, George Bernard, 11.
Shekhar, Indu, 184.
siddhi, 86-7, 105.
Śilālin, 26, 29, 30.
Singal, R.L., 215.
Sītā, 46.
Śiva as dancer, 73, 74.
skene, 129, 130, 139-40.
skinnis, 157.
Smṛtis, 19, 21.
social reformism, 11.
śobhanikās, 24.
Socrates, 95.
soma, 22, 43.
song, 171, 173.
Sophist, 94.
Sophocles, 109.
sparagmos, 53, 215.
śrāddha, 48.
śruti, 24, 180, 187, 199, 202.
stambha, 114, 116.
Stanford, W.B., 115-6, 171-72, 179-80, 202, 248-52.
stasimon, 148.
sthāna, 24.
sthāpaka, 161.
sthāyī bhāva, 86-7, 99, 114, 253-4, 261-70.
stoikhoi, 145.
strophe, 146, 157, 175.
sūcā, sūcya, 160, 161, 193, 206.
sukumāra, 165, 206, 211.
sunafe, 177.
supplicant, 49.
Supplices, 50, 147, 228.
sustema, 177.
sūtradhāra, 70, 159-60.
sūtra period, works, 25, 26.
Svapnavāsavadattam, 207.
svara, 86-7, 105.
svarabheda, 114.
svarita, 105, 187, 198.
svarūpas, 118.
Svāti, 29, 31.
sveda, 114.

Tāla, 111, 159, 171.
Taṇḍu, 31, 73, 112.
Tāpasavatsarāja, 244.
tārākarma, 107.
techne, 94.
Tertullian, 7.
theatre-house, 77, 78.
theatron, 125-134.
theokrasis, 54.
thumos, 44.
timee, 45, 46.
tonos, 177-8.
tragadoi, 76.
tragedy, 13, 46, 86, 90, 147, 169, 173, 203-5, 218, 255-6.
transformation, 8, 233-6.
Tripuradāha, 209.
Trojan Women, 147.
Troy, 50.
Tumburu, 20, 25, 29, 31.
turbasia, 155.
Turner, Victor, 79.

Ubhaisārikā, 212.
udātta, 105, 187, 198.
universal egg, 54.
Urubhaṅgam, 49, 210, 223.
Udbhaṭa, 91.
Urvaśī, 23.

utsṛṣṭikāṅka, 165, 209, 212, 216, 246.
Uttararāmacaritam, 54, 207.

Vācika abhinaya, 106, 112-3, 181.
vāgabhinaya, 181-2.
vāk, 21, 169.
vākyābhinaya, 87, 160.
Vālmīki, 15, 21, 24, 200.
vāraṇa, 135.
Vararuci, 82.
varṇaka ahārya, 120.
vartanā, 109.
Vatsarāja, 209.
Vātsya, 29.
Vātsyāyana, 27, 28.
Vātsyāyana's *Kāmasūtra*, 81.
Vātsyāyana, Kapilā, 238.
Vedas, 21, 175, 224.
Vedic dialogues, 70.
Vedic ritual, 71.
Vedic sacrifices, 71.
Veṇīsaṃhāra, 49, 196, 207, 221.
vibhāva, 87, 90, 261-70.
vedika, 136.
Vibhīṣaṇa, 60.
vilakṣaṇa pratīti, 265, 270.
vīṇā, 20, 21, 24.
vipañcī, 21.
virāma, 193.
Viśvāvasu, 21, 22, 31.
vīthī, 139, 165, 210, 222.
Vṛddhabharata, 29.
vṛtti, 86, 105, 212, 214.
vyabhicārī bhāva, 90, 253-4, 261-70.
vyañjaka, 269.
vyāpāra, 217, 220.
vyāyoga, 165, 207, 222.

Wells, Henry, W., 214.

Xuga, 145.

Yajña, 224-6.
Yājñavalkya Smṛti, 58, 200.
Yājurveda, 53.
yakṣas, 120, 162.
Yakṣagāna, 237.
Yavanas, 120.
yavanikā, 73, 158-9.
yonyantarī bhāṣā, 184.
Yudhiṣṭhira, 49.
yuga, 56-7.

Zeus, 55, 56.
Zeus Katharsios, 51, 60.